CENTRAL BANKERS, BUREAUCRATIC INCENTIVES, AND MONETARY POLICY

FINANCIAL AND MONETARY POLICY STUDIES

volume 13

For a list of the volumes in this series see final page of the volume.

CENTRAL BANKERS, BUREAUCRATIC INCENTIVES, AND MONETARY POLICY

Edited by

Eugenia Froedge Toma
Department of Economics, Auburn University
Mark Toma
Department of Economics, Miami University

1986 **KLUWER ACADEMIC PUBLISHERS**
DORDRECHT / BOSTON / LANCASTER

Distributors

for the United States and Canada: Kluwer Academic Publishers, P.O. Box 358, Accord Station, Hingham, MA 02018-0358
for the UK and Ireland: Kluwer Academic Publishers, MTP Press Limited, Falcon House, Queen Square, Lancaster LA1 1RN, UK
for all other countries: Kluwer Academic Publishers Group, Distribution Center, P.O. Box 322, 3300 AH Dordrecht, The Netherlands

Library of Congress Cataloging in Publication Data

Central bankers, bureaucratic incentives, and monetary policy.

(Financial and monetary policy studies ; v. 13)
1. Board of Governors of the Federal Reserve System (U.S.) 2. Monetary policy--United States. 3. Banks and banking, Central--Decision making. I. Toma, Mark. II. Toma, Eugenia Froedge. III. Series: Financial and monetary policy studies ; 13.
HG2565.C33 1986 332.1'12'0973 86-12572

ISBN-13:978-94-010-8473-4 e-ISBN-13:978-94-009-4432-9
DOI: 10.1007/978-94-009-4432-9

ISBN 90-247-3366-9 (this volume)
ISBN 90-247-2605-0 (series)

To

Gordon Tullock

FOREWORD

By now it has become obvious that Federal Reserve actions have an immense impact on the functioning of our economy. As a result, a great deal of research has been done on the Fed and on monetary policy. Much of this work is normative; it tells us what the Fed *should* do. Positive work on the Fed has usually tried to elucidate particular Fed policies, and has not tried to present a theory of why the Fed behaves the way it does.

The dominant theory of Fed behavior is that the Fed does what it believes to be best for the public welfare. This theory – usually left implicit – is so simple, and seemingly so obviously correct, that it has received widespread credence without extended discussion or tests. When thinking about government in general many observers doubt that it nearly always acts in the public interest. However, they ascribe this unfortunate state of affairs mainly to political pressures. Since the Fed is *relatively* removed from such pressures, the public interest theory of government seems more applicable to it.

But some economists have challenged this public interest view of Fed behavior, and have interpreted Fed behavior in accordance with the economic theory of bureaucracy. Their papers are scattered in various journals. This book brings them together in one place, so that the strengths and weaknesses of this approach can more easily be appraised. In brief, these papers assert that the Fed frequently acts to enhance its own status and welfare, rather than the public welfare. Man is driven by self-interest, and appointing him to the Board of Governors does not change his nature.

Given the appeal that the assumption of rational utility maximizing has for economists one might expect that the bureaucratic theory of Fed behavior would find ready acceptance among economists, and might even appear in elementary textbooks as an example of the insights that economics can provide. But this has not happened. Perhaps, somewhat cynically, one might mention as one reason that economists may well consider the Fed to be 'one of us'. Most of its policymakers are economists. No other U.S. government agency can – or would like to – make this statement. Another reason is probably that this theory seems to conflict with what we *know*: that Fed officials are fundamentally decent people. Both from our personal contacts with them, and from what we imagine we would do if we were in their position, we form a belief about their value system. Specifically, we believe that to make themselves slightly better off, they do not say, condemn several thousand people to unemployment. To be plausible the self-interest approach to the Fed has to tackle this objection.

There are several ways to do so. One is to challenge the 'decent officials' view head-on. Various books on World War II have argued that generals sometimes interfered with the war effort, thus needlessly sacrificing troops, to gain the glory that would otherwise go to another general. Moreover, a study of the development of the nuclear bomb hinted at a similar behavior by a scientist. But all the same, this seems a weak defense of the Fed self-interest theory.

A more plausible approach is to argue that a policymaker need not be selfish to act in the interest of his agency rather than in the public interest. He or she may honestly believe that the public interest is served by increasing the power, autonomy and prestige of the agency. To serve the public's welfare in the future one needs power, and if the price of this power is to make a small sacrifice of the public's welfare right now, this may be worth doing. Given the obvious tendency of officials to overestimate the good that their agency can do, even good officials concerned with the public's welfare may act in ways that are better explained by the bureaucratic self-interest approach than by the public welfare approach. Means tend to become ends. As literature, in the conventional sense of the term, teaches us, it does not take bad people to generate bad deeds.

The temptation to do bad now in order to enhance the power to do good subsequently is more easily resisted if it is obvious that the current action is bad. But our knowledge of monetary policy is limited. We are frequently far from certain that the seemingly bad action is really bad. Consider the following example: The incoming data suggest that the money growth rate is too high, but lowering it, and allowing interest rates to rise temporarily would call down the wrath of Congress on the Fed. Fed officials might be more willing to suffer the consequences of lowering the money growth rate if they were not afraid that a subsequent revision of the money growth rate data might show that it actually was not excessive. In a field in which so little is known an intelligent person can always find a good reason for doing the wrong thing.

For these reasons the bureaucratic self-interest theory cannot be dismissed out of hand. Its validity can only be determined by empirical tests, and this is what the papers in this volume provide.

Evaluating the evidence for the bureaucratic theory is a tricky matter. Even those who reject this theory will probably admit that among the multitude of Fed actions there exist a few cases in which their theory can explain the Fed's actions. Similarly, adherents of the bureaucratic theory do not deny that the Fed ever acts in the public interest rather than its own interest. The real question is how much, and what part, of the Fed's behavior is explained by each theory. This is an extraordinarily difficult question. It invites the type of evidence that consists of showing that certain Fed behavior is consistent with the preferred theory. However, such evidence is not fully convincing because it does not deny that the same Fed behavior could also be explained by the other theory. For example, the Fed's use of vague targets certainly fits the bureaucratic theory. But the Fed might argue that, given the uncertainties that accompany monetary policy-making, it also fits the public interest theory. To decide whether this is correct, one has to resolve some of the main disputes about monetary policy. If, on the other hand, the proponents of the bureaucratic theory pick a narrow issue that has little to do with monetary policy, their opponents might respond that the Fed's pursuit of its self-interest on this issue does not matter, as long as the Fed follows the public interest approach in its important decisions.

Hence, I believe that the bureaucratic theory of the Fed should be interpreted as an interesting approach that has something to teach us, and not as the final answer to the question of what motivates Fed behavior. One might go beyond this theory and ask, not what motivates the FOMC per se, because the FOMC per se, does not act; but in accordance with methodological individualism, one might ask what motivates the individual members of the FOMC. They may sometimes be more concerned with their own self-image than with the Fed's prestige. Thus, they may vote for that policy that minimizes the probability that they will subsequently feel guilty for having made a mistake. Hence they may prefer vague policy statements to more meaningful ones. The trouble with such an hypothesis is that it does not allow one to use the tools that economists have available and requires the use of less developed tools from other social sciences. Hence, there is much to be said for seeing first how much of the puzzle of Fed behavior can be explained by the economic theory of bureaucracy.

Thomas Mayer

PREFACE

Past studies of the decision-making process at central banks have focused on the technical relationship between the production of the monetary base and the resulting rate of inflation. An implicit assumption in most of this work is that central bankers act in a way that is consistent with the so-called public interest. Only recently have economists started to go beyond this mechanical analysis and begun to focus attention on the incentives created by the institutional structure of the bank. This book contains a collection of these recent works that look at central bank behavior by first examining the constraints confronting bank members.

To this point these works have appeared in two sets of unrelated literature. Some of the contributions have been addressed to traditional monetary theorists while others have emphasized the public choice approach. There have been no previous attempts to explicitly tie together these works that apply bureaucracy theory to central bank behavior and that is our purpose in this book.

We do not intend this book to represent the final word on this subject. Rather we have selected works for this collection that help to lay the foundation for research in this area. We can only hope that this book will promote further interest in understanding *why* central bankers behave as they do.

Many of the chapters included in this book are reprints of previously published papers. We have made only minor stylistic changes in the papers as they originally appeared. Permission to reprint the papers was granted by the copyright holders. We are grateful to all the authors and the publishers for allowing us to include their works. Also we express our thanks to Judy Thommesen for her efforts in typing this book. Milton Friedman's, 'Monetary Policy: Theory and Practice,' initially appeared in the *Journal of Money, Credit and Banking* 14 (February 1982): 98-118. Mark Toma's

'Inflationary Bias of the Federal Reserve System,' originally appeared in the *Journal of Monetary Economics* 10 (September 1982): 163-90. William Shughart and Robert Tollison's paper 'Preliminary Evidence on the Use of Inputs in the Federal Reserve System,' initially appeared in the *American Economic Review* 73 (June 1983): 291-304.

The paper by Keith Acheson and John Chant, 'Bureaucratic Theory and the Choice of Central Bank Goals,' originally appeared in the *Journal of Money, Credit and Banking* 5 (May 1973): 637-55. The remaining papers in this section first appeared in *Public Choice*. John Chant and Keith Acheson's 'The Choice of Monetary Instruments and the Theory of Bureaucracy,' appeared in 12 (Spring 1972): 13-33. Eugenia Froedge Toma and Mark Toma's paper, 'Research Activities and Budget Allocations Among Federal Reserve Banks,' was in 45(2) (1985): 175-91. Neil Skaggs and Cheryl Wasserkrug's article, 'Banking Sector Influence on the Relationship of Congress to the Federal Reserve System,' was in 41 (1983): 295-306.

The paper, 'Politics and Fed Policymaking' by Edward Kane initially appeared in the *Journal of Monetary Economics* (April 1980): 199-211. 'Central Bank Independence,' by King Banaian, Leroy O. Laney, and Thomas Willett was published originally in the *Economic Review: Federal Reserve Bank of Dallas* (March 1983): 1-13. Gary Santoni's paper, 'A Private Central Bank: Some Olde English Lessons,' initially appeared in *The Federal Reserve Bank of St. Louis Review* 66 (April 1984): 12-22.

CONTENTS

Foreword vii
Thomas Mayer

Preface xi

1. Central Bankers, Bureaucratic Incentives, and Monetary Policy: An Introduction 1
Eugenia Froedge Toma and Mark Toma

I. Structure of Central Bank Financing and Bureaucratic Rents

2. Monetary Policy: Theory and Practice 11
Milton Friedman

3. Inflationary Bias of the Federal Reserve System: A Bureaucratic Perspective 37
Mark Toma

4. Preliminary Evidence on the Use of Inputs in the Federal Reserve System 67
William Shughart and Robert Tollison

5. Human Capital and Bureaucratic Inertia: The Use of Inputs by the Federal Reserve 91
Stewart Mounts and Clifford Sowell

II. The Organization of Central Bank Bureaus and the Problems of Control

6. The Choice of Monetary Instruments and the Theory of Bureaucracy — 107
John Chant and Keith Acheson

7. Bureaucratic Theory and the Choice of Central Bank Goals — 129
Keith Acheson and John Chant

8. Research Activities and Budget Allocations Among Federal Reserve Banks — 151
Eugenia Froedge Toma and Mark Toma

9. Banking Sector Influence on the Relationship of Congress to the Federal Reserve System — 169
Neil Skaggs and Cheryl Wasserkrug

III. Political Pressures, Bureaucratic Incentives, and Monetary Policy

10. Politics and Fed Policymaking — 185
Edward Kane

11. Central Bank Independence: An International Comparison — 199
King Banaian, Leroy O. Laney, and Thomas D. Willett

12. A Private Central Bank: Some Olde English Lessons — 219
Gary Santoni

IV. Conclusion

13. Central Bankers and the Issue of Independence — 243
Eugenia Froedge Toma and Mark Toma

Contributors — 251

Chapter 1

CENTRAL BANKERS, BUREAUCRATIC INCENTIVES, AND MONETARY POLICY: AN INTRODUCTION

by Eugenia Froedge Toma and Mark Toma

The idea that institutional structures, or property rights, affect individual behavior is not a new one. In fact, this idea has been the focus of much of the public choice/property rights literature of the past two decades. What is relatively new is the application of this principle to central bank behavior. Until recently, economists have tended to analyze central banks in a utopian framework. The implicit assumption has been that central banks conduct their operations to maximize the public interest. Any deviation from the optimal rate of inflation could be attributed to technical problems associated with unanticipated changes in the money multiplier or money demand. Because of the assumptions employed, the economist's role is that of a technician, one who identifies the precise relationships between the monetary base, the money supply, and the resulting inflation rate.

As the works in CENTRAL BANKERS suggest, the traditional approach leaves a void in our understanding of the behavior of central bankers and the conduct of monetary policy. Filling this void entails explicitly accounting for the reward structure facing central bank bureaucrats. In many countries central bankers are not subject to a legislative appropriation process, and they may enjoy relatively long tenures in office during which they are subject to a minimal degree of legislative oversight. If this institutional structure is taken as given, and a utility-maximizing framework adopted, certain questions arise that do not present themselves to the traditional technician. For instance, how does a particular reward structure affect the bureaucratic payoffs to different monetary strategies? Does a change in the set of

Toma, E.F. and Toma, M. (eds.) Central Bankers, Bureaucratic Incentives, and Monetary Policy

ISBN 90 247 3366 9

bureaucratic incentives have any systematic effect on a central bank's propensity to generate inflation?

In addressing these questions, the chapters in this book are organized into three parts. Section one presents a collection of works that highlights the one institutional feature of the Federal Reserve System that distinguishes it from other U.S. government agencies. Rather than going to Congress each year for an appropriation, the Fed finances its operation primarily from open market earnings. Acknowledging this institutional peculiarity provides insights into the Fed's propensity to produce inflation that tend to be obscured by the traditional technician's approach.

Instead of focusing on the novel aspects of the institutional framework, the second section emphasizes that the *internal* organization of central bank bureaucracies is similar to that of many other government agencies. For this reason, the approach employed by public choice theorists in studying the internal operation of typical government agencies can be readily applied to the various layers within the central bank hierarchy. Generally, the works in this section argue that the internal dynamics of the central bank bureaucracy can be understood best by adopting the hypothesis that individual bureaucrats engage in rent-seeking behavior. Finally, section three broadens the analysis by considering how political factors influence central bank officials' behavior. What distinguishes the works in this section from other 'political pressure' theories is that the legislative influence is evaluated strictly in terms of its impact on the reward structure of the central bank.

In the opening chapter of section one, Milton Friedman states the case for a shift in research agenda from the utopian model to the public choice approach. In practice central banks are not automatons that follow the advice of some economic authority. Instead, many of the Fed's past decisions can be better understood by recognizing its institutional structure. The one feature that stands out is that the Fed operates without a bottom line. 'The Fed is not subject to an effective budget constraint. It prints its own money to pay its expenses' (Chapter 2 in this volume, p. 27).

The Fed has operated without a 'budget constraint' throughout its history. From 1914 to 1933, the Federal Reserve Act required the System to transfer excess earnings to the Treasury after financing its own operations. With the Banking Act of 1933, this transfer requirement was eliminated so that for the first time the Fed could retain all revenue. Finally, in 1947 the Fed started voluntarily transferring excess revenue to the government. Although the details have varied over time, some form of what might be called the revenue structure has always governed the Fed's finances.

Chapters 3 and 4 contrast this financing method with others and conclude that the revenue structure produces an inflationary bias in the Fed's decisions. Empirically, both the paper by Mark Toma and the one by William Shughart and Robert Tollison focus on the type of bureaucratic payoffs associated with the revenue structure. Shughart and Tollison used System employment as a proxy for Federal Reserve rewards, but Toma used the size of System spending itself.

In investigating the impact of the revenue structure on Federal Reserve official behavior, Toma isolates the post-1947 period. He hypothesizes that during years when base changes generated extraordinarily high open market revenue, a Fed interested in bureaucratic amenities would transform some portion of these higher earnings into discretionary spending. To test this proposition, Toma regressed changes in annual expenditures by the System from 1947 to 1979 against changes in its open market wealth and other (non-monetary) output variables. Open market wealth proved to be a significant factor in explaining expenditures of the Fed.

Shughart and Tollison explore the bureaucratic hypothesis by testing whether the Fed uses its powers of base expansion to increase its size as measured in terms of System employment. Focusing on the base-employment relationship over the entire 1915-81 period, their regression analysis implies that increases in System employment cause expansions in the monetary base. As they summarize the results, 'every time the Fed hired one more worker, the stock of high-powered money rose by about $362,000' (Chapter 4 in this volume, p. 81). This finding further supports the notion that the Fed's pursuit of rents within the revenue structure helps drive the money supply process.

William Stewart Mounts and Clifford Sowell (Chapter 5) criticize the aggregative empirical approach taken by Toma and Shughart and Tollison. Because the Board, and not the entire System, conducts monetary policy, the Board technically 'earns' the excess revenue . . . and may act as if it 'owns' the excess by appropriating it for its use. If it is correct to measure the monetary base-amenities relation through a size variable then, within this property rights perspective, the effects would be specified correctly through Board employment as opposed to System employment. (Chapter 5 in this volume, p. 101). In measuring the base-amenities relationship, Mounts and Sowell explicitly isolate the period 1933-47 – the years the Fed retained all its 'excess' earnings and returned nothing to the Treasury. Arguing that this particular variation of the revenue structure closes off an avenue through which congressional monitoring could influence Board activities, Mounts and Sowell conclude that the connection between Board employment and base expansion should be particularly strong during this subperiod. Their regression results support their hypothesis as well as the proposition that the absence of any direct monitoring of the Board of Governors has a predictable effect on bureaucratic rents.

While section one focuses on the behavior of the central bank's upper management, section two explores the structure of rewards that connects the layers of a central bank. Here the hierarchy of the central bank system becomes the object of analysis. Consider the Federal Reserve System as an example of an hierarchical organization. At the top of the hierarchy are members of the Board of Governors. Next in line are the Presidents and general employees of the twelve Reserve Banks. Financial institutions (in particular the member banks) represent a final hierarchical layer.

Like any bureaucratic head, the Board of Governors confronts a control problem in conditioning the behavior of its agents. Noting that the Board has a direct budgetary link to the individual Reserve Banks, Eugenia Froedge Toma and Mark Toma hypothesize in chapter 8 that Banks producing adverse publicity for the System would be penalized by budget reductions. At least in the long run, this adverse publicity would tend to have a negative effect on the discretionary spending opportunities of the Board in particular and the System in general. Two Reserve Banks, St. Louis and Minneapolis, were identified as experiencing periods (1968-80 for St. Louis and 1974-79 for Minneapolis) in which they published adverse information. Regressions were run to explain the annual budget changes of the Reserve Banks with the adverse publicity periods treated as dummy years. After controlling for other factors, Toma and Toma found that the budget growth rates in the St. Louis and Minneapolis Banks during their dummy years were lower than for other Banks in the System over the same time periods. The hypothesis that the Board uses budget allocations to protect the Fed's pool of spending opportunities could not be rejected.

Reserve Banks are not the only organizations whose activities pose a potential control problem for the System. The private financial sector that is regulated by the Federal Reserve System is in a similar position. The Board, however, has no direct budgetary control over financial institutions. Instead, a quid pro quo relationship has emerged. In an attempt to uncover such a relationship, Neil Skaggs and Cheryl Wasserkrug (Chapter 9) investigated a 1974 congressional vote on whether to institute comprehensive outside audits of the Federal Reserve System. They found that financial institutions provide valuable support for the Fed on this issue. In particular, the scope of the financial sector in a congressional district was a significant factor in explaining a congressman's opposition to a comprehensive audit.

Two pioneering papers by Keith Acheson and John Chant (chapters 6 and

7) used the Canadian Central Bank as an example of the financial sector's role in insulating the central bank from public criticism. They note that the central bank can choose from a broad spectrum of tools in conducting monetary policy. It can use a single instrument, such as open market operations; or by employing a variety of tools and using both direct and indirect procedures, it can raise the cost to the public of obtaining information about its operations. Acheson and Chant argue that the Canadian Bank has opted for this more obscure route of conducting policy. In doing so, it often relies on the cooperation of the private financial sector. For example, rather than using only open market operations, the Bank has also changed the base by transferring government deposits between itself and chartered banks. The banks cooperate with the central bank because it has extensive regulatory powers such as determining the eligibility of day-to-day loans for money market dealers.

The final section of the book explores how political considerations shape the incentive structures facing monetary decision makers in different countries. Edward Kane in chapter 10 examines the political responsiveness of Federal Reserve officials. He emphasizes that the Fed is only as independent as Congress wants it to be. Fed officials, of course, are fully aware of that and act as a political scapegoat in order to insure their continued independence in terms of financing and long tenure in office. According to Kane, the Fed's nebulous goals and the incomplete information given to the public can be explained once we recognize that in the final analysis this behavior provides benefits to elected politicians.

In chapter 11, King Banaian, Leroy Laney, and Thomas Willett examine the degree to which short-run political considerations influence central bank policy. Their analysis applies not only to the Fed but to the central banks of other industrial countries as well. Banaian, Laney, and Willett consider several ways in which central banks' incentive structures vary considerably. They include the procedure for appointing central bank officers, the term of office, and whether the bank stock is privately or publicly held. They conclude that the central banks of West Germany, Switzerland, and the United States are among the most independently structured and have been subjected to fewer political pressures to inflate the money supply. The relatively 'dependent' central banks have shown a greater tendency to accommodate the inflationary pressures that originate from the legislative branch.

Finally, Gary Santoni takes an historical approach to the question of how political pressures shape central bank incentive structures. From 1694 to the early 1930s, the Bank of England was operated as a private-for-profit institution virtually independent of government. 'Further, the Bank was immersed in a set of institutional arrangements that related the wealth of the Bank's owners inversely to the rate of inflation' (Chapter 12 in this volume, p. 220). Control over money supply was temporarily seized by the government during the period 1793-1821, and the private structure was permanently abolished by the English government in 1931. Santoni finds that while the inflation rate was not significantly different from zero during the purely private regime, it surged during the periods when the Bank was subject to political pressures.

In summary, the central bank structures considered in this book differ significantly across time and across countries. At one extreme, we have Santoni's description of the early Bank of England. The private-for-profit central bankers faced a reward structure that tied profits directly to the demand for (real) central bank money. Given the unique set of institutional arrangements that prevailed as well as the unattenuated property rights structure, relatively low rates of inflation were a predictable outcome.

At the other extreme are those countries (or those time periods) where monetary decisions are made by a legislative body that is granted a monopoly franchise over base production, but without the unusual reward system that characterizes the Santoni private bank setting. Real world legislatures may be viewed as valuing additions to government revenue from many sources – including money creation. To the extent that political rules of the game imply that legislative representatives in these countries have limited tenures, their political discount rate may be relatively high. Greater weight will be placed on increasing the revenue from money creation in the short run, thereby leading to relatively high inflation rates.

The institutional structure examined in the first section represents the intermediate setting. Those chapters indicated that modern U.S. central bankers enjoy a high degree of financial autonomy with relatively long terms of office. If these institutional features cause appointed Fed officials to be less short-sighted than elected legislative bodies, there will be a predictable consequence of shifting power to Fed officials. Federal Reserve officials will tend to take into account the public's ability to alter its real money holdings over time as a means of adjusting to inflation. This would tend to mitigate the inflationary bias that is produced by myopia on the part of legislators. Money production rates, nevertheless, would still be excessive compared to some reference ideal of price stability.

Taken together, this collection of works makes an effective argument that incentives matter. Fundamentally, these studies show that the degree to which central banks produce inflation depends upon the extent to which they are rewarded for this behavior. A better understanding of monetary policy can be achieved by explicitly recognizing the institutional structure surrounding central banks' decision-making processes.

I. STRUCTURE OF CENTRAL BANK FINANCING AND BUREAUCRATIC RENTS

Chapter 2

MONETARY POLICY: THEORY AND PRACTICE

*By Milton Friedman**

In respect of the theory of monetary policy, I am reminded of the comment that Jacob Viner made many years ago at a meeting of the American Economic Association about Alfred Marshall's economics: 'What is new is highly unlikely at this late date also to be true and significant.'(1) Consequently, I shall restrict my remarks on theory to trying to summarize what I regard as the present intellectual position.

I want to devote most of my time to two other topics: first, the actual practice of monetary policy, with special reference to some examples from American experience; second, the reasons why the practice has been what it has been. In these areas, history keeps on turning up new evidence about old principles. It's still true that much of what's true is not new. But it's no longer true that what's new is not true.

1. THE THEORY OF MONETARY POLICY

The role for monetary policy depends on what James Buchanan has called the monetary constitution, in particular, the domestic monetary standard, and international monetary arrangements.

*I am indebted to Robert D. Auerbach, William G. Dewald, David E. Lindsey, Allan H. Meltzer, and members of the audience when this lecture was delivered for comments on the initial version of this paper. I hardly need emphasize that not all comments reflected agreement.

Toma, E.F. and Toma, M. (eds.) Central Bankers, Bureaucratic Incentives, and Monetary Policy

ISBN 90 247 3366 9

If a domestic money consists of a commodity, a pure gold standard or cowrie bead standard, the principles of monetary policy are very simple. There aren't any. The commodity money takes care of itself. The analysis of the factors that determine the price level in terms of the commodity money is largely an exercise in conventional price theory. However, a pure commodity standard has little relevance, either today or for much of the past. Even when an international gold standard was regarded as the norm, it involved a large admixture of fiat elements. And today, throughout the world, the domestic monetary standard is a fiat standard, a standard in which money is issued by governments backed only by the words that are written on pieces of paper.

With respect to international arrangements, three basically different types can be distinguished: a single commodity standard internationally; a system of managed, fixed exchange rates such as prevailed during the Bretton Woods period, in which the domestic monetary standard is fundamentally a fiat standard, but in which exchange rates between countries are fixed by some kind of an agreement; and, flexible exchange rates among domestic currencies.

The rest of this lecture deals with the current system, namely, a domestic fiat currency plus a system of flexible exchange rates. A system of flexible exchange rates does not in practice mean a system of completely unmanaged, floating rates. I wish it did, but it doesn't. It means in practice dirty floating of fixed rates. (As a believer in cleanliness, I'm in favor of both clean fixed rates and clean floating rates.)

Let me emphasize, however, that the system we now take for granted – a domestic fiat standard plus flexible exchange rates among currencies – is a relatively recent arrival, though I believe that it will prevail for a long time. That combination has become the norm in the United States only since August 15, 1971, the day that President Nixon closed the gold window and thereby ended the Bretton Woods period. Even then it took several years before the notion that the exchange rates were to be fixed once again was really given up, and we embarked on the present system. Moreover, the current Administration is the first to adopt and announce a policy of avoiding governmental intervention into the exchange rate market, except it is said, under 'extreme circumstances.'

The theory of monetary policy under the present monetary constitution reduces to two parts: the strategy of monetary policy and the tactics that should be followed by the people who guide monetary policy. Put differently, what should be the ultimate objectives of monetary policy? What should be the proximate targets and instruments? Both issues have generated much discussion and given rise to an extensive literature. Also, views on both have converged remarkably, so that today opinions differ little on either strategy or tactics. Let me emphasize at once that the convergence of views did not arise from the persuasiveness of the theoretical arguments advanced by people like myself, Allan Meltzer, Karl Brunner, and others, or by people who differed with us. The convergence is due not to theoretical reasoning, but to the brute force and impact of actual experience.

A. Strategy

With respect to ultimate objectives, it's easy to cite the holy trinity that has become standard: full employment, economic growth, and stable prices. However, reciting the Holy Trinity begs the fundamental question. What is the special role of monetary policy in contributing to these objectives? Three views have been held about the appropriate strategy: first, that monetary policy should be directed specifically at promoting full employment; second, that it should be directed at promoting growth through cheap money, through keeping interest rates low; and third, that it should concentrate on price stability.

Experience and not theory has demonstrated that the first two strategies are not feasible, that monetary policy is not an effective instrument for achieving directly either full employment or economic growth. As a result, there is today a worldwide consensus, not only among most academic economists but also among monetary practitioners, that the long-run objective of monetary policy must be price stability, or, to put it more generally, control of the absolute level of prices, because the objective could be a specified rate of inflation or deflation. Such a long-run objective is in principle consistent with the short-run objective of pursuing the long-run policy in a manner that contributes to minimizing economic fluctuation, that avoids introducing unnecessary elements of disturbance into the economy.

B. Tactics

With respect to proximate instruments and targets, the fundamental issue is the one that was raised by Henry Simons nearly fifty years ago, namely, 'Rules versus Authorities.'(2) Should the tactics be determined by relatively mechanical rules that are publicly promulgated, or by the discretion of authorities instructed to follow the right policy at the right time for the right objective?

Whatever way the fundamental issue is decided, there remains the operating question of what rules should be adopted, or, how authorities should be guided. Here too there is a trinity of possible tactics: first, using what are called euphemistically money market conditions, which really means interest rates, both as a target and also as an instrument; second, using monetary aggregates as a target, but money market conditions or interest rates as an instrument for achieving that target; third, using monetary aggregates as a target and control over the monetary base, that is, the obligations of the monetary authority, as the instrument.

On tactics, too, opinion has converged remarkably, again not due to persuasive theoretical reasoning but to experience. Experience has demonstrated that it is simply not feasible for the monetary authority to use interest rates as either a target or as an effective instrument. Were it feasible for the Federal Reserve to adopt and achieve a target interest rate, it is inconceivable that the prime rate would ever have risen to over 20 percent. In principle, given sufficient knowledge about market behavior, it is possible to use market instruments to achieve monetary aggregate targets. However, experience had demonstrated that monetary authorities are in practice unable to achieve in this way the degree of control over monetary aggregates that seems hypothetically possible. Hence, there is now wide agreement that the appropriate, short-run tactics are to express a target in terms of monetary aggregates, and to use control of the base, or components of the base, as an instrument to achieve the target. The end result is widespread rhetorical agreement by central banks around the world to what has come to be called a monetarist policy. (I may say that personally I do not like the term 'monetarism.' I would prefer to talk simply about the quantity theory of money, but we can't avoid usages that custom imposes on us.)

A monetarist policy has five points: first, the target should be growth in some monetary aggregate – just which monetary aggregate is a separate question; second, monetary authorities should adopt long-run targets for monetary growth that are consistent with no inflation; third, present rates of growth of monetary aggregates should be modified to achieve the long-run target in a gradual, systematic, and preannounced fashion; fourth, monetary authorities should avoid fine-tuning; fifth, monetary authorities should avoid trying to manipulate either interest rates or exchange rates.

Almost every central banker in the world today agrees verbally to at least the first three of these five points, and most also to the fourth. The fifth is unquestionably the most controversial. However, in many cases, the profession of faith is simply lip service, and does not carry over to actual practice, which brings me to the second part of my lecture.

2. PRACTICE

Rhetoric is one thing. Performance is often a very different thing. The fascinating and challenging question, I believe, is how to explain the frequent wide discrepancy between rhetoric and practice.

A. International

Internationally, those countries that have broadly followed the five-point monetarist policy have succeeded in controlling inflation and have done so while achieving relatively satisfactory economic growth.

Among the advanced countries of the world, the outstanding example is Japan. In 1973, Japan's inflation rate was around 25 percent per year, following monetary growth at a similar rate. Japan brought the rate of monetary growth down drastically, to the neighborhood of 10 to 15 percent, and has continued to reduce it still further. After an intervening recession – by Japanese standards, not necessarily ours – of about eighteen months, inflation started to come down. It came down gradually and steadily, reached a level below 5 percent, then temporarily went up after the most recent oil shock. Since then, it is starting to come back down again, and clearly seems under control. And the reduction of inflation has been accompanied by a growing economy.

West Germany is another example, not quite as successful, not quite as dramatic, but still, on the whole, successful with respect to both inflation and economic growth because it has followed a policy of controlling the quantity of money along monetarist lines.

Among the less developed countries, Chile provides an even more dramatic case. In 1975, Chile had an inflation rate of about 800 percent per year. It has brought that down to under 20 percent a year, has now pegged its exchange rate to the U.S. exchange rate, having decided that, bad as U.S. monetary policy is, it is likely to be more successful than their own. They are therefore reconciled to achieving, or suffering, our rate of inflation.

In Chile, as in Japan, an initial period of about a year and a half of great difficulty was followed by highly satisfactory real growth along with declining inflation. Real growth in Chile has been in the neighborhood of something like 6 to 10 percent a year during the past three or four years.

In my experience, these countries are exceptions. In most countries that I know about, lip service, not actual adherence, has been paid to monetarist policies. Essentially every major country, and many a minor one, proclaims monetary growth targets annually and pronounces its determination to stick to them. However, any relation between the targets and actual monetary growth is purely coincidental. The United States is a particularly egregious case. So I propose to concentrate on experience in the United States.

B. United States

Ever since the establishment of the Federal Reserve System, every chairman of the Federal Reserve Board, indeed, I suspect every member of the board, has proclaimed that the Federal Reserve will not be an engine of inflation. Yet the Federal Reserve was an engine of inflation during both world wars and has been one in peacetime since at least 1960.

My examination of that experience impresses me with the unbelievable strength of bureaucratic inertia in preventing the system from learning from experience. The inertia has prevailed not only since 1960, but for the whole sixty-seven years of the Federal Reserve's existence. With perhaps a few minor exceptions, the system has repeatedly been unable or unwilling to change its methods of operation in order to benefit from its own experience.

I stress the long duration of bureaucratic inertia for a very important reason. All of us tend to personalize issues, to say, if only the right person were chairman of the Federal Reserve its policy would be fine; or if only the right person were president or secretary of the Treasury. No doubt it makes a difference, and sometimes a big difference, who is in charge of the system, or the Treasury, or the White House. However, so far as the Federal Reserve System is concerned, the same inability to learn from experience has prevailed under a succession of personalities. Information about the name of the chairman of the Federal Reserve is of little or no use in describing the behavior of the Fed – though the name of the president apparently is.(3) I conclude that the problem is somehow rooted in the institutional structure of the Federal Reserve System.

I shall sketch very broadly the basis for my conclusion about the Fed's longstanding inability to learn from experience, and then turn to some more specific examples.

In our book on U.S. monetary history, Anna Schwartz and I found it possible to use one sentence to describe the central principle followed by the Federal Reserve System from the time it began operations in 1914 to 1952. That principle, to quote from our book, is: 'If the "money market" is properly managed so as to avoid the unproductive use of credit and to assure the availability of credit for productive use, then the money stock will take care of itself.'(4) The principle is, of course, the Real Bills doctrine of the nineteenth century – so the continuity extends not only back to 1914, but even to the early nineteenth century when Henry Thornton had already given a correct theoretical analysis of the problem and had indicated the fallacy of this approach.(5) It also, unfortunately, extends forward to the present – manifested most recently in the 1980 credit controls instituted by President Carter.

From 1952 to October 1979, the system gradually began to pay lip service to monetary aggregate targets. However, there was no change in procedures, only in the wording of the Federal Open Market directives. From October 1979 to date, there has been no real improvement in performance. But something more than lip service has been paid to changing procedures.

In preparing for this talk, I reread the proceedings of a conference held at Nantucket under the auspices of the Boston Federal Reserve Bank in June 1969. Out of that conference came a book entitled *Controlling Monetary Aggregates*.(6) It was a depressing experience to reread those proceedings. The same people are now saying the same things they were saying then. The people who were then talking about the difficulty or impossibility of controlling the quantity of money through controlling the base are still saying much the same thing. Parts of those conference proceedings could be interchanged bodily with large sections of the most recent Federal Reserve's apologia, to which I shall return, and no one would notice the difference. Indeed, I was surprised to find that Allan Meltzer had proposed, at that conference, the procedure that the Federal Reserve has recently adopted, of setting a monetary aggregates target subject to a specified numerically wide range of Federal Funds rates. Of course, in his defense, I should note that he considered such a procedure a transitory expedient. He wanted the range to be widened and widened until it disappeared. However, it is a sign of how little progress we have made that hardly a point entering today's discussion is absent from that 1969 discussion.

I want to consider four specific examples: first, the policy of pegged interest rates followed during World War II (I include this example to emphasize again that the issue is not one of particular personalities, but rather of institutional structure); second, the movement from controlling money market conditions to trying to control monetary aggregates; third, lagged reserve requirements and its adoption; fourth, defensive open market operations.

1. *Pegged Bond Prices.* The Great Depression shocked the Fed into inactivity. From 1933 to 1941, the Federal Reserve essentially followed a wholly passive policy, devoting all its energy to keeping its bond portfolio

unchanged. Insofar as there was any active monetary policy, it was conducted by the Treasury Department. The passive policy finally degenerated in 1942 into an explicit policy by the Federal Reserve of pegging the prices of government securities, that is, of establishing a pattern of rates on securities of different maturities – short-term bills, long-term bonds, and so on – and maintaining it there by standing ready to buy, or sell, any amounts offered or demanded at those rates.

In 1947, five years later, some tentative steps were taken that did not change the principle but simply changed slightly the difference between the short-term rate and the long-term rate.

In 1951, nine years after the program had been adopted, the famous Federal Reserve-Treasury accord was negotiated, under which the Federal Reserve was freed from its commitment to pegging government bond prices. However, the Fed continued to do so. It did not really unpeg the prices of government securities until 1953. So it took all told eleven years from the inception of that policy until its termination, though at no point in that whole eleven years was any valid intellectual argument presented in favor of the policy. The policy was not even consistent with the Federal Reserve's own view because, after all, adherence to the Real Bills doctrine does not call for pegging interest rates. It calls for distinguishing between productive and unproductive uses of credit.

Why was that program ended? Did the initiative to end it come from within the system? Not at all. It was ended entirely as a result of three courses of outside pressure. One was the Korean War, which produced a change in anticipations that in turn led to a sharp jump in monetary velocity and to the emergence of inflation. The second, and, in my opinion, unquestionably the more important in terms of the immediate effect, was pressure from Senator Paul Douglas, the famous University of Chicago economist – the first recent example of the influence of the Chicago school of monetary policy. Senator Douglas conducted a series of hearings on monetary policy. Throughout those hearings, he kept hammering away on the undesirability of pegging bond prices. I have very little doubt that his pressure played a critical role in finally producing the Federal Reserve-Treasury accord.(7) The third source of outside pressure came, after 1952, from the Eisenhower White House.

2. *Money Market Conditions to Monetary Targets.* The gradual transition from money market conditions to monetary targets from 1953 to 1979, a period of twenty-six years, is a more complex story.

The unpegging of government bond prices in 1953 was followed by lip service by the Federal Reserve to monetary growth as a long-run target.

However, to the best of my knowledge, it did not set any specific monetary growth targets for itself until 1975, when Congress required it to do so. The phrase that really mattered was one that was popular at the time, namely, that the Federal Reserve should 'lean against the wind' as a short-run policy without any very clear specification of what wind or when.

The first sign of movement by the Fed came in 1966 when it introduced into its directive to the manager of the Federal Open Market Account (the 'desk') a proviso clause that instructed the desk to maintain specified money market conditions provided that doing so did not lead to an undesirable expansion of credit. Even that minor step, which was just words and had no significance in practice, was produced by external pressure arising from the Vietnam War and the emergence of inflation rates of something like 2 or 3 percent – regarded at the time with great horror.

In 1969, the conference on controlling monetary aggregates that I have already referred to was organized by the Boston Federal Reserve Bank. That was the first real step from within the system to bring in outside people to explore the question of the operating procedures that would best control monetary aggregates.(8)

In that same year, I wrote a letter to William McChesney Martin, then chairman of the Federal Reserve, noting that two issues were under discussion: first, whether a monetary aggregate ought to be the policy target; second, whether, if it were the target, the system could control it. I suggested that the issues be separated, and that there be carried out at the New York Fed 'a dry run to test the possibility of achieving money supply targets and to develop and calibrate the necessary techniques.'(9) Such procedures would then be available when and if the first issue was decided in favor of monetary aggregates.

I refer to this letter, not to advertise the suggestion I made, but rather because of the reply I received from Chairman Martin. I quote from his reply: 'I seriously doubt that we could ever attain complete control [of monetary aggregates], I think it's quite true that we could come significantly closer to such control than we do now – if we wished to make that variable our exclusive target. But the wisdom of such an exclusive orientation for monetary policy is, of course, the basic question.'(10)

That's a very instructive statement. First of all, it says what the Fed had repeatedly denied and was to deny throughout the rest of the period that I'm talking about, that it could control the monetary aggregates. But second, the Fed didn't really mean it. The reply was simply designed to immobilize me – as I later learned from an economist in the Fed's Research Division, who boasted to me about his cleverness in constructing that reply. And of course it did immobilize me. Why conduct a study to figure out how to do something the Fed already knew how to do?

Almost simultaneously, at the Nantucket conference, Alan Holmes, who ran the desk in New York, and Sherman Maisel, who was at that time a member of the Federal Reserve Board, were proclaiming that the Fed could not in fact control the money supply. Yet also, to show the conflicting currents within the system, Richard Davis, a member of the research staff at the New York Federal Reserve Bank, wrote in the course of a long piece dated 1969, 'The system is likely in the future to judge its behavior more on the basis of . . . monetary and bank credit growth rates than it has in the past and less on the basis of money market conditions.' He went on to say: 'It can be argued that the use of money market targets has in practice deprived the system of any effective means of controlling aggregates.'(11) So within the system in 1969, twelve years ago, people were recognizing the problem.

In 1970, the directive was changed again after Arthur Burns became chairman. Monetary growth was put first and money market conditions second. However, that change turned out to be pure lip service, and was later deemphasized.

In that same year (November 26, 1970), I repeated to Arthur Burns the recommendation I had made to Chairman Martin.(12) I also recommended that the Fed establish two committees of outside and inside people, one to study procedures for controlling the money supply, the other to study the measurement of the money supply. The first committee was never established; the second was appointed three years later (January 31, 1974) and turned in its report in early 1976. Some minor recommendations were adopted, and this committee provided part of the stimulus to the redefinitions of the monetary aggregates in 1980 and 1981. However, its two major recommendations have still not been adopted.(13) With respect to one of these, the treatment of seasonal, another committee was appointed, which has just recently turned in a report.(14)

In 1972, George Kaufman wrote: 'The Federal Reserve has increased its own difficulty in controlling the stock of money. Ironically, these actions have coincided with a tendency toward greater Federal Reserve emphasis on monetary aggregates as intermediate targets. However, to the extent the increased difficulty supports the long voiced contention of some Federal Reserve officials that they are unable to control the stock of money even if they so wished, the actions truly represent a self-fulfilling prophecy.'(15)

In 1975, Congress passed Concurrent Resolution 133, which expressed 'the sense of the Congress' that the Fed 'maintain long-run growth of the monetary and credit aggregates commensurate with the economy's long-run potential to increase production,' and provided that the Fed 'consult' Congress at regular intervals about its 'objectives and plans' for monetary growth and 'report to the Congress the reasons' for any subsequent departure from the objectives.(16)

At the time, I believed that this resolution was a major breakthrough, describing it as 'perhaps the most important change [in the structure of monetary policy] since the banking acts of the mid-1930s.' In justifying this judgment, I wrote: 'Though superficially innocuous [because it has no teeth], the resolution represents the first time since the Fed began operation in 1914 that the Congress has (1) specified monetary and credit aggregates as the Fed's immediate target, (2) enjoined it to produce steady monetary growth in line with output growth, (3) required it to state its objectives publicly in advance, and (4) required it to justify publicly any departure from them. All four elements are major changes. The Fed has shifted among alternative targets – monetary aggregates, interest rates, exchange rates; it has produced widely varying rates of monetary growth; it has never specified long-range numerical objectives and has decided its short-term objectives in camera, making them public long after the event; it has reported to Congress in vague terms that have resisted strict accountability.'(17)

In the event, my judgment proved wide of the mark. The Federal Reserve had strongly opposed the resolution and had tried to prevent its passage. When it was passed, it pledged cooperation, but then proceeded to undermine it so subtly and effectively that the resolution has proved to be a noteworthy minor step rather than the major breakthrough that I had mistakenly interpreted it as being. James Pierce, who served on the research staff of the Board of Governors for many years, made a more accurate assessment of the likely effect of the resolution in 1977 – two years after it was adopted – when he wrote: 'Whatever can be said for Congressional supervision of monetary policy, it has not produced closer control over the monetary aggregates and it has not lessened the Fed's penchant for stabilizing movements in short-term interest rates. It appears safe to conclude that increased Congressional oversight has not altered the conduct of monetary policy.'(18)

As Pierce explains, the Fed undermined the resolution in two ways. First, 'It appeared before the banking committees armed with growth rate ranges for five different measures of monetary and credit aggregates. With this menu of aggregates it was able to create confusion and to direct attention away from policy objectives and toward the technical question of who has the best M.'(19) Moreover, it could shift attention back and forth from one M to another, depending on which one put the Fed in the best light. In general, the various M's show similar movements but at times there have been sharp differences, primarily as a result of 'disintermediation' or 'reintermediation' produced by the varying impact of Regulation Q – a particular example of George Kaufman's 'self-fulfilling prophecy.'(20)

A second way in which the Fed undermined the resolution was by 'introducing a shifting base for its projections for the various M's'(21) – what has come to be known as base drift. It reported its targets each quarter (alternately to House and Senate committees) in terms of a range of rates of monetary growth (for example, 4 to 6 percent per year for the next year). The implication for the level of the money supply depends on the base figure to which these targets are applied. The Fed proceeded to apply them each quarter to the actual (not targeted) level of the prior quarter, thereby essentially burying any failures to achieve the target in the base. In effect, this meant that, in statistical terms, the money supply was a random walk, and the target rates of growth were essentially irrelevant, or, at most, applied to the next quarter rather than the next year.

It was repeatedly suggested to the Fed – by the Shadow Open Market Committee, members or staff of congressional committees, myself and other academic economists – that the targets be expressed in terms of the absolute level of the money supply with a constant band (of say 1 percent) around the targeted level. This change, which required no legislation, would have eliminated base drift. The Fed consistently expressed interest in such suggestions but equally consistent did not implement them. In 1978, the Humphrey-Hawkins Act reduced base drift by restricting changes in the base to once every half year instead of every quarter.

Finally on October 6, 1979, the Federal Reserve made a dramatic announcement of a change in procedure. Like all previous major moves by the Fed, this one too was a delayed reaction to external events or pressure, on this occasion, a collapse of the dollar abroad because of a lack of confidence in monetary policy and rising U.S. inflation. Chairman Volcker flew back from the meeting of the International Monetary Fund in Belgrade, where the foreign pressure came to a head, in order to issue the announcement. Despite that announcement of a change in operating procedures, the Fed reverted briefly to a straight Federal Funds target in the spring of 1980.

My final item is that the Fed in late 1980 deployed some of its ablest technicians to examine the operation of the new procedures. The result was a two-volume, 685-page study published in early 1981 containing an excruciatingly detailed analysis of the experience since October 6, 1979, plus an examination of earlier experience as a basis for judging the new procedures.(22) The two volumes contain some highly competent and relevant technical studies.

However, Stephen H. Axilrod's initial 'Overview of Findings and Evaluation' skims lightly over any negative conclusions about current procedures (see next section) and, instead, stresses that 'the variability in money growth of the past year appears to be related to an unusual combination of circumstances,' and that while 'a number of modifications to the operating procedures . . . might be considered . . . these modifications all have certain disadvantages.'(23)

In reporting the results to Congress, the Fed stated that 'the research suggests that the basic operating procedure represents a sound approach to attaining the longer-run objectives set for the monetary aggregates. However, the Federal Open Market Committee and the Board of Governors will be considering modifications', – a familiar tune to those of us whose professional work has imposed the dreary duty of reading the periodic reports of the Fed to the Congress over the years.(24) As has occurred repeatedly, there is a striking contrast between highly professional and competent staff studies, and the platitudinous and self-serving conclusions drawn from them by the Fed's leaders – not only for public consumption, but judged by the failure to implement the conclusions of such studies, as a guide to their own actions.

Nonetheless, the very massiveness of the two-volume apologia is significant. It testifies to the Fed's recognition that its prestige and credibility are at an all-time low and to its own uneasiness about its procedures.

3. *Lagged Reserve Requirements.* Member banks calculate required reserves for a reserve period (now one week for all banks, before 1968, two weeks for some) on the basis of average daily deposits during that period. Before 1968, reserves held to satisfy requirements were calculated for the same reserve period.(25) This system of contemporaneous reserve accounting was changed in 1968 so that reserves held to satisfy requirements for any week consisted of vault cash held during that week plus deposits at the Fed two weeks later. At the time, internal memos in the Fed, one of them prepared by George Kaufman whom I've already referred to and who at the time was employed by the Chicago Federal Reserve Bank, pointed out that lagged reserve accounting would make it more difficult to control the quantity of money. The measure was adopted nonetheless in the belief that it would be welcomed by small banks and might help to stop their departure from the system – a constant concern of the board.

From 1970 to 1972, Warren Coats did a doctoral study at the University of Chicago on the impact of lagged reserve accounting. That study documented decisively that the introduction of lagged reserve requirements had substantially increased the variability of almost anything of interest, roughly doubling the variability of free reserves, of the Federal Funds rate, of borrowing – you name it.(26)

In 1970, I wrote to Arthur Burns summarizing the initial findings of Coats. My letter was analyzed by Stephen Axilrod. I quote one sentence of a long reply: 'It may well be that the two-week lag has not produced the benefits that were attributed to it.' Most of the rest of the reply went on to minimize the importance of the issue – the precise stance that the system has adopted from then to now. One sentence from my reply to Arthur Burns in reaction to Axilrod's memorandum is equally applicable to most subsequent Fed memos that I have seen on the subject: 'Frankly, what bothered me about Steve's response was less its lack of rigor than its defensive tone, a tone which I have repeatedly encountered in Federal Reserve responses over many years.(27)

In 1975, I testified before the Senate Banking Committee on problems of monetary control. One of the items I referred to was lagged reserve accounting. Senator Proxmire asked the Federal Reserve Board for comment. The Federal Reserve Board sent one of its apologia in which it wrote that 'Lagged reserve accounting . . . would appear to have little, if any, adverse effect on monetary control if the Federal Funds rate is the day-to-day target. Even if reserve aggregates were given more emphasis as an operating target . . ., the lag in reserve accounts would present only a minor problem. It does appear to limit the precision of monetary control through reserves in the very short run, but a two-week lag poses no real impediment to monetary control over a more relevant longer period' – an exact echo of Chairman Martin's letter to me of 1969, and of Stephen Axilrod's memo of 1970.(28)

Nearly two years later, responding to a letter from Congressman Reuss, head of the House Banking and Currency Committee, urging the end of lagged reserve requirements, Arthur F. Burns wrote: 'None of the evaluative work done by the Board staff suggests that lagged reserve accounting seriously impedes the management of the monetary aggregates or contributes to disruptive money-market conditions' (July 20, 1977). That letter was followed, several months later, by a detailed, 23-page Fed memorandum (dated October 6, 1977) which reached 'essentially the same conclusions as in earlier reports.'

Reuss sent the Fed's memorandum to a number of outside experts other than myself to ask for their judgment. The four who replied were unanimous in rejecting the Fed's reply as a valid justification for lagged reserve accounting and in urging that lagged reserve accounting should be terminated.(29) On April 18, 1978, Reuss sent those results to G. William Miller, who had replaced Burns as chairman of the Fed. In that letter, Reuss also referred, as he had in previous letters to Burns, to four experts within the Federal Reserve System who had published articles critical of lagged reserve requirements. In congressional testimony on July 28, 1978, Miller said: 'In terms of operations, it would be preferable to be on a current basis' and that the system would consider restoring contemporary reserve accounting, 'once we can alleviate some of the membership problems.'

On April 3, 1980, Chairman Reuss wrote to Paul Volcker, who has replaced Miller as chairman of the Fed, repeating his earlier endorsement of three reforms: ending lagged reserve requirements, staggering closing dates, and tying the discount rate to a market rate. In making the letter public on April 9, Reuss noted: 'The Federal Reserve has said in the past that they have been unable to adopt these reforms because of the membership problem. With the passage of the Depository Institutions Deregulation and Monetary Control Act of 1980, there are no longer valid excuses for waiting.'

In June 1980, the system circulated a proposal to eliminate lagged reserve accounting. In its early 1981 Summary Report to Congress, it said, 'The Board has already indicated its inclination to switch from the present system of lagged reserve accounting to a system in which required reserves are posted essentially contemporaneously with deposits and will continue to study the technical feasibility of such a system' – this, thirteen years after the mistake was made, and almost as long after the measure was essentially unanimously recognized, inside and outside the Fed, as a hindrance to effective control of the quantity of money. Moreover, is it really necessary 'to study the technical feasibility of . . . a system' that was in operation for the first fifty-four years of the Fed's operating life? Have computers that seriously reduced the capacity of banks to keep track of deposits and reserves?

On January 1, 1981, the number of institutions reporting to the Fed weekly was nearly tripled under the new act.(30) Personally, I regard it as utterly inexcusable for the Federal Reserve to have delayed the elimination of lagged reserve accounting until after this major increase in the number of institutions subject to their requirements. How can it justify requiring all of those additional institutions to enter under one method of reporting and then a year later require them to change to another?(31)

The contrast between the technical staff papers in the February 1981 two-volume Fed study and the policy pronouncements of the Fed is particularly sharp with respect to lagged reserve requirements. The staff papers contain twelve references to lagged reserve accounting, and a fairly detailed examination of their quantitative effect on the stability of monetary multipliers. Without exception the statements are adverse to lagged reserve accounting by comparison with contemporary reserve accounting.(32) Yet that apparently has had no impact on the Fed's resolve to 'continue to study' the issue.

To avoid misunderstanding, let me emphasize that I do not regard the ending of lagged reserve accounting as the be-all and end-all of improvements in operating procedures. It would be possible for the Fed to control monetary growth more effectively than it has even with lagged reserve accounting. Other changes in procedures could produce an equal or larger improvement. Moreover, I agree with the Fed's conclusion that lagged reserve accounting has a more serious effect on the controllability of week-to-week or month-to-month monetary growth than of the longer-term growth which is basically more important.

I have nonetheless stressed lagged reserve requirements for two reasons. First, it is such a crystal clear case of a mistake made by the Fed which it has stubbornly refused to rectify under four different chairmen despite the weight of evidence, from inside and outside the system, on its adverse effects on monetary control. Second, short-term swings in monetary growth do no great harm if they are not only actually reversed but also *widely expected to be reversed.* But there's the rub. The wide short-term swings, partly due to lagged reserve accounting, have eroded the credibility of Federal Reserve policy statements and that credibility can only be restored by actions.

4. *Defensive Open Market Operations.* What is the problem here? In the year 1980, the Federal Reserve made gross open market purchases of securities of something over $800 billion, and gross transactions, including sales or maturities being rolled over, of more than double that amount. The net change in the portfolio was $4.5 billion. The open market desk therefore made $184 worth of purchases gross and roughly twice that amount of transactions (purchases plus sales) in order to add one dollar to its portfolio. Why all this churning? It accounts for something like one-quarter to one-half of all the transactions of U.S. government securities dealers other than the Fed itself. It generates millions of dollars of fees for the dealers involved. But what function does it have for monetary policy, and why has it occurred? It has occurred for only one reason: the mode of operations the Fed has adopted, including a reserve accounting period under which every bank in the United States settles on Wednesday.(33)

In 1964, Albert Cox and Ralph Leach proposed one partial solution to this problem.(34) They proposed lengthening the reserve period to a month and staggering settlements so that a quarter of the banks would settle each week. I proposed at the same time keeping the weekly settlement period but having a fifth of the banks settle each day, so a fifth of the banks would settle on

Monday, Tuesday, Wednesday, Thursday, Friday, and simultaneously calculating actual and required reserved on a per-working-day basis so that Friday would not, as now, count for three days. In 1966, both solutions were rejected by a Fed subcommittee. In the years since, economists and others have repeatedly proposed something along this line.

In 1978, Chairman Reuss proposed staggering the reserve accounting periods to Chairman Miller. It was rejected. On January 12, 1981, Representative St. Germain, the new chairman of the House Banking, Finance and Urban Affairs Committee, wrote to Anthony Solomon, president of the New York Federal Reserve Bank, referring to the 'huge amount of repurchase agreement transactions' and asking for information about them.(35) In my opinion, there is no reason for gross purchases to exceed the net change in the portfolio plus whatever purchases are necessary to replace maturing securities. As I shall spell out more fully below, I believe that this buying, selling, and churning serves no useful function. All it does is to muddy the waters, introduce uncertainty and speculation, and generate commissions for bond dealers and activity for people in the system.

3. EXPLANATION

The preceding pages have documented an extraordinary record of bureaucratic inertia, of mistakes that have not been corrected despite their widespread recognition. What is the explanation?

As I noted at the outset, I do not believe an answer can be found in terms of the particular personalities who have been in charge because the resistance to learning from experience has persisted for more than six decades. Moreover, similar bureaucratic inertia is present everywhere. Every large bureaucratic organization knows that the way it has been conducting things is the only way its task can be performed. That's true for private business. It's true for government. However, in general, bureaucratic inertia is subject to check by a bottom line. In private business, the check is provided by monetary losses. When losses occur, something has to be done. People get fired. In government, the check is much more limited, but at least so far as Congress is concerned, there is a bottom line, namely, getting elected. Hence Congress has to respond to voter disenchantment.

I believe that the fundamental explanation for the persistence and importance of bureaucratic inertia in the Federal Reserve System is the absence of a bottom line. The Fed is not subject to an effective budget constraint. It prints its own money to pay its expenses.(36) The Federal Reserve does not have to face the voters. The members of the board are appointed by the president. If appointed for a full fourteen-year term, they are not eligible for reappointment. If appointed to complete an unexpired term, they may be reappointed for a full term, and hence do face something of a bottom line.

Mark Toma has recently written an interesting paper directed at examining 'the role played by a particular factor – discretionary profits – in motivating the actions of Federal Reserve officials.'(37) His approach is along the lines that have been developed by economists such as James Buchanan, Gordon Tullock, William Niskanen, George Stigler, of analyzing bureaucratic behavior, not in terms of stated objectives, but in terms of the self-interest of the bureaucrats.(38) He takes Anna Schwartz's and my analysis of monetary policy as exemplifying the straw man that he is attacking. His criticism is largely justified. In the analysis of monetary policy in our book, we paid only passing attention to the self-interest of the people conducting monetary policy. More recently, we have all become familiar with the idea of applying to governmental performance the same approach that we apply to private business enterprises. The social function of business or government is one thing; the forces that control behavior may be very different.

Toma examines what he describes as 'revisions in the country's "monetary constitution" ' in the mid-1930s and 1947. His approach is, I believe, even more directly applicable to the kind of issues that I have been discussing. For example, why is it that over its whole history, the Federal Reserve has been so much concerned with retaining members? As noted, that concern was the reason for introducing lagged reserve accounting.

Monetary theorists have demonstrated that the conduct of monetary policy does not require that the Federal Reserve System have any member banks. I have argued frequently that it would be desirable to separate the regulatory and monetary control activities of the Fed. The latter requires simply that the monetary authority have a monopoly on the printing press or its equivalent to control the total amount of high-powered or base money. Control over the base exerts about as much influence on nonmember commercial banks as on member banks, on thrift institutions as on commercial banks, and so on in unending circle.

The Federal Reserve's concern with membership, though it always cites monetary control grounds, cannot be explained on those grounds. It derives rather from the prestige, sense of importance, power, and effective lobby that the system gains by supervising many thousands of banks and other financial institutions – 5,422 member banks before January 1, 1981; more than 22,000 institutions subject to Federal Reserve requirements since then.

Member bank support of the Fed's actions has played a major role in giving the Fed influence on Congress.(39)

Why the enormous resistance of the Fed to moving to monetary aggregates? Fundamentally, I believe, because monetary aggregates permit far more effective monitoring of performance and accountability for achieving targets than money market conditions.

Who of us wants to be held responsible for our mistakes? It's not very nice to have a bottom line. If we don't have a bottom line, why should we introduce one?

The annual or more frequent statements by chairmen of the Federal Reserve to congressional committees have a common script. If things have gone well in the economy, the Fed takes full credit and the chairman explains that it was all due to the wise policies followed by the Fed. If things have gone badly in the economy, the chairman explains that the reason was the limited powers of the Fed to offset external disturbances that were beyond the Fed's control. He then assures the committee that the Fed will now be able to correct any of its own past deviations for desirable policy, and that next year, all will be well – subject of course to unpredictable external events. The statements of general principles and desirable policies are always excellent – both wise and theoretically sound. The explanation of defects in past performance is always ad hoc and exculpates the Fed.

Why the opposition to staggering settlement dates or to other devices for reducing gross market transactions? Because the churning gives people who are involved in it a sense of importance, makes them involved in big deals. Why even, to get down to picayune details, the resistance to the prompt issuance of open market directives? I and others have argued over the years that the open market directives ought to be issued promptly after it is reached, and not much later – it used to be postponed for six months, then three months, now one month.

Why? Because stressing that these directives are so enormously important that immediate knowledge about them would give speculators an opportunity to make a killing, gives the board a sense of importance. Secondarily, it offers very good jobs to ex-officials who are hired by firms in Wall Street because they are believed able to read the tea leaves and figure out what the Fed is really doing.

To avoid misunderstanding, let me emphasize that I am not saying that people in the system deliberately pursue these measures for these reasons. Not at all. As economists, we treat a business enterprise as if it were solving a large number of complex simultaneous equations even though the person running that business enterprise never went to school and learned mathematics. We justify that procedure by saying that if we analyze them as if they are rationally and knowingly pursuing the maximization of profit, we'll get a good approximation of their behavior. In the same way, I am trying to analyze the forces at work, and not to describe the detailed motivation or personal behavior of the people involved. All of us know that what's good for us is good for the country. We all know that what we are doing is important, that it performs a real and useful function. How can a person be in a position of buying and selling billions of dollars of securities every day, subject to pressure and influence from important people – and resisting that pressure – and yet believe that it is 'full of sound and fury, signifying nothing'? So I am not criticizing specific individuals, I have often argued that the human species is distinguished from animals much more by its ability to rationalize than by its ability to reason.

Finally, to suggest the importance of what I've been saying, consider the effect of adopting the following policy – one that is not ideal, but could be put into effect within a few weeks or months if the Fed decided to do so, and, in my opinion, would produce a stabler monetary environment that would enable inflation to be eliminated with relatively little interim adverse effect on output and employment.

1. Replace lagged reserve accounting with contemporary reserve accounting
2. Make the discount rate a penalty, and tie it to a market rate so it automatically moves
3. Eliminate any attempt to introduce a seasonal into the money supply. One of the greatest sources of obfuscation has been the talk about seasonally adjusted money supply. There is no seasonal in the money supply except what the Fed permits
4. Set a target path of several years ahead of a single aggregate – for example, M2 or the base. It is less important which aggregate is chosen than that a single aggregate be designated as the target
5. Make reserve requirements uniform for all components of that aggregate
6. Estimate the change over an extended period, say three or six months, in the Fed's holdings of securities that would be necessary to approximate the target path over that period. Divide that estimate by 13 or 26. Let the Fed purchase precisely that amount every week in addition to the amount needed to replace maturing securities
7. Eliminate all repurchase agreements and similar short-term transactions
8. Finally, announce in advance and in full detail the proposed schedule of purchases and stick to it.

Such a policy would assure control over the monetary aggregates – not from day to day but over the longer period the Fed now insists is all that matters. It would remove uncertainty about Fed policy and establish credibility for that policy. It would leave to the market the day-to-day and seasonal adjustments that the market is well qualified to handle – and could do so far more effectively if it knew precisely what the Federal Reserve intended to do, than in the present state of uncertainty, with the weekly guessing game about Fed intentions that follows each Friday's release of the figures on money supply.

But it would have other effects as well. The open market desk could be replaced by the part-time activity of one employee to make the designated purchases. He would be buying roughly $100 million a week, not as now $184 hundred million or more than $18 billion. The Federal Open Market Committee could meet once every three or six months instead of monthly. The research staff at the Federal Reserve and at the twelve banks could be cut drastically. A large fraction of those research staffs – for the most part highly trained and competent economists – have as their main function preparing their presidents for the monthly open market meetings.

The Federal Reserve governors, who now devote 90 percent of their time, not to monetary control, but to their regulatory functions, could spend 99 percent of their time on such regulatory functions. They would do far less harm that way than the harm which they have been doing with the additional 9 percent they now spend on monetary control.

Again, I am not criticizing individuals. You or I would react in the same way if we were in their position. That's why, unfortunately, this policy, however desirable it might be in the abstract, is not likely to be adopted, if left to the discretion of the Fed.

There is, I believe, only one realistic alternative. That is somehow to establish a bottom line. One such policy proposed by the Shadow Open Market Committee that would do so is to require by law that the Federal Reserve Governors submit their resignations at the end of the year in which the growth of a specified monetary aggregate has departed from the advance target by more than a designated amount. Unfortunately, I do not really think that's feasible. The only two alternatives that do seem to me feasible over the longer run are either to make the Federal Reserve a bureau in the Treasury under the secretary of the Treasury, or to put the Federal Reserve under direct congressional control. Either involves terminating the so-called independence of the system.(40) But either would establish a strong incentive for the Fed to produce a stabler monetary environment than we have had.

A simple version of congressional control would involve a congressional directive to the Fed to adopt and implement the eight-point policy outlined above. That policy incorporates principles that are widely accepted and too which the Fed itself pays lip service. It is practicable and achievable within a matter of months. Its adoption would terminate promptly and credibly a policy course that has reduced the Fed's prestige and credibility in the financial markets of the world to an all-time low.

NOTES

1. 'Marshall's Economics, The Man and His Times,' *American Economic Review*, 31 (June 1941): 224.
2. 'Rules versus Authorities in Monetary Policy,' *Journal of Political Economy*, 44, (1936): 1-30, reprinted in Henry C. Simons, *Economic Policy for a Free Society*, (Chicago 1948), pp. 160-83.
3. See Robert E. Weintraub, 'Congressional Supervision of Monetary Policy,' *Journal of Monetary Economics* 4 (April 1978): 341-62.
4. *A Monetary History of the United States, 1867 to 1960*, National Bureau of Economic Research Studies in Business Cycles, no. 12 (Princeton: Princeton University Press, 1963), p. 629.
5. *An Enquiry into the Nature and Effects of the Paper Credit of Great Britain* (1802), ed. by F. A. v. Hayek (Augustus M. Kelley, 1965), pp. 86-87, 244, 252-53.
6. The Federal Reserve Bank of Boston, 1969.
7. For a discussion of this episode and full references to the relevant congressional hearings, see Friedman and Schwartz, *A Monetary History of the United States, pp. 595, 621-27. See also George S. Tavlas, 'The Chicago Tradition Revisited: Some Neglected Monetary Contributions, Senator Paul Douglas (1892-1976),' Journal of Money, Credit, and Banking* 9 (November 1977): 529-35.
8. Prior and subsequent to this time, outside persons were invited to meet with the members of the board in Washington from time to time. I attended many such meetings of so-called academic consultants. They were interesting experiences, no doubt instructive to the many Federal Reserve personnel who sat around the sides of the boardroom, where the meeting was invariably held, without participating. However, I finally concluded that the meetings were called purely for window-dressing purposes. I was unable to detect any influence whatsoever exerted by the consultants' comments on the system's action. Indeed, the choice of the particular consultants invited to attend seemed designed to guarantee offsetting and contradictory advice, leaving the Fed free to pursue its own devices. However, even on those rare occasions when something approaching a consensus emerged, I could detect no subsequent effect on policy.
9. The letter went on to say: 'This experiment could be conducted entirely by the Fed. However, if for any reason you would prefer it to be a cooperative effort with academic scholars, I would be very pleased to have our Workshop in Money and Banking at the University of Chicago cosponsor the experiment and share its cost. It would fit very well indeed into our program of research.' Letter from Milton Friedman to William McChesney Martin, January 29, 1969.
10. Letter from William McChesney Martin to Milton Friedman, April 7, 1969.

11. 'Short Run Targets for Open Market Operations,' unpublished paper dated December 1969.
12. Chairman Burns adopted a different tactic than Chairman Martin, replying 'There is merit in his [Steve Axilrod's] suggestion that a study of the operational uses of reserve aggregates be undertaken in your money and banking workshop with whatever help he and other of the Board can render to make the project realistic.' (Letter from Arthur F. Burns to Milton Friedman, January 18, 1971.)

    I replied that I had decided that a project by our workshop alone was not desirable. 'The problem is to develop workable operating procedures, not to study basic monetary relations. That fits neither our academic function nor our research competence. It is a job for the Fed not for us.' (Milton Friedman to Arthur F. Burns, March 15, 1971.)
13. *Improving the Monetary Aggregates: Report of the Advisory Committee on Monetary Statistics*, by George L. Bach, Chairman (Washington, D.C.: Board of Governors of the Federal Reserve System, June 1976).
14. The other, a revised method of consolidating data from different financial institutions, was never implemented, presumably because it would have reduced reported M1 by a large sum, and the Fed's research staff never succeeded in explaining the source of the discrepancy between the proposed method and the method currently in use.
15. The actions stressed by Kaufman as increasing the difficulty in controlling the stock of money included: '1. Encouraging proliferation in the number of deposit categories subject to different reserve requirements, 2. . . . [and] different interest rate ceilings, and 3. Unintentionally promoting a proliferation in the number of on deposit categories excluded from the definition of money supply.' In a footnote, he added 'the introduction of lagged reserve requirements,' George G. Kaufman, 'Federal Reserve Inability to Control the Money Supply: A Self-Fulfilling Prophecy,' *Financial Analysts Journal* 28 (September-October 1972): 22, 57, 58.
16. Quoted from the text of the resolution. The substance of the resolution was later incorporated in the Federal Reserve Act in the form of an amendment to the act passed in late 1977. (See Weintraub, 'Congressional Supervision of Monetary Policy,' p. 344.)
17. Milton Friedman, 'Congress and the Federal Reserve,' *Newsweek*, June 2, 1975.
18. James L. Pierce, 'The Myth of Congressional Supervision of Monetary Policy,' *Journal of Monetary Economics* 4 (1978): 363-70; quotation from p. 369.
19. Ibid., p. 364. For the Fed's opposition, see Arthur F. Burns, testimony to Congress, February 25, 1975, *Federal Reserve Bulletin*, May 1975, pp. 280-88.
20. In recent years, but only in recent years the Fed has favored eliminating the ceilings, at least for time and savings deposits. So have many commercial banks.
21. Pierce, 'The Myth of Congressional Supervision of Monetary Policy,' p. 364.
22. *New Monetary Control Procedures*, Federal Reserve Staff Study, Board of Governors of the Federal Reserve System, February, 1981.
23. Ibid., pp. A6, A24.
24. Quoted from *Monetary Policy Objectives from 1981*, Summary Report of the Federal Reserve Board, p. 15.
25. Because deposits and vault cash were calculated on a beginning of day basis, but reserves at the Fed on an end of day basis, there was, to be precise, a one-day lag instead of the present two-week lag.
26. Warren L. Coats, 'The September, 1968, Changes in "Regulation D" and Their Implications for Money Stock Control,' Ph.D. dissertation, University of Chicago, 1972.
27. Letter of Milton Friedman to Arthur F. Burns, October 13, 1970.

The rest of the paragraph from my letter which began with the sentence quoted in the text is equally applicable to most late responses: 'Of course, there were good and what seemed like sufficient reasons for going to lagged reserves. Of course, any possible change is going to have adverse as well as favorable effects that must be weighed against one another. But it is equally true that the ablest and best intentioned of men can make mistakes and that the most important task is not to defend and rationalize what has been done, but to explore open-mindedly ways of improving the existing system of operation.'

28. Yet at about the same time, an economist in the Division of Research and Statistics, Board of Governors, Federal Reserve System, wrote a comment pointing out the adverse effects of lagged reserve accounting compared with contemporaneous accounting: Daniel E. Laufenberg, 'Contemporaneous vs. Lagged Reserve Accounting,' *Journal of Money, Credit, and Banking* 8 (May 1976): 239-45.
29. The four were: Edgar L. Feige, with collaboration of Robert T. McGee; William Poole; Warren L. Coats, Jr.; and George G. Kaufman.
30. On December 31, 1980, 5,422 banks were members of the Federal Reserve System and required to report. On July 1, 1981, the number of institutions reporting weekly numbered 14,169. An additional 8.544 reported to the Fed quarterly.
31. The numbers in the preceding footnote overstate the size of this problem, since many small institutions satisfy reserve requirements wholly by vault cash, which is now on a contemporaneous basis.
32. For example, 'Ignoring the short-term problem created by lagged reserve accounting,' Richard G. Davis, p. 33.

    In re a penalty or a tied discount rate, a 'system of this type would not be possible under the existing system of lagged reserve accounting' and 'under a contemporaneous reserve accounting system, tying of the discount rate to the current level of the federal funds rate would create less of a problem,' Peter Keir, pp. 43, 47.

    All references are to *New Monetary Control Procedures*.
33. The effect of same-day settlement on so-called 'defensive open market operations' was greatest when the Fed was using the federal funds rate as its day-to-day target. It has far less effect on 'churning' under current procedures. However, it still has a very important effect on the variability of the federal funds rate, and therefore, indirectly, on the variability of other short-term interest rates.
34. Albert H. Cox, Jr., and Ralph F. Leach, 'Defensive Open Market Operations and the Reserve Settlement Periods of Member Banks,' *Journal of Finance* 19 (March 1964): 76-93. The same proposal has been repeated and urged in *Morgan Guaranty Survey* (July 1981): 7-10, but without reference to the Cox-Leach article.
35. Letter from Fernand J. St. Germain to Anthony M. Solomon, June 12, 1981.
36. Its recorded income is a large multiple of its expenses. However, that is a pure bookkeeping operation. Since the Fed is essentially a branch of the government, the bonds it holds are obligations of one government agency to another. The economic essence of the situation is that the Fed prints the money (or makes equivalent bookkeeping entries) to pay itself the interest, part of which it uses to pay its expenses, part of which it turns over to the Treasury, that is, in effect cancels.
37. 'Inflationary Bias of the Federal Reserve System: A Bureaucratic Perspective,' chapter 3 in this volume.
38. After the lecture was delivered, I learned that this approach has been applied to the Bank of Canada in a sophisticated and persuasive fashion by Keith Acheson and John F. Chant in three articles published in 1972 and 1973: 'The Choice of Monetary Instruments and the

Theory of Bureaucracy,' chapter 6 in this volume; 'Mythology and Central Banking,' *Kyklos* 2 (1973): 362-79; and 'Bureaucratic Theory and the Choice of Central Bank Goals,' chapter 7 in this volume.

39. In return, the member banks have received many and varied benefits.
40. See Milton Friedman, 'Should There Be An Independent Monetary Authority?' in Leland B. Yeager, ed., *In Search of a Monetary Constitution* (Cambridge: Harvard University Press, 1962), pp. 219-43.

Chapter 3

INFLATIONARY BIAS OF THE FEDERAL RESERVE SYSTEM
A Bureaucratic Perspective

Mark Toma

1. INTRODUCTION

The creation of the Federal Reserve System coincides with a turning point in the inflationary history of the United States. Before 1914 there was no overall trend in the price level. Generally, during war time periods the consumer price index increased significantly, but during the intervening periods prices gradually declined to appṙoximately their former levels. However, since the creation of the Fed, there has been an unmistakable, and almost continuous, upward trend in prices.(1)

While there appears to be a growing recognition, both academically and publicly, that the Federal Reserve System's open market operations are related to this phenomena, the explanation for the Fed's behavior is less clear. Any such explanation requires an examination of the incentives confronting Federal Reserve officials in their decision-making capacity. To the extent this incentive structure has been investigated in the past, analysts generally have focused on the influence of individuals, or groups, outside the Fed. Special interest groups, that differentially benefit from an expansionary monetary policy, are depicted as using the political process to place pressure on the Fed to increase the money supply.(2) Surprisingly, this demand side approach, which I label the political pressure approach, has not been complemented by an explicit supply side theory. Instead, studies often have assumed, at least implicitly, that monetary policy is formulated according to Reserve officials' perception of what will prove beneficial for the

Toma, E.F. and Toma, M. (eds.) Central Bankers, Bureaucratic Incentives, and Monetary Policy

ISBN 90 247 3366 9

general public.(3) Taken together these approaches construe monetary policy as an outcome of a struggle between interest groups pursuing special benefits and Federal Reserve officials searching for the 'public interest'.

This paper attempts to go beyond the robot-like caricature of Federal Reserve officials. By relaxing the passive bureaucrat assumption, an explicit supply side theory of Federal Reserve official behavior will be developed. This analysis will be based upon a literature that has developed over the last decade as economists have started to apply microeconomic tools to the operation of government bureaucracies. Most of this work on the economics of bureaucracy characterizes bureaus as non-profit monopoly firms whose members are utility maximizers.(4) Even though the Federal Reserve System largely has been overlooked in this literature, it would seem to be an interesting subject of analysis, since there are several institutional features unique to the Fed as a bureau. The feature of particular interest in this paper is the fact that the Fed presently does not receive a budget from Congress. Instead, the Fed may keep, as 'earnings', interest payments on the portfolio of federal securities it acquires through open market operations.

The next section will describe the evolution of the Fed's financing structure over time. Then, using this description as a foundation, I shall attempt to establish theoretical links between the utility-maximizing behavior of Federal Reserve officials, the Fed's budget (revenue), and the rate of inflation. The implications derived from this bureaucratic model will be contrasted with the implications following from the traditional (passive-bureaucrat) model. In the final section of the paper, these implications will be used as a basis for testing the two theories.

2. EVOLUTION OF THE FED'S BUDGETARY PROCESS

Historically, the dominant form of Federal Reserve funding has not been through the regular appropriation process. This method was used only before 1933, and then, exclusively to finance the expenses of the Federal Reserve Board. In these early days, the individual Reserve Banks had to rely on income from their assets. Since 1933, the entire System's operation has been funded in this latter way; revenue is acquired primarily through interest payments on government security holdings. In describing the different stages in the evolution of the Fed's revenue scheme, three different subperiods will be delineated: (1) 1914-1933, (2) 1933-1947, and (3) 1947 to the present.

The Federal Reserve Act of 1914 states that the Federal Reserve Banks first were to use earnings for paying their expenses and for paying dividends to member banks. Then half of their yearly net earnings were to be paid to the United States government in the form of a franchise tax, and the other half could be retained by the System as long as its surplus was less than 40 percent of paid-in capital.(5) Any funds turned over to the government 'shall, in the discretion of the Secretary, be used to supplement the gold reserve held against outstanding United States notes, or shall be applied to the reduction of the outstanding bond indebtedness of the United States under regulations to be prescribed by the Secretary of the Treasury' (Federal Reserve Act, Section 7).

The first significant transformation in the method of financing took place in 1933. While called upon to provide a one-time grant for the creation of the Federal Deposit Insurance Corporation, the Fed was more than compensated by repeal of the franchise tax. Legally, all earnings now could be spent or retained by the Fed. This change in the distribution of revenue was accompanied by related changes in the System's revenue-raising process. Federal Reserve open market operations became more important as a source of earnings and also more centralized in nature. Originally, buying and selling of securities could be undertaken only at the initiative of the individual Reserve Banks. But, as early as 1915, the New York Federal Reserve Bank began taking and executing the transactions of several Banks at one time to avoid competition between them. Later, Reserve Banks were required to notify the New York Bank any time they wanted to conduct open market operations independently. Complete centralization of open market transactions was achieved with the Banking Act of 1935. This act created a new committee, the Federal Open Market Committee (FOMC), which had absolute open market powers. With this measure, decision-making power was taken out of the hands of one of the Reserve Banks and placed under the authority of a political organization based in Washington, D.C. The individual Reserve Banks now possessed no means of influencing the government securities market, except through their minority representation on the FOMC. This final step in the centralization process occurred at a time when interest earnings from the System's bond portfolio comprised the major share of earnings.(6)

World War II provided the Fed with the opportunity of making considerable open market purchases, thereby expanding its revenue. Although operating expenses more than doubled from 1940 to 1947, they did not keep up with the almost four-fold rise in earnings. These 'excess' earnings sparked congressional interest which the Fed feared might be expressed in the form of a legislative measure, mandating a particular disposition of excess earnings. This fear, at least partially, accounted for the Fed's 'voluntary' transfer of a portion of its revenue to the Treasury in 1947.

The Federal Reserve Act contained no section or amendment which directly provided for such a transfer from the Fed to the Treasury. However, the System interpreted an obscure clause (fourth paragraph of Section 16) in the original act as providing them with this authority. This clause allowed an interest payment to be levied on outstanding Federal Reserve notes, not backed by gold certificates. Although the Fed's interpretation of the clause was questioned,(7) the fact that no one challenged it in the courts was significant. In the absence of a successful challenge, the Fed's interpretation effectively served to redefine the monetary constitution. It was as if the Federal Reserve Act for the first time contained a clause which specifically authorized the transfer of funds to the government at the Fed's initiative.

During 1947, $75 million out of $159 million in current earnings were transferred to the Treasury. Similar transfers have continued annually throughout the fifties and sixties and up to the present. Whereas this payment was required by law in the early days of the Fed's existence, in 1947, as well as today, these annual transfer payments are initiated by the Fed. Currently, out of yearly earnings in the neighborhood of $10 billion, approximately $9 billion are returned to the Treasury.

To summarize, this survey indicates that the revenue setting has characterized the financial structure of the Fed throughout its existence. Furthermore, this particular financing structure was found to have evolved through several distinct stages. The (two) demarcation lines between the stages corresponded to periods when the nation's monetary constitution was undergoing revision. In the first case (mid-1930's), the FOMC was created and the Federal Reserve Act was amended to allow the Fed to retain all revenue. Then later, in 1947, a second constitutional change enabled the Fed, at its own discretion, to begin redistributing a portion of its earnings to the Treasury.

3. CENTRAL BANK AS A BUREAU

Given the peculiar nature of the Federal Reserve System's funding structure, this section provides a framework for assessing its impact. Specifically, a theoretical model of Fed production will be developed in order to compare the output and spending consequences under a conventional appropriation structure versus the revenue structure. Several assumptions will be employed throughout this investigation: (1) The Fed's output is the monetary base (high-powered money), which equals reserves plus currency outside the banking system. Taxpayers value the Fed's operation according to the degree of price stability (or instability) associated with the base rate . . . of growth (B), (2) The inflation rate (P) equals B and the general public accurately anticipates the rate of inflation, (3) Federal Reserve officials strive to maximize discretionary profits or, more informally, shirking, (4) The Fed's sponsor (Congress) passively reflects the desires of taxpayers who are alike with respect to the net benefits they derive from the Fed's operation, and (5) Congress does not monitor the activities of the Fed.

Assumption (1) implies that taxpayers ultimately hold the Fed responsible for the degree of price stability prevailing in the economy because of its role in the creation of high-powered money.(8) This assumption represents a simplification of reality, in the sense that there are many other services and goods besides price stability (or more directly, monetary base) that the system can, and does, provide.(9) Price stability is isolated in an effort to demonstrate how pursuit of this goal influences the Fed's operation. The analysis built upon this assumption illustrates the central tendency of Federal Reserve officials' behavior only to the extent that the public perceives price stability as the major good being provided by the Fed.

The purpose of assumption (2) is to make the relationship between the Fed's open market operations and inflation as simple as possible. In order for B to equal P at any point in time, inflation must be proceeding at a constant rate and real income, velocity and the money multiplier must not change over time. The analysis ignores the transition stage from one inflation rate to another, by assuming that such adjustments are instantaneous.

With assumption (3), I assume that bureaucrats attempt to maximize the difference between the budget (or revenue) and the least cost of operation. This difference, called discretionary profits, may be used by bureaucrats through a wide range of activities including perquisites of office, shirking and larger salaries and staff. Of course, bureaucrats may have other arguments in their utility functions, not related to discretionary profits. Federal Reserve officials, for instance, may obtain a certain degree of satisfaction from knowing their policies have contributed to the well-being of others in the economy. The discretionary profit assumption is offered in an effort to isolate the impact of this type of maximizing activity on the Fed's operations. Ultimately, the fruitfulness of this approach depends on whether it provides insight into real world monetary policy decisions.

Traditionally, bureaucratic sponsors have been legislative committees within Congress. Because of the focus on the operation of the Federal Reserve System as a bureau, I make the simplest assumption [(4) and (5)] concerning the role of the sponsor. The extreme assumption of zero monitoring implies that the sponsor obtains no information on the Fed's cost of operation. Under these circumstances, bargaining between the Fed and its sponsor will result in a budgetary outcome most preferred by bureaucrats. Individual taxpayers will find that expenditures of the agency have been increased to the point where the net benefits they obtain from the existence of the present Fed management approach zero. In the last part of this section, I relax assumption (5) and consider the consequences of monitoring activities which may be initiated by members of Congress or some other entity.

3.1. Budget Setting

In the budget setting, the Fed must periodically approach Congress for a budget since, by assumption, no payments are made by the Treasury on any government securities in the Fed's portfolio. A Federal Reserve purchase of securities simply erases the interest obligations with respect to those securities. As with any bureau, the constraints imposed on the Fed's operation depend on the costs and benefits (to the general public) of its actions. To derive the benefits, first consider fig. 1a which depicts the total amount of real money balances demanded as a function of the nominal rate of interest. From an individual's perspective, the nominal interest rate, which equals the real interest rate (r_0) plus the (anticipated) inflation rate ($\dot{P}$), represents the cost of holding real balances. With an inflation rate of $\dot{P}_2$, no one demands money balances and the total benefits from money holdings are zero. Lower rates of inflation increase the amount of real balances demanded along with the public's total benefits. Price stability ($\dot{P}_0$), for instance, causes the public to demand $(M/P)_0$ of real money balances; in this case, the public obtains benefits from money provision equal to the area under the demand curve up to $(M/P)_0$.[10] Notice that total benefits are maximized when the nominal rate of interest approaches zero [Friedman (1969)]. In fig. 1a a deflation rate of P_3 generates benefits equal to triangle ade.

Generally, the Fed will not confront the total demand curve abe. The Fed's demand function would be this total curve only if there were no conceivable alternative(s) to money supply management by the present set of Federal Reserve officials. As Niskanen (1975, pp. 620-621) indicates, 'if there is any effective competition from other sources of supply or from another management team . . . the demand function facing a bureau will be both lower and more elastic than the total demand curve for the service'.

Consider the simplest case where Congress has access to an alternative source at zero cost. If Congress judges that this source would produce an inflation rate equal to $\dot{P}_1$, then the present management team need not fear replacement as long as their open market operations result in an inflation of $\dot{P}_1$ or less. Over this range the present Federal Reserve bureau confronts the total demand curve for real money balances. Once this bureau contemplates increasing the inflation rate incrementally beyond $\dot{P}_1$, however, Congress will threaten to turn to the alternative source; inflation rates higher than $\dot{P}_1$ will not be viable option to the Fed.(11) Under these circumstances, the Fed's demand curve will be only the portion eb in fig. la, and hence, the public's benefits from that particular bureau's operation will be different than if abe had been the relevant demand curve.

The relationship between the total benefits and the Fed's creation of monetary base is shown directly in fig. 1b. Because of the assumption that $\dot{B} = \dot{P}$, a rightward movement along the horizontal axis corresponds to a vertical movement along the nominal interest rate axis in fig. 1a. When the Fed confronts the total demand curve abe, the negatively sloped TB_0 curve indicates the public's total benefits from the Fed's operation. Notice how the availability of an alternative source alters the benefit function. Suppose as suggested above, this alternative promises an inflation rate of $\dot{P}1$, and thus, benefits equal to the area of the trapezoid abcd. Then, at best, the benefits which could be obtained from the present Fed's existence (over and above the benefits from the alternative) would be equal to the area of triangle bce. In fig. lb this maximum amount is shown by the distance fg and the resulting total benefit curve under these circumstances is TB1.

On the cost side of the ledger, the TC curve in fig. 1b indicates the least cost of the Fed's operation.(12) Because the Fed creates additional high-powered money simply by writing a check on itself, the cost function has zero slope. The height of this curve depends on the amount, and price, of inputs (e.g., staff, telephone, ink) required to conduct any level of open market bond acquisitions.

To derive the bureaucratic solution in this setting, consider the general case where the present management team must compete with other (potential) suppliers, and a curve like TB_1 indicates the total benefits to the public. Because this section assumes that the sponsor devotes no resources to monitoring, the Fed will be able to increase its budget subject only to the condition that its existence does not make taxpayers worse off. In this case, points on the TB_1 curve indicate the maximum budget the Fed can succeed in obtaining at any output level. Bureaucratic profits will be equal to the vertical distance between the TB_1 and TC curves.

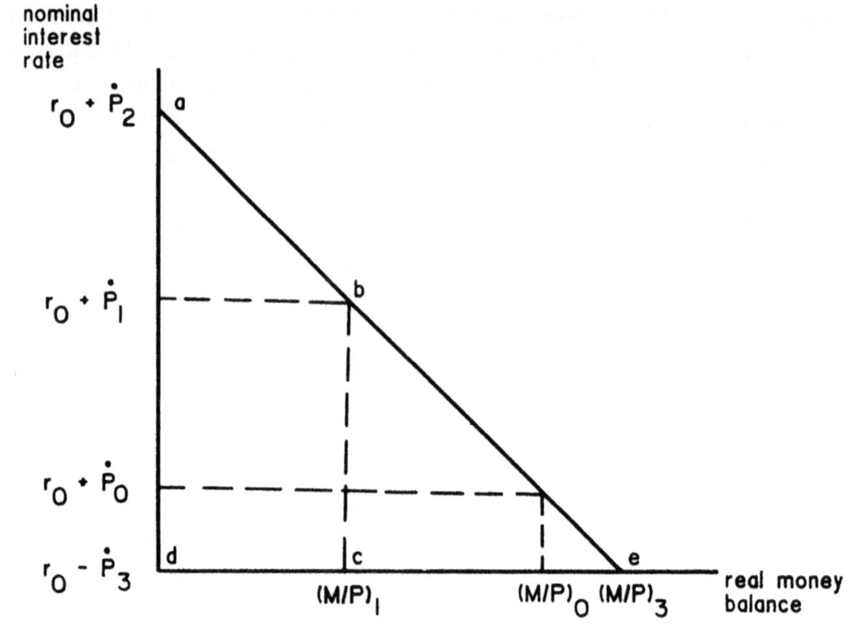
nominal interest rate
$r_0 + \dot{P}_2$
a
$r_0 + \dot{P}_1$
b
$r_0 + \dot{P}_0$
$r_0 - \dot{P}_3$
d
c
e
$(M/P)_1$
$(M/P)_0$
$(M/P)_3$
real money balance

Fig. 1a

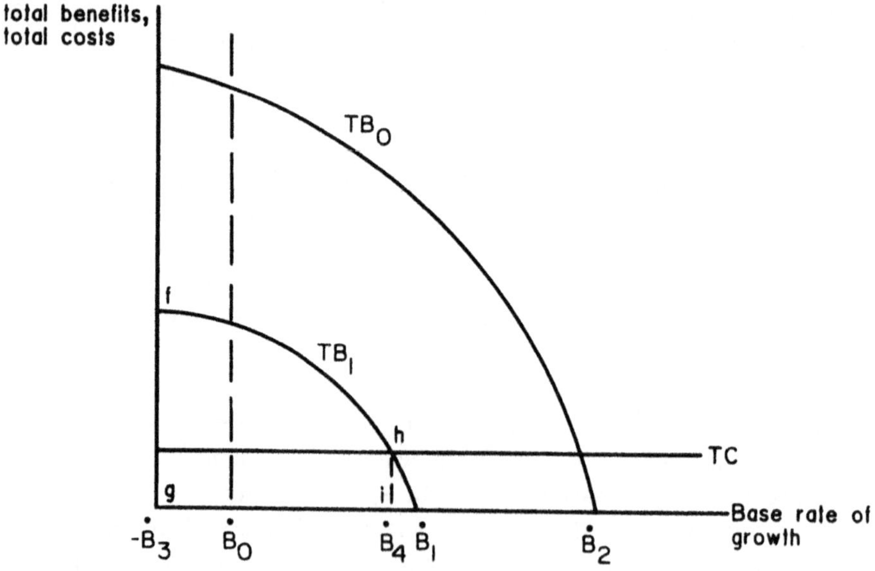
total benefits, total costs
TB_0
f
TB_1
h
TC
g
i
$-\dot{B}_3$
$\dot{B}_0$
$\dot{B}_4$
$\dot{B}_1$
$\dot{B}_2$
Base rate of growth

Fig. 1b

No special significance attaches to the point where the TB_1 curve intersects the TC curve. At point h the Fed has pursued an inflationary policy to the point where taxpayer benefits are no larger than the least cost of the Fed's operation. Clearly, trading an output of B_4 for a budget of ih dollars is not in the interest of a shirking maximizing bureau, since nothing is left over for discretionary spending. The Fed will have an incentive to reduce the rate of base growth below B_4. Discretionary profits are maximized with a rate of $(-B^3)$ and budget of fg dollars. Taxpayers find themselves no better off with this deflationary outcome than they would have been at position h.

In all important respects this solution corresponds to the conventional appropriation outcome in bureaucracy theory. According to this literature, a shirking monopolist will be motivated to provide the optimal output since at this point (potential) taxpayer surplus will be at a maximum. Bureaucrats will be able to extract this surplus through their ability to bargain for larger budgets. In confronting basically the same reward structure, the central bank of this section also provides the optimal output, $(-B^3)$. As with the conventional approach, net taxpayer benefits are eroded as Federal Reserve bureaucrats bargain for a budget which allows them to maximize utility through engaging in activities that raise the cost of production.

3.2 Revenue Setting

The method of financing bureaucratic activity constitutes the primary difference between the setting of this subsection and the previous one. Instead of obtaining an appropriation from Congress, the Fed keeps as 'earnings' the interest on government securities it acquires through open market operations. Under these circumstances, the Fed does not have to give up the claim to resources represented by a security purchase; any time Federal Reserve officials create high-powered money simply by writing a check on themselves, wealth is transferred from the general public to the Fed.

If the base equals the money supply, then the real wealth transfer would equal the inflation rate times the amount of real balances held.(13) In fig. 2a, this inflation tax equals the area of the slanted line rectangle, given an inflation rate of $\dot{P}_1$. Generally, however, one dollar of Fed-created money generates more than one dollar in the total money supply. The relationship between the real base B/P and real money balances M/P is given by

$$B/P = (1/m)(M/P),$$

where m is the money multiplier. When m is greater than one, the Fed does not capture all of the inflation tax. For instance, if m equals two, then with an inflation rate of $\dot{P}_1$, the Fed's revenue equals one half of the rectangle in fig. 2a.

Given a particular money multiplier magnitude, the relationship between the public's wealth loss and different output levels can be derived. Such a relationship is depicted by the wealth transfer curve, WT, in fig. 2b. When the base rate of growth equals zero or $\dot{B}_2$ (the inflation rate equals either zero or $\dot{P}_1$ in fig. 2a), the Fed's revenue yield is zero. The wealth transfer is greatest where the elasticity of demand for real money with respect to the inflation rate equals one. In the absence of any other constraints, the Fed will produce an amount of base growth (B1) that corresponds to the high point of the wealth transfer curve. This outcome will be the one preferred by discretionary profit maximizing officials because at $\dot{B}_1$ the difference between the Fed's revenue and the least cost of operation (broken horizontal line) is maximized.

This solution holds only when the total benefit curve does not serve as an effective constraint on the Fed's high-powered money creation. For instance, when the present Fed management is considered to be the only possible source of money provision, then TB_0 is the relevant total benefit curve and the Fed can do no better than $\dot{B}_1$. However, if the Fed confronts demand curve eb then the total benefit curve, TB_1, intersects the WT curve to the left of its high point. In this case output will be increased to this intersection point. Although the Fed has an incentive to extend base creation further, any incremental increase beyond $\dot{B}_5$ results in the total costs of the Fed's operation to taxpayers exceeding the total benefits.

Notice how the dual solutions in fig. 2b compare to the outcome in the appropriation setting. First, note that the base creation outcomes categorically differ in the two settings. While the Fed's open market operations generated an optimal deflation rate in the appropriation case, now with revenue tied to bond holdings, the Fed extends bond purchases past the price stability point. Inflation is a predictable outcome in the latter setting.(14) Somewhat paradoxically, the possibility exists that taxpayers could receive net benefits from the (present) Fed's existence in the revenue case, even with the inflationary outcome. Given TB_0, for instance, the Fed maximizes net earnings at an output level ($\dot{B}_1$) that enables taxpayers to obtain net benefits from the Fed's operation equal to jk dollars. This possibility arises from the fact that the Fed's 'budget' depends solely on the size of its bond portfolio.

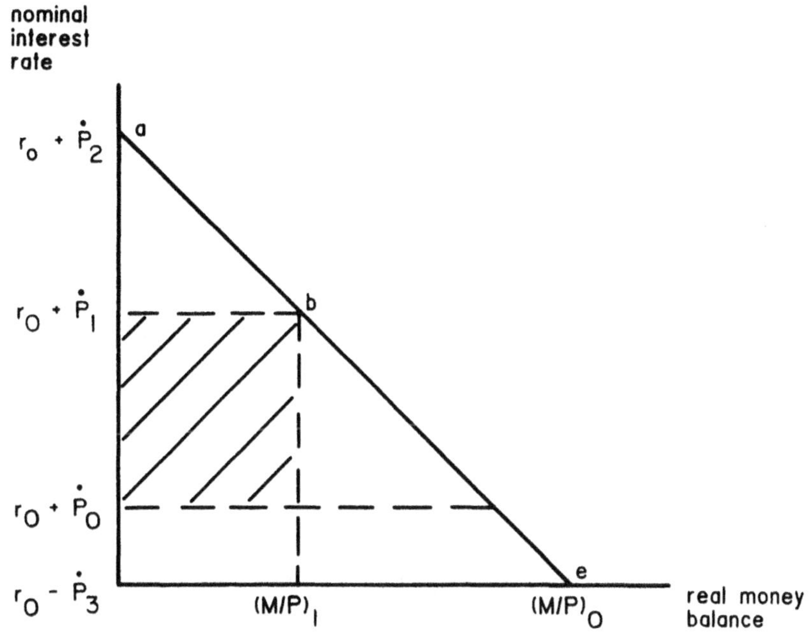

nominal interest rate
$r_o + \dot{P}_2$
a
$r_O + \dot{P}_1$
b
$r_O + \dot{P}_O$
$r_O - \dot{P}_3$
e
$(M/P)_1$
$(M/P)_O$
real money balance

Fig. 2a

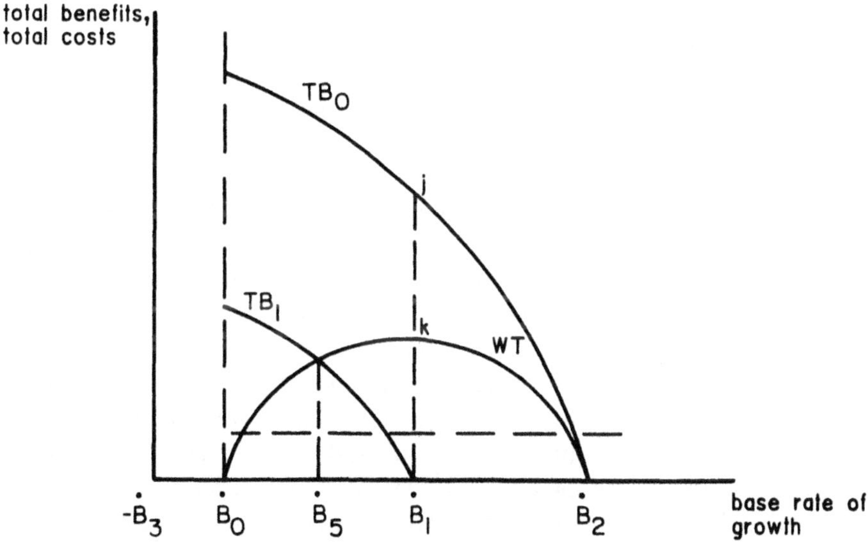

total benefits, total costs
TB_O
j
TB_1
k
WT
$-\dot{B}_3$
$\dot{B}_O$
$\dot{B}_5$
$\dot{B}_1$
$\dot{B}_2$
base rate of growth

Fig. 2b

If the maximum wealth transfer does not happen to exhaust total taxpayer benefits, there is no institutional mechanism that allows the Fed to bargain for a larger budget.

Put differently, the institutional structure that ties revenue to Fed-created base money represents the least cost method of governmental money issue, as long as we assume no effective competition, and remain in the no-monitoring environment. To see this, again consider total benefit curve TB_0. Under the budget setting the Fed bargains for a budget that equals total benefits; hence, the TB_0 curve shows the actual taxpayer cost of producing any $\dot{B}$. In contrast, the revenue setting implies that WT will be the actual total cost curve. Note that for any base rate of growth, WT lies below the total benefit curve.

3.3 Monitoring

To this point, I have been assuming that the Fed is constrained in its shirking activities either by its open market revenue, or (in the budget setting) by the condition that its actions do not make taxpayers prefer zero output from that particular management team. Specifically, I assumed that no organization within the government monitored the Fed's operation in an effort to reduce the level of discretionary profits. In this subsection the appropriateness of this assumption will be explored. A brief investigation of the monitoring process will provide a basis upon which the limits of the previously derived appropriation and revenue outcomes can be specified further.

Ordinarily, monitoring of a bureau's operations would be undertaken by the legislative committee responsible for determining the bureau's budget. Some form of monitoring seems to be a necessary ingredient of the appropriation process; if nothing else, a bureau's attempt to justify its budget request involves at least a crude reckoning of costs and benefits. However, as Niskanen (1975) points out, monitoring has the characteristics of a public good. If a legislator (or group of legislators) reduces bureaucratic shirking by a certain amount, his constituents do not capture the entire gain. Instead, the benefits are spread across the entire population. For this reason, the probability that any monitoring will be undertaken by members of the appropriate legislative committee is reduced.

When the Fed is not subject to the appropriation process, but instead obtains revenue from open market operations, this tendency is reinforced by the fact that the monitoring task does not fall naturally within the jurisdiction of any group in Congress.(15) However, the Fed may confront monitoring efforts from another source in this case. Because of its close ties with the Fed and the fact that it issues an asset ultimately purchased by the Fed, the Treasury can obtain information on the Fed's cost of operation at relatively low cost. If the Treasury reports this monitoring information, then Congress, acting upon this information, will force the Fed to give up a portion of its earnings. The Treasury Department captures benefits from this transfer whether the funds supplement the Treasury's budget or go into the government's general fund. In the latter case, the beneficial nature of the transfer stems from the fact that one of the primary tasks of the Treasury is to collect and raise funds to finance government expenditures. A transfer of earnings from the Fed to the general fund reduces the cost of fund raising, and thereby offers the opportunity for more discretionary spending by Treasury officials.

Regardless of where the funds end up, the Treasury will have an incentive to monitor the Fed's activities and report its findings to Congress. Under certain circumstances, however, a Treasury report on monitoring may not be necessary to achieve its purposes. For instance, suppose that the net gains from monitoring and reporting would be X dollars. The simple threat of revealing the Fed's shirking activity may be enough to induce the Fed to 'voluntarily' turn over an amount of excess earnings that generates (at least) X dollars worth of net benefits for the Treasury. These transfers may take place even if they are not required by the legal structure surrounding the Fed's operation.

Introduction of the monitoring factor does not change the conclusions of the earlier analysis in any substantive way. Within the revenue framework, monitoring, or the threat of monitoring, implies that a one dollar increase in Fed revenue will not benefit Fed officials by the entire one dollar. At least a portion of this increase will be turned over to the government. However, only if one assumes that monitoring is perfectly efficient (that is, only if one assumes costless monitoring) will the Fed receive zero benefits from incremental increases in earnings. More generally, when these benefits are positive, the Fed will have an incentive to push money supply creation to the point that generates the maximum possible (pre-monitoring) wealth transfer. On this basis, the base growth rate conclusions from the last section fully hold.(16)

3.4 Qualifications and Implications

The implication that Fed officials will be motivated to maximize the wealth transfer depends upon a bureaucratic utility function that contains discretionary profits as the only argument. Certainly other variables are possible. As one out of an assortment of possibilities, Fed officials might value praise from the President of the United States. In an effort to win favorable public pronouncements, monetary policy could be conducted to promote the re-election prospects of the President. If this type of consideration is relevant, then the simple wealth maximization hypothesis does not hold in its strong form. Decision-makers in the Fed will confront trade-offs between discretionary profits and other arguments in their utility functions. Monetary policy will depend upon how the different variables are weighted.

Once this point is acknowledged, the pertinent question concerns not whether Fed officials are wealth maximizers, but whether the wealth factor influences policy. In other words, do bureaucrats place any value on discretionary profits? The model presented in this paper responds in the affirmative, whereas the traditional model posits a purely 'public interest' motivation. To test the theories, two types of Federal Reserve official behavior can be identified. At one level, officials might strive to change the institutional framework surrounding the money creation process. The specific rule changes that would be promoted depend upon whether officials are bureaucratic or traditional prototypes. At a second level, the institutional structure is given, and behavior within this framework is the object of study. Here, the everyday expenditure decisions of the Fed might be used as a means of discriminating between the two theories.

Consider, first, the incentives Federal Reserve officials have to change the institutional structure, itself. Broadly stated, the bureaucratic model implies that Fed officials will favor those changes in their institutional environment which increase their revenue yield (all other things constant) from open market operations. One such element of their environment, over which Reserve officials may be able to exert some influence, would be the money multiplier. With a reduction in the money multiplier, the high point of the wealth transfer curve in fig. 2b will lie somewhere on the vertical line above point k. While the general public will be left with lower net benefits for any $\dot{B}$, the Fed will be able to capture a larger fraction of the inflation tax.(17)

The second type of implication concerns the expenditure outcomes of the Federal Reserve decision-making process. Of prime interest is the possible influence of Fed revenue in explaining these outcomes. Fig. 3 depicts the relationship between annual expenditures and revenue, while abstracting

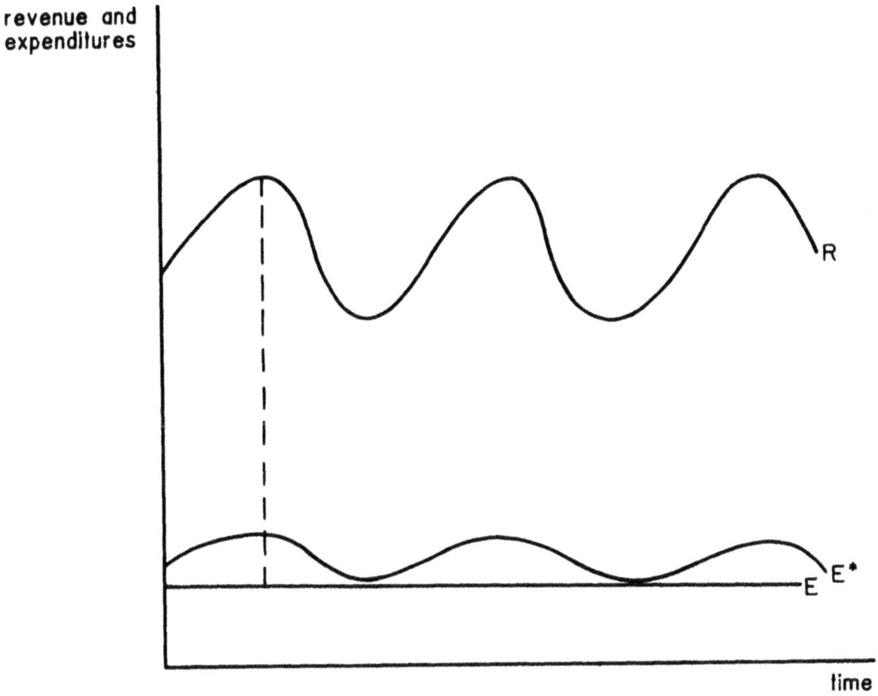

Fig. 3

from any time trend in the variables. Both theories of Federal Reserve official behavior imply that revenue (R) will fluctuate over time. In the traditional approach, this variation results from changes in the Fed's government security portfolio as it attempts to fine tune the economy; the bureaucratic theory highlights the fact that the Fed will increase or decrease the base rate of growth as the demand for money increases or decreases over the business cycle.

While both theories lead to the conclusion that Fed revenue fluctuates in the short run, they generate different predictions about the behavior of expenditures, and its movement with revenue. Under the traditional approach, Federal Reserve officials are motivated to produce their output in the least cost fashion. Since the Fed creates money simply by writing a check on itself, least cost expenditures, E, will be independent (all other things constant) of the amount of monetary base, and also the level of open market revenue.(18) This means that during periods of extraordinarily high revenue, a 'public interested' Fed simply will transfer a larger amount of its earnings to the Treasury. The broken line in fig. 3 shows the Treasury transfer under these circumstances.

The bureaucratic approach implies that total expenditures include a component that does not reflect least costs. Bureaucrats are able to transform (at least a portion of) open market revenue increases into discretionary profits. Therefore, when revenue is relatively high (low), total expenditures, E*, also should be relatively high (low).(19) In contrast to the traditional assumptions, discretionary profit bureaucrats do take advantage of high revenue periods by consuming additional perks. On this basis, the analysis implies that there should be no correlation between changes in revenue and changes in expenditures if the traditional model holds, but a positive correlation if bureaucrats value discretionary profits.

The next section confronts both the expenditure and money multiplier implications with the real world. First, in determining whether the Fed has promoted wealth-increasing changes (money multiplier decreases) in its environment, I shall focus on periods of constitutional change in the Fed's financing structure, and the accompanying policy changes. Subsequently, regression analysis will be employed to investigate the nature of the relationship between Fed revenue and expenditures. Throughout this analysis, the implications of the traditional model will be compared and contrasted with those of the discretionary profit model to determine which provides the better explanation of Federal Reserve bureaucrats' actions.

4. TESTING: THE TRADITIONAL VERSUS THE BUREAUCRATIC MODEL

4.1 Changes in the Monetary Constitution

The historical description in section 2 highlighted the fact that there were two important changes in the Fed's method of finance which represented revisions in the country's 'monetary constitution'. These changes may, or may not, have behavioral implications depending on which Federal Reserve model is adopted. The traditional model draws no link between changes in the financing structure and changes in Federal Reserve official behavior. However, if the discretionary profit model holds, then the two revenue-related alterations in the monetary constitution (mid-1930's and 1947) have a predictable impact. Each constitutional revision affected the Fed's costs and/or benefits of undertaking activities to reduce the money multiplier (m).

Consider first the benefit side of the ledger. Before 1933, the Federal Reserve Act outlined a formula that specified the terms under which the Fed would share its revenue with the government. The amendment in 1933, entailing a transformation in the financing structure, effectively eliminated the sharing requirement. With this change, the Fed became the sole claimant to earnings accruing from the open market process. This provided an added stimulus for the Fed to engage in activities which reduce m, since now, the Fed would capture all the extra revenue that would be generated.

This benefit was reinforced by the other part of the mid-1930's constitutional revision. Generally, the Fed can decrease the money multiplier through two methods. Either the Fed unilaterally takes actions which serve to decrease m, or it may bargain with another entity for such a change. The centralization of open market operations in the mid-1930's reduced the costs to the Fed of the second type activity. Under the original organizational structure, any agreement between the Fed and a second party required the consent or cooperation of twelve Reserve Banks. After 1935 only one organization, the FOMC, was involved. As with any type of joint action, the costs of securing agreement decrease with the size of the group.(20)

By enabling the Fed to initiate a direct transfer of revenue, the 1947 constitutional change had a similar cost-reducing impact. Prior to this change, any agreement the Fed made with an outside party involved a form of bartering; for instance, the Fed might make some sort of policy concession in exchange for a corresponding concession from the other party. However, barter is a relatively costly means of exchange. With the 1947 revision the Fed no longer had to rely on indirect exchange since the Fed's revenue could be used as a bargaining chip. The possibility of this direct monetary transaction serves to reduce the costs to the Fed of 'purchasing' money multiplier changes.

If Reserve officials are discretionary profit seekers, then monetary policy procedures during the thirties and forties would be expected to reflect these constitutionally induced changes in the cost/benefit calculus. Note that the Fed agreed to cooperate with an outside agency in two monetary policy programs during this period. A program to sterilize gold inflows was arranged jointly with the Treasury in 1936, immediately following the mid-1930's constitutional change. Additionally, the Fed and Treasury embarked on a program during World War II to stabilize interest rates; this program eventually created pressures which resulted in a 1947 agreement to take one step toward more flexible rates.(21) The remainder of this subsection explores these programs in an effort to assess the explanatory power of the bureaucratic model in comparison with the traditional model.

Prior to 1936, the Treasury legally could create new balances for itself by issuing gold certificates to the Fed for every dollar's worth of Treasury gold. This meant that any time gold flowed into the nation and was acquired by the Treasury, the monetary base automatically would go up by the dollar value of the new gold certificate. The continued inflow of gold, along with the corresponding increase in high-powered money, gave birth to the gold sterilization program at the end of 1936. In December, the Treasury and Fed agreed that the Treasury would change the procedure through which gold was acquired. Instead of automatically increasing its deposits at the Fed through a gold certificate issue, the Treasury would be required to purchase gold by selling securities to the general public. Under this procedure, the Treasury's acquisition of gold would not lead to the creation of new high-powered money, and in this sense, the gold inflows would be sterilized. The gold sterilization program had an effective life of approximately three years.(22)

Any attempt to explain the Fed's cooperation in this program must identify the Fed's objective, and furthermore, must explain why the Fed would desire sterilization as the means of accomplishing this end. Ultimately, the resolution of these issues depends on the analyst's model of bureaucratic behavior. The traditional approach is best represented by Milton Friedman's and Anna Schwartz's (1971) discussion of this period. A careful reading of their description of the Fed reveals a bureau inhabited by individuals who are motivated to manage the economy according to their perception of what is best. On this basis, the identification of the Fed's objective poses no particular problem. According to Friedman and Schwartz (FS), the Fed's desire to offset the gold inflows stemmed from a concern about the undesirable inflationary side effects of this inflow.

However, the sterilization program was not the only alternative available; an open market sale of securities would accomplish the same purpose. As FS correctly note, the outcome of the two programs are identical in terms of their effect on high-powered money. This being the case, FS pose a 'means' puzzle: 'why did it (the Fed) ask the Treasury to take actions that the System could equally well have taken?' (1971, p. 532). Why, in other words, would the Fed allow the Treasury to assume the central bank's traditional role of implementing monetary policy? Ultimately, FS's traditional model provides no satisfactory answer.(23) The Fed's behavior is judged to be anomalous since a central bank that consents to the sterilization program, instead of conducting open market security sales on its own, narrows its sphere of influence and thereby reduces its ability to intervene on behalf of the economy in the future.

Notice that when the traditional approach is replaced with the discretionary profit approach the whole cost/benefit structure facing Federal Reserve bureaucrats changes in a way that makes the Fed's behavior explicable. From the bureaucratic perspective, the most important feature of the presterilization environment is that the Treasury's issue of gold certificates, in effect, represented an additional source of money issue. From February, 1934 (after gold officially was revalued), to December, 1936, the \$3.82 billion gold inflow resulted directly in a 45.5 percent increase in high-powered money. This inflow served to increase the ratio of the total money supply to Fed-created money, and on this basis reduced the portion of the inflation tax going to Federal Reserve officials. The discretionary profit approach suggests that the major concern to Reserve officials at this time was not simply that gold inflows would result in inflation, but that the Fed would not reap the full benefits from the inflation tax.

With this in mind, the mid-1930's period can be construed as a turning point in Federal Reserve official's decision-making strategy. Not only were gold inflows having an increasingly adverse impact on the Fed's wealth position, but as mentioned earlier, the constitutional revision at this time increased the Fed's incentive to strike some bargain which would reverse this effect. The sterilization program can be interpreted as a direct outcome of such a bargain, since Treasury acquisition of gold no longer adds to the money supply with sterilization.(24) Once the analyst acknowledges the constitutional change that occurred just before sterilization, and once the traditional bureaucrat is replaced with one who values discretionary profits, then the Fed's consent to sterilization can be shown to be consistent with a deliberate wealth-increasing strategy.(25)

The second agreement between the Fed and Treasury in 1947 can be understood only within the context of a wartime policy to stabilize interest rates. In April, 1942, the Federal Open Market Committee announced that it would keep the yields on Treasury bills at 3/8 percent by freely buying and selling bills at the proposed rate. With respect to longer-term securities, the Fed's objective was to keep rates from rising above a certain level, rather than pegging them at this level. This stabilization policy continued throughout the war years; however, the Fed began lobbying for relaxation of the policy in the early post-war years. Specifically, in 1947 the Fed pushed for elimination of the fixed 3/8 percent bill rate.

The orthodox explanation for the Fed's behavior at this time focuses on the fact that in its policy pronouncements, relating to the stabilization program, the Fed repeatedly warned of the 'danger of inflationary forces'.(26) Implicit in these types of pronouncements is the presumption that the original stabilization program did not allow Federal Reserve officials to do what they perceived best for the economy; that is, it did not allow for a sufficient degree of monetary restraint to combat inflation. In this sense, the orthodox explanation used the traditional bureaucrat as its prototype.

Other features of the economic environment at this time pose problems for this orthodox interpretation. Consider, for instance, the expectations of the general public with respect to future price changes. Friedman and Schwartz present evidence from this period which indicates that the public expected deflation, not inflation. This being the case, it seems paradoxical that Fed officials would have different expectations.(27) Furthermore, the rate of growth in Federal Reserve credit declined sharply in early 1947 and, if the Fed had desired, the monetary contraction could have been even more severe since the yields on long-term securities were below the support levels. Both the price expectation factor and the money supply record tend to belie an explanation which implies that the fixed 3/8 percent bill rate was part of a larger program that prevented the Fed from acting on its fear of an over-expansionary monetary policy.

According to the bureaucratic model, the costs imposed on the Fed were different in nature than implied by the orthodox explanation. As long as government security rates were not allowed to rise above a certain level, holders of these securities had the option of reselling their asset at a price no lower than its original purchase price. By increasing the liquidity of securities in this fashion, the stabilization program resulted in an increased willingness on the part of commercial banks to exchange excess reserves for securities. This effect was significant. From April, 1942, to July, 1947, the ratio of demand to reserves increased from 3.96 to 6.61. Taken by itself, this factor would have caused an increase in the money multiplier from 2.714 to 3.535 over the period.(28) On this basis, the stabilization program served to decrease the portion of the inflation tax going to the Fed. To the extent revenue (discretionary profits) enters positively into their utility function, the decline in the yield from the inflation tax will influence the well-being of Federal Reserve officials in a negative fashion.

The first step in altering the stabilization policy coincided with the constitutional change which allowed Federal Reserve transfer payments to the Treasury. According to the discretionary profit model, the temporal juxtaposition of these events was no accident. Any change in the bills rate policy required the consent of the Treasury and, as described earlier, the 1947 constitutional revision reduced the cost to the Fed of winning this consent. The link between the bills rate policy and the constitutional change was formulated explicitly in the March 1, 1947, meeting of the FOMC. Here, the Fed announced it was willing to transfer a large portion of its earnings (over 75 million dollars) to the Treasury in return for the elimination of the pegged bill rate. As the record of policy actions of the FOMC revealed, Fed officials anticipated that this agreement would enable the Treasury to share in 'the increased earnings of the Federal Reserve Banks which would result from an increase in the bill rate' [Board of Governors (1947, p. 89)].(29)

While the bureaucratic model suggests that this joint action can be interpreted as an outcome of the Fed's strategy to bargain for an institutional change that enhances revenue (by decreasing m), the magnitude and timing of the transfer was influenced by one other factor. During and after the war, open market revenue increased so rapidly that few individuals inside (or outside) the Fed pretended this revenue equaled only the least cost of operation. This growing surplus presented the government with the opportunity of capturing a significant amount of revenue at relatively low monitoring cost. On this basis, the 'voluntary' transfer of revenue in 1947 to some extent may be interpreted as an attempt by the Fed to pre-empt a congressional effort outlining a formula which would specify the exact dollar transfer for any given year. The fear of such congressional action helps explain why transfers of this nature have continued on an annual basis up to the present.

4.2 Expenditure Outcomes

By focusing on structural changes in the Fed's environment, the last subsection provided insights into the explanatory power of the two competing models of Federal Reserve official behavior. This is not the only basis upon which the bureaucratic and traditional theories can be evaluated. Recall that the two theories generated different implications concerning the impact of the annual open market wealth transfer on Federal Reserve System expenditures. According to the traditional model, expenditures should be independent of changes in Federal Reserve revenue. In contrast, the bureaucratic model implies a positive relationship between revenue and total expenditures since the latter variable contains a discretionary profit component.

In order to test the budgetary implications of the two models, a time series study from 1947 to 1979 was conducted.(30) I estimated a first difference expenditure equation which took the following general form:

$$\triangle EXP_i = a_0 + a_1 \triangle W_i + \sum_{j=1}^{3} b_j \triangle X_{ji} + c_1 \triangle PW_i + d_1 TM_i + e_i,$$

$$i = 1, \ldots, 32,$$

where EXP_i denotes the real Federal Reserve System expenditures in year i, a_0, a_1, b_j, c_1, and d_1 are estimated coefficients, W_i is an independent variable representing Fed open market wealth in year i, X_{ji} is an independent variable which represents the (non-monetary) output of the Fed in year i, PW_i is a wage variable which influences the (least) cost conditions of providing output, TM_i is a time variable, and finally, e_i is an independent and identically distributed error term with mean zero and finite variance 2.

The set of independent variables, X, reflects the fact that the Fed performs services other than the creation of money. Check clearing operations, the currency function and fiscal agency operations are the three major functions of the Fed as revealed by the fact that in 1979 they comprised 36.6, 23.7, and 11 percent of total Federal Reserve Bank expenditures, respectively. To serve as proxies for these operations, X includes the number of checks handled, NCH;(31) the amount of currency and coin received and counted, NCU; and the number of government securities issued, redeemed, and exchanged, NGS. Fed expenditures are expected to vary directly with changes in both NCH and NCU. The sign on the NGS variable is more problematic. While an increase in the amount of government securities handled leads to an increase in expenditures, the Fed receives reimbursement from the Treasury. Whether expenditures (net of reimbursement) go up or down depends on the magnitude of the reimbursement relative to the change in the Fed's operating costs associated with these fiscal agency operations.

The independent variable, PW, is the real adjusted annual hourly earnings in the private non-agricultural sector. PW is used as a proxy for the cost of producing Federal Reserve output. On this basis it should have a positive coefficient. TM captures the effect of any improvements in production technology which may have occurred over time. Since such changes would reduce costs of production, a negative relationship should exist between $\triangle$EXP and TM.

With respect to variable W two measures of Fed open market wealth were employed. The most obvious and readily available measure is the annual real revenue (REV) the Fed receives primarily from its open market operations. However, under certain circumstances, REV may not capture the true open market wealth position of the Fed. To illustrate, consider two open market transactions that provide the same amount of current income, but different future income streams.(32) In this case REV would be appropriate only as long as Federal Reserve decision-makers ignore the future income differences of the transactions. If, on the other hand, the behavior of Fed officials is influenced by the anticipation of higher revenue in future years, then a measure broader than REV is required.

One such candidate would be a variable, WEA, that includes the annual real revenue plus the (recorded) real value of the Fed's security portfolio.(33)

Even where appropriate, this measure tends to overstate wealth for several reasons. First, although the magnitude of daily open market transactions is enormous, the Fed's security holdings are not subject to continuous sale/repurchase orders. If (some) securities lie dormant over a period of declining bond prices, then the reported value of the portfolio would be greater than the market value. The time span between 1947 and 1979 was characterized by periods of declining bond prices. Furthermore, Fed decision-makers do not enjoy all the benefits that a typical security holder enjoys. Generally, a security offers two ownership rights to its holder: the right to a future income stream and the right to transform the (current) value of a security into some other form of wealth. With respect to the first right, the number of years left in the term of a Fed decision-maker may preclude him from enjoying all future income prospects. This possibility is compounded by the fact that the Fed does not possess the second ownership right. The Fed, for instance, cannot simply sell a $10,000 security and acquire $10,000 of furniture. The sales transaction, in effect, causes $10,000 of monetary base to disappear. Because of this attenuation of ownership rights, possession of a $10,000 security is not worth as much to the Fed as, say, $10,000 of cash.

In short, REV and WEA offer approximations to the Fed's true open market wealth position. 'Real' Fed wealth depends on the institutional structure (e.g., rules that define the average tenure of decision-makers) surrounding the Federal Reserve System. REV will be a better approximation when these institutional factors cause Fed officials to disregard future open market revenue prospects. To the extent these prospects are reflected in the behavior of decision-makers, WEA becomes the more appropriate measure.

With these qualifications in mind, two specific forms of the expenditure equation were run in order to test the impact of REV and WEA. The traditional model of bureaucratic behavior predicts that $\triangle$ REV and $\triangle$ WEA will have no influence on System expenditures. A finding that the coefficients on one (or more forcefully, two) of the wealth variables is significantly positive provides evidence against the traditional model, while supporting the bureaucratic model. Table 1 reports the results. Both $\triangle$ REV and $\triangle$ WEA are significantly positive at the 0.05 level. Moreover, the higher R^2 of the WEA equation indicates that Federal Reserve officials do consider future interest revenue in formulating today's expenditure decisions.

Although the results should be interpreted with some caution, it is interesting to note the information yielded by the coefficients on the two wealth variables. These coefficients indicate that spending goes up as a direct result of changes in the Fed's revenue/wealth. If, as the bureaucratic theory suggests, these spending changes are pure discretionary profit changes, then for any given year the increase in discretionary profits induced by a revenue/wealth increase can be estimated. Note that the average annual revenue change over the course of the sample period is $138 million. During this 'typical' year, Federal Reserve officials would enjoy an estimated $2,559,019 of additional discretionary spending over that which they would have enjoyed, had there been no increase in revenue. The WEA measure leads to a somewhat more conservative figure of $1,908,025. Of course, how much this means to individual Fed officials depends on the size of the relevant sharing group. If the sharing group is 500 members for instance, then the REV (WEA) measure indicates an average member share of $5,118 ($3,816).(34) Not only do these results provide evidence in support of the bureaucratic model, but they also suggest that the cost to Federal Reserve officials of pursuing a purely 'public interest' operating strategy may be substantial.

Table 1
Federal Reserve System Expenditures, Fed Revenue/Wealth, and other Variables (t-statistics in parentheses).[a]

Independent Variables	Eq. (1)	Eq. (2)
△ REV	+0.0185	
	(1.819)[b]	
△ WEA		+0.0024
		(2.468)[b]
△ NCH	+2.448	+3.216
	(2.299)[b]	(3.362)[b]
△ NCU	−0.169	−0.100
	(1.138)	(0.7036)
△ NGS	−0.393	−0.219
	(2.205)[b]	(1.605)[c]
△ PW	+155.211	+69.779
	(3.317)[b]	(1.324)[c]
TM	−354.934	−881.924
	(0.915)	(2.334)[b]
Constant	−1707.29	6072.70
R^2	0.4677	0.5154

[a] Sources: Board of Governors of the Federal Reserve System, *Annual Report*; Board of Governors of the Federal Reserve System, *Banking and Monetary Statistics 1941-1970*; Board of Governors of the Federal Reserve System, *Annual Statistical Digest*; U.S. Department of Labor, Bureau of Labor Statistics, *Employment and Earnings, United States*, 1979 (Government Printing Office, Washington, DC).

[b] Denotes significance at 0.05 level.

[c] Denotes significance at 0.10 level.

5. CONCLUDING REMARKS

This paper examined the role played by a particular factor – discretionary profits – in motivating the actions of Federal Reserve officials. The traditional approach has ignored this factor, and thereby, implicitly assumed that Federal Reserve officials are automatons which do not respond to changes in the cost/benefit structure of their environment. Making this traditional assumption, however, leaves much unexplained about present-day monetary policy. Once it is recognized that the Fed operates in an open market revenue financing setting, many insights can be gained by explicitly accounting for the discretionary profit seeking propensities of its members. Both the traditional and bureaucratic models were used in an attempt to explain the interactions of the Fed and Treasury during two episodes of constitutional change. Elements of two monetary policy agreements, which appear puzzling within the context of the traditional Fed model, were interpreted as wealth-increasing strategies within the framework of the alternative model. Subsequently, regression analysis was employed to test the relationship between Fed expenditures and revenue/wealth. The outcomes, while preliminary, were consistent with the hypothesis that Federal Reserve officials conduct open market operations with an awareness of their wealth transfer effects.

While the analysis of this paper represents a fundamental step in the development of a general theory of the Federal Reserve System's operations, it is only a first step. Future research efforts could be directed toward (1) providing additional evidence concerning the importance of the discretionary profit motive, (2) examining more thoroughly, the Fed's incentive to raise the costs of the sponsoring agency of gathering information on the performance of alternative money-issuing institutional structures, (3) considering the intrabureaucracy dynamics of the Fed; for instance, what are the specific decision-making rules confronting individuals on the Board of Governors, and how do member banks enter into the decision-making process, and (4) integrating the theory of demand for money changes with the supply side theory developed in this paper.

With respect to this last consideration, the political pressure approach most recently has been offered as a demand side explanation of inflation. According to this approach, politicians increase government spending (without raising explicit taxes) and then place pressure on the Fed to finance the spending through increases in the money supply. This strategy provides political payoffs for politicians because taxpayers either (1) underestimate the inflation tax, or (2) fail to attribute inflation to the actions of the politicians. The latter possibility arises because of the indirect and complex link between the actions of politicians and the actions of an 'independent' Fed.

This type of argument ultimately must confront one nagging question: Why would the central bank ever submit to these demand side pressures? True, the Fed must be wary of the possibility that an impatient Congress will alter the rules of the game by changing the Bank's 'independent' structure. But this ready response does not get at the heart of the matter. The political pressure approach implies that politicians benefit from the present framework. They have no real incentive to eliminate the Bank's 'independent' structure, and thereby increase their responsibility for the money supply effects of the Fed's actions. My focus on the Fed's method of financing suggests a more fundamental reason for the Fed's cooperation in the production of inflation – Federal Reserve officials benefit from inflation. As a supply side phenomenon, inflation is a predictable consequence of an institutional structure that ties Fed revenue to bond holdings.

NOTES

1. There were short periods of deflation after World War I and during the Great Depression, but they were insignificant in comparison to the length of the earlier deflationary periods. For instance, the deflationary episodes after the War of 1812 and the Civil War each lasted in excess of three decades. For a graphical depiction of the inflation record throughout the history of the United States see David and Solar (1977).
2. This approach is developed fully in Gordon (1975). The thesis of Gordon's paper is that 'accelerations in money and prices are not thrust upon society by a capricious or self-serving government, but rather represent the vote-maximizing response of government to the political pressure exerted by potential beneficiaries of inflation' (1975, p. 808). More recently, Kane (1980) examines the way in which political forces shape the policy strategies of the Federal Open Market Committee.
3. Although this traditional perspective pervades much of the monetary policy literature, later I single out Friedman and Schwartz (1971) as representative of this approach.
4. See particularly works by Niskanen (1971, 1975) and Migue and Belanger (1974). Acheson and Chant (1972, chapters 6 and 7 in this volume) have examined the operation of the central bank in Canada from a bureaucratic perspective. However, unlike the above works, they do not explicitly posit utility-maximizing behavior by bureaucrats as the driving force behind their theory.
5. A 1919 amendment to the Federal Reserve Act changed the required surplus from 40 percent of paid-in capital to 100 percent of subscribed capital. When this condition was satisfied, 10 percent of net earnings could be added to surplus and 90 percent was to be paid to the government.
6. Federal Reserve earnings from bonds did not comprise half of total earnings until 1932. During the next few years security holdings increased in importance, so that in 1935 earnings on government securities were over 90 percent of total earnings. Presently, this figure is over 99 percent.

7. See Spahr (1947a, b).
8. The analysis in this paper is long run in nature and it is on this basis that I assume the Fed's monetary policy actions are responsible for the inflation record.
9. Besides other possible macroeconomic goals, the Fed provides services such as clearing checks for the commercial banking system.
10. To simplify matters, I do not consider one beneficial consequence of price stability emphasized in the works of F. A. Hayek. According to Hayek (1978), any deviation from price stability impairs economic calculation, and thereby, takes the form of a negative sum move. Inclusion of this factor in the analysis would tend to increase the total benefits associated with price stability.
11. Of course, in the real world the institutional structure surrounding the Fed does not allow Congress to change management teams costlessly.

    However, this consideration does not alter the analysis in a fundamental way; it simply means that the Fed will be able to push the inflation rate beyond P_1 before Congress will be induced to do something.
12. Generally, there are two types of costs to an individual from holding money balances. First, in a world inflation, there is a wealth transfer from the public to the money issuer. However, the money issuer (the Fed) does not keep the proceeds from the transfer in the budget case. Implicitly, I assume that this revenue is redistributed to the general public in a way that cancels out the initial transfer. The foregone real interest return also does not represent a cost of money provision since it 'is a cost to the individual of altering his cash balances that confers a precisely compensating benefit on others . . . If he reduces his consumption, all others will be able to consume a bit more' [Friedman (1969, p. 20)].
13. See Friedman (1953, 1971), and Bailey (1956) for a detailed explanation of inflation as a tax. As Friedman (1971, p. 846) notes, 'the rate of price rise is the rate of the tax. The real stock of money is the base of the tax. By strict analogy with an excise tax on a commodity, the yield is the product of the two'. This calculation of the revenue yield to the Fed holds only if real income is constant.
14. Technically speaking, inflation is not a necessary outcome of the revenue setting if one of the assumptions is relaxed. In a growing economy Friedman (1971) has shown that under certain circumstances deflation generates the (long-run) maximum wealth transfer.
15. Also, the monitoring task is made more difficult by the fact that a bureau has an incentive to take actions which tend to raise the cost of obtaining information about the least cost of production. See Acheson and Chant (1972a) for a discussion of how the Bank of Canada uses this technique to frustrate monitoring efforts.
16. This section focused exclusively on the possibility that the sponsor would monitor the Fed's operation in order to reduce discretionary profits directly. However, this is not the only type of monitoring activity. The sponsor may use monitoring devices which are designed to reduce the amount of output (monetary base) produced by the bureaucratic agency. Even in this case the general thrust of the conclusions hold. A discretionary profit maximizing Fed will increase the wealth transfer to the extent allowed by the sponsor's use of output monitoring devices.
17. The Fed directly can reduce the money multiplier by increasing reserve requirements. However, the Fed may not desire this particular change because of other consequences. An increase in the reserve requirement would decrease the profitability of banking, and thereby, make commercial bank membership in the System less attractive.
18. As outlined in a later section, the Fed provides services in addition to the creation of monetary base. Even taking these other services into account, the traditional approach

posits no relationship (all other things constant) between changes in revenue and changes in expenditures.

19. Under certain circumstances, annual revenue may not capture the true open market wealth position of the Fed. This point is discussed fully in the empirical section.
20. Olson's *The Logic of Collective Action* (1965) was an early work that emphasized the relationship between voluntary action and group size.
21. Generally, the agreement to stabilize interest rates has been interpreted as an emergency measure to help finance the war effort.
22. Although the Treasury began issuing gold certificates to the Fed in September, 1937, this procedural change had no immediate effect since the Treasury did not spend the newly created balances. Effective desterilization was not implemented until the end of 1939, when Treasury cash and deposits were reduced to approximately their presterilization levels. The prospects of World War II at least partially may account for the demise of the sterilization program. Facing significant increases in defense spending at the turn of the decade, with even larger increases looming on the horizon, the Treasury made use of any readily available funds, including 'excess' balances at the Fed.
23. In attempting to explain why the Fed did not sell securities to reduce excess reserves, Friedman and Schwartz mention the 'problem of earnings'. However, FS interpret earnings as a constraint on Fed behavior, rather than a motivating factor. 'Sales of securities large enough to reduce reserves to levels regarded as appropriate would also have reduced the income of the Reserve Banks to negligible amounts' (1971, p. 519), and thereby threatened the continued existence of the System.
24. In other words, this bargain decreased the money multiplier, if m is defined with respect to Fed-created base. Reserve requirement increases in August, 1936, March, 1937, and May, 1937, served to reinforce this effect of the sterilization program.
25. Interestingly, Friedman and Schwartz report that the first step toward desterilization was taken at the initiative of the Fed. FS (1971, p. 9) cite the Federal Reserve's Annual Report of 1937 as the source for this statement. If true, an implication of the revenue framework seemingly would be contradicted, since desterilization implies a smaller Federal Reserve bond portfolio for any given monetary base rate of growth. However, the Fed's statement in its *Annual Report* was misleading according to acting Secretary of Treasury, Henry Morgenthau. At the time desterilization was being considered, the Board of Governors preferred to have high-powered money increase through an alternative (revenue-increasing) method, open market operations. When Morgenthau finally insisted that the Treasury was going through with desterilization, the Chairman of the Fed, Marriner Eccles, asked the Secretary to implement the change in a way that would not suggest to the press that the Treasury was placing pressure on the Fed. Morgenthau arranged to let Eccles tell the story to the newspapers and to report that desterilization had been the Fed's idea [Blum (1959, p. 378)].
26. As the *Annual Report of 1947* [Board of Governors (1947, p. 5)] states in reference to the 3/8 percent policy, 'beginning in July the Federal Reserve System and the Treasury adopted measures to permit some rise in interest rates on short term Government securities in order to increase their attractiveness to banks and other investors and to place an additional restraint on further monetary expansion'.
27. As Friedman and Schwartz (1971, pp. 583-584) point out, a belief that prices will go up in the future should result in an increase in the price (decrease in the yield) of stocks relative to bonds because 'of the hedge which stocks provide against inflation'. FS provide data on the yields of Baa corporate bonds and one hundred and twenty-five industrial common stocks for the first quarter of 1946 and the fourth quarter of 1948. Over this period the yield on

stocks grew much more rapidly than the yield on bonds, indicating that the public generally expected deflation. When considered in conjunction with the Fed's professed expectation of inflation, this outcome is puzzling because it implies there were opportunities for mutually beneficial exchange in these asset markets which remained unexploited over time.

28. The increase in the deposit-reserve ratio would have made the percentage increase in the stock of money approximately 1.6 times the percentage increase in high-powered money. Note that in 1942 reserve requirements on net demand deposits in central city banks in New York and Chicago were reduced from 26 to 20 percent. This reduction occurred in three stages, effective August 20, September 14, and October 3. However, the impact of this change appears relatively small since the deposit-reserve ratio increased from 4.34 to only 4.6 by the end of October, and to 4.67 by the end of the year.
29. The Board of Governors officially announced, in its April 23 meetings, the new policy of voluntarily paying a portion of earnings to the Treasury. Three months later (July 1947) the Secretary of Treasury felt the Treasury 'could prudently consider taking steps toward higher short-term rates' and at this time the Fed and Treasury took joint action which resulted in a change in the bill rate [Joint Committee on the Economic Report (1952, p. 62)].
30. 1947 was chosen as the starting point, since this year corresponds to the revision in the monetary constitution discussed earlier.
31. NCH does not include U.S. Government checks handled or postal money orders handled.
32. Suppose, for instance, that the Fed enters the period with a $10,000 government security in its portfolio. This security has ten years left to maturity and promises annual interest payments of $500. On the one hand, the Fed may sell this security at the beginning of the period for a $500 capital gain. Alternatively, the Fed simply may hold the security in its portfolio throughout the year. In both cases, the revenue collected during the year would be $500. However, the Fed may not be indifferent between the two alternatives since in the latter case the Fed still has a $10,000 security in its portfolio.
33. The value of the Fed's portfolio is measured by the average daily holdings of loans and securities during a year.
34. Keep in mind that this figure is an average. Individual portions within the sharing group generally will differ.

REFERENCES

Acheson, Keith and John F. Chant, 'Mythology and Central Banking,' *Kyklos*, 1972, 16, 362-379.

Acheson, Keith and John F. Chant, 'The Choice of Monetary Instruments and the Theory of Bureaucracy,' chapter 6 in this volume.

Acheson, Keith and John F. Chant, 'Bureaucratic Theory and the Choice of Central Bank Goals,' chapter 7 in this volume.

Bailey, Martin J., 'The Welfare Cost of Inflationary Finance,' *Journal of Political Economy*, 1956, April, 93-110.

Blum, John Morton, *From the Morgenthau Diaries* (Boston: Houghton Mifflin), 1959.

Board of Governors of the Federal Reserve System, *Annual Report*, 1937.

Board of Governors of the Federal Reserve System, *Annual Report*, 1947.

Breton, Albert and Ronald Wintrobe, 'The Equilibrium Size of a Budget-maximizing Bureau: A Note on Niskanen's Theory of Bureaucracy,' *Journal of Political Economy*, 1975, 83, 195-207.

David, Paul A. and Peter Solar, 'A Bicentenary Contribution to the History of the Cost of Living in America,' *Research in Economic History*, 1977, 2, 1-80.

Friedman, Milton, 'Discussion of the Inflationary Gap,' *Essays in Positive Economics*, University of Chicago Press: Chicago, 1953.

Friedman, Milton, *The Optimum Quantity of Money and Other Essays*, Aldine: Chicago, 1969.

Friedman, Milton, 'Government Revenue from Inflation,' *Journal of Political Economy*, 1971, 79, July/August, 846-856.

Friedman, Milton and Anna Jacobson Schwartz, *A Monetary History of the United States, 1867-1960*, Princeton University Press: Princeton, 1971.

Gordon, Robert J., 'The Demand for and Supply of Inflation,' *Journal of Law and Economics*, 1975, 18, 807-836.

Hayek, F. A., *Denationalization of Money*, London: Institute of Economic Affairs, 1978.

Joint Committee on the Economic Report, Monetary Policy and the Management of the Public Debt, Washington, DC: United States Printing Office, 1952.

Kane, Edward J., 'Politics and Fed Policymaking,' *Journal of Monetary Economics*, 1980, 6, 199-211.

Migue, Jean-Luc and Gerard Belanger, 'Toward a General Theory of Managerial Discretion,' *Public Choice*, 1974, 17, Spring, 27-43.

Niskanen, William A., *Bureaucracy and Representative Government*, Chicago: Aldine-Atherton Press, 1971.

Niskanen, William A., 'Bureaucrats and Politicians,' *Journal of Law and Economics*, 1975, 18, 617-643.

Olson, Mancur, *The Logic of Collective Action*, Cambridge, MA: Harvard University Press, 1965.

Spahr, Walter E., 'Federal Reserve Board Out of Bounds Again,' *The Commercial and Financial Chronicle*, 1947a, June 19.

Spahr, Walter, E., 'More on Reserve Board's Illegal Distribution of Federal Reserve Bank's Earnings,' *The Commercial and Financial Chronicle*, 1947b, Sept. 18.

Chapter 4

PRELIMINARY EVIDENCE ON THE USE OF INPUTS BY THE FEDERAL RESERVE SYSTEM

by William F. Shughart II and Robert D. Tollison

Because the main objectives of the Federal Reserve System (the Fed) concern what Milton Friedman (chapter 2, p. 12) describes as the Holy Trinity – full employment, economic growth, and stable prices – scholarly evaluations of the central bank's performance understandably center most often on the behavior over time of macroeconomic variables such as the aggregate price level, interest rates, and national income. Recently, however, Friedman and others have been drawn to the view that an explanation for the Fed's monetary policy record may be found in the bureaucratic incentives faced by central bank officials.

To illustrate this approach, Friedman observes that the Fed's historical concern with the number of banks in the system cannot be rationalized on the basis of monetary control: 'it derives rather from the prestige, sense of importance, power, and effective lobby that the system gains by supervising many thousands of banks and other financial institutions . . .' (chapter 2, p. 28). Mark Toma argues that the Fed's independence of the normal congressional budgetary process introduces an inflationary bias to monetary policy. Specifically, he finds a positive relationship between the Fed's income from open market operations and the size of Fed operating expenses.

Keith Acheson and John Chant adduce evidence that several of the Bank of Canada's policy initiatives during the 1950's and 1960's were more consistent with minimizing the cost of government debt than with the Banks' publicly stated goal of extending Canadian financial markets. Chant and Acheson also produce data to support their thesis that the Bank of Canada's

Toma, E.F. and Toma, M. (eds.) Central Bankers, Bureaucratic Incentives, and Monetary Policy

ISBN 90 247 3366 9

'. . . decisions to emphasize covert instruments, to acquiesce in preserving a concentrated banking system and to maintain an excessive battery of tools appear rational' (chapter 6, p. 123) only when viewed in the context of bureaucratic behavior. Finally, they (chapter 7) find the public pronouncements of the Bank of Canada to be consistent with the bureaucratic goal of avoiding accountability for policy failures.

In this paper we present evidence on Fed behavior that focuses on its use of inputs. Using data that cover the entire period over which the Fed has been in existence, we find a positive and statistically significant ceteris paribus relation between the monetary base and the size of the Fed. 'Size' is measured in terms of the number of employees. This result suggests that one motiviation for expansions in the money supply is to finance the growth of the Fed's bureaucracy. That is, the Fed, which operates under a requirement that it return excess income to the Treasury, 'pads' its operating expenditures by increasing the number of employees on its payroll. The employment effect does not explain all (or even most) of historical money supply values. Our empirical results indicate, rather, that bureaucratic incentives play a role in the formulation of monetary policy and perhaps explain in part the Fed's apparent inflationary bias.

Our presentation is organized as follows. Section I contains a discussion of the constraints placed on the Fed's income-earning abilities and indicates how the Fed adjusts to those constraints. In particular, we argue that because the Fed can retain profits denominated in people but not in dollars, it has an incentive to hire more employees than would a for-profit central bank not operating under such a constraint. The basic data and empirical evidence are presented in Section II. Additional findings and implications are reported in Section III, and concluding remarks are offered in Section IV.

I. THE FED AS A BUREAUCRATIC AGENT

As Friedman has suggested, the Fed operates much like any other bureaucracy. As such it seems useful to treat the central bank within a principal-agent context where the Fed carries out a menu of activities for a sponsor. For example, the Fed may pursue the Holy Trinity, it may generate the rate of monetary growth that maximizes inflationary tax revenue, it may be in the business of disrupting private contracts denominated in nominal dollars, it may underwrite budget deficits, and so forth.(1) Whatever functions it performs, and without excluding the possibility that the central bank also serves as agent for the executive branch, we assume that the Fed's sponsor is the Congress and that the Fed's activities are geared toward assisting the legislature in attaining its political goals. The latter may be wealth transfers or macroeconomic stability. In any case, the actual objectives of government are not crucial to our theory of bureaucratic control.

Operationally, the Fed produces and then sells money through commercial banks and a select group of government securities dealers. In carrying out such open market transactions, the Fed operates under several constraints, one of which is that it may purchase only a restricted set of assets. Allowable purchases include U.S. government securities (Treasury bills, notes, certificates, and U.S. bonds) and certain kinds of commercial paper.(2) This securities portfolio represents the principal asset on the central bank's balance sheet; major liabilities include outstanding Federal Reserve notes and member bank reserves.(3)

In an open market purchase of securities, the Fed exchanges the Federal Reserve notes that it has produced at very low resource cost for assets that generate a stream of interest payments.(4) In contrast, open market sales involve the trade of income-earning securities for non-interest-bearing currency. Thus, securities purchases raise the Fed's profits while open market sales reduce its profits.

The Fed pays its current operating expenses out of current interest income, and then returns any excess revenue to the Treasury. The Fed's operating expenses, which are quite similar to those of a typical commercial bank, include maintenance and depreciation of the premises and equipment owned by the Federal Reserve district and branch banks, as well as the offices of the Board of Governors; the costs of operating an extensive check-clearing network; and member bank supervision costs. In most years, the funds turned over to the Treasury are a large multiple of the Fed's current expenses.(5)

How well the Fed assists the legislature in achieving its political goals depends in part on the ability of Congress to monitor its agent. In a bureaucratic setting, economic theory suggests that the degree to which principals can exercise control over the behavior of agents is a function of such factors as the real prices of technical inputs, including accounting and computer services, and political variables such as the size of congressional staffs or the number of committees overseeing the bureau. Of particular importance is that the cost of monitoring any given bureau will depend on the overall number of bureaucratic agents which the principal seeks to control. In the case of Congress, we expect that the secular growth of political margins controlled by the legislature, has raised the costs of monitoring

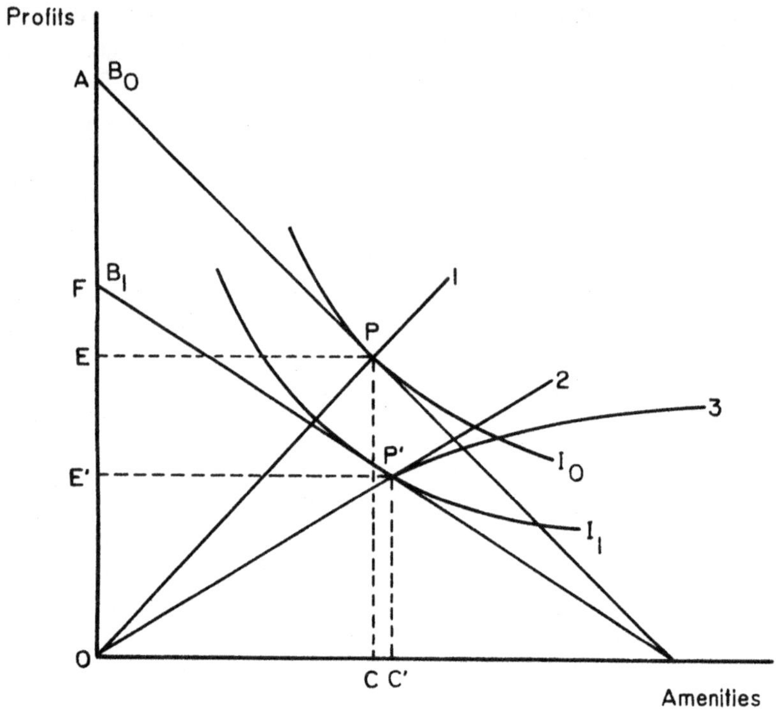

Figure 1. The Fed's Profits-Amenities Tradeoff.

individual bureaus substantially. Moreover, the effect on monitoring costs of increased numbers of departments, bureaus, and agencies is likely to swamp any cost-reducing effects arising from lower technical input prices or from improved technologies for reaching consensus among monitors. In this context, it is useful to remember that as government has grown in size over the modern period, the number of legislators/monitors has remained virtually fixed.

As we noted earlier, the Fed's excess income is turned back to the budget. Such a requirement facilitates political equilibrium. If, for example, the Fed does not generate the appropriate level or pattern of transfers, including payments to the Treasury, then at least one political margin will fail to clear: a particular group's tax bill will be 'too high'; the gain realized by certain parties to private contracts (debtors, for example) will be 'too large'; a government project will receive 'too little' funding; and so forth. In that event, some congressmen will be revealed to be inefficient monitors of the Fed and will be replaced with new monitors who are able to constrain the central bank to the equilibrium level or pattern of transfers.

The policing problem with respect to the Fed is not qualitatively different from that of any other principal-agent relation, except that the 'bottom line' is political survivorship rather than profits. In the typical analysis of agency problems, it is difficult to obtain empirical surrogates for the relevant variables. Because of the Fed's profit constraint, however, we can formulate a simple agency cost model in which variations over time in monitoring costs affect, and are revealed in, the central bank's use of inputs.

The tradeoff faced by the Fed in allocating its gross income is illustrated in Figure 1. We assume that the Board of Governors maximizes a utility function which includes as arguments the profits earned from open market operations and amenities appearing on the Fed's income statement as operating expenses.(6) The latter includes goods such as salaries, office space, funds for employee travel, and other perquisites. In addition, salaries of the Governors and other officers will depend to some extent on the number of workers they supervise. For simplicity, we assume that the dollar value of amenities is a monotone transformation of Federal Reserve System employment.

Indifference curves labeled I_0 and I_1 show the expense preferences of the Fed's managers, that is, the various combinations of amenities and profits that yield a given level of utility. The rate at which profits can be transformed into amenities in the market is given by the budget lines B_0 and B_1.

The opportunity set, B_0, represents the constraint that would prevail if the Congress did not require the Fed to return excess income to the Treasury. In that case, equilibrium would obtain at a point such a P where an indifference curve, I_0, is just tangent to B_0. Here, the Fed earns profits in the amount OE, and purchases OC amenities with foregone profits, AE.

Now suppose that Congress designates the Treasury as residual claimant of the Fed's excess income. To the extent that such a constraint is effective, the budget line will become less steep, indicating that the Fed now faces smaller costs for amenities in terms of foregone profits. In essence, the constraint allows the Federal Reserve System to retain profits that are denominated in employees or other amenities, but not those denominated in dollars. A new equilibrium consequently occurs at P′ where I_1 is tangent to B_1. The Fed now foregoes FE′ in dollar profits and purchases OC′ amenities. Funds in the amount OE′ are turned over to the government's general revenue account.(7) Comparing this solution to the equilibrium with no constraint on how profits may be allocated, it is plain that the Fed buys more noble premises, hires more employees, and takes advantage of more perquisites than before.

The comparative statics result depicted in the diagram of course depends on the assumption that amenities are a normal good. In that case, a fall in the price of amenities in terms of dollar profits will lead the Fed to purchase more of them if the substitution effect dominates the income effect. In general, however, the overall effect on the quantity of amenities is indeterminate a priori.

Congress certainly recognizes that the profit constraint induces the Fed to over-purchase amenities, but it will generally not pay to eliminate entirely such effects if the opportunity cost of monitoring the central bank is positive. As we noted before, as the size of government grows, a fixed number of legislators/monitors must monitor more political margins, and the cost of policing any individual agency consequently rises.

Expansionary open market operations enlarge the Fed's opportunity set, that is, shift B_1 to the right, raising potential profits (and therefore potential amenities) for the central bank. If the relative prices of profits and amenities remain constant over time, each successive shift in B_1 will be parallel to the previous budget line. In that case, the Fed's 'expansion' path would be given by ray 2, which lies to the right of the path that would be followed by a bank whose choices were constrained only by market prices (ray 1). On the other hand, rising congressional monitoring costs will cause counterclockwise rotations in the constraint as the Fed's opportunity set moves to the right. These successively flatter budget lines will yield an expansion path for amenities, such as ray 3, which lies to the right of and below the path that would obtain if relative prices remain constant. That is, increasingly higher policing costs resulting from government growth will generate a clear 'amenities bias' in the Fed's input purchases.

Figure 1 illustrates two general consequences of requiring the Fed to turn back its excess income to the Treasury. In a timeless setting, the constraint changes the relative prices of amenities and profits, leading the Fed to purchase more amenities if the substitution effect dominates the income effect. Over time, rising monitoring costs cause the Fed's input choices to diverge increasingly from the path that would be chosen by a central bank not operating under the postulated conditions.

As expansionary monetary policies enlarge the Fed's potential profits-amenities choices, the Fed faces higher real costs of operating the monetary system. That is, expansions in the money supply undoubtedly require additional inputs for the purposes of, for example, clearing a larger number of checks, engaging in a larger number of open market transactions, and so forth. Under a fiat standard, however, these incremental production costs will be trivial in comparison to the nominal value added to the money stock.

Our model predicts in addition that the Fed will tend to purchase more amenities than would be justified by cost-minimizing money production, that is, to incur 'fake' costs.

That the Fed does not expend all of its income, but chooses to return some profits to the Treasury, implies a survivorship strategy. Our purpose here is not to explain the political constraints that guide such strategies, but rather to examine Fed behavior under the postulated conditions. Moreover, it is important to emphasize that the tendency of the Fed to purchase more amenities than would a for-profit producer of money is not due to the 'waste' or lack of efficiency sometimes attributed to monopoly, but is in addition to such agruments.(8) Rather, the Fed chooses a combination of amenities and payments to the Treasury that maximizes its utility subject to the profit-confiscating political constraint.

The Fed's incentive to enlarge its purchases of amenities conflicts with its mandate to promote macroeconomic stability only part of the time. When engaging in expansionary policies, the Fed can both increase the supply of money and increase the size of its bureaucracy because the two goals are served by open market purchases of securities. In contrast, contractionary policies force the Fed to lower its profits when it undertakes open market sales to reduce the rate of growth in money. It is an empirical question whether the Fed's concern with the size of its bureaucracy is useful in explaining the way in which monetary policy is carried out. It is to that question that we now turn.

II. EMPIRICAL EVIDENCE

We have outlined a hypothesis which suggests that the Federal Reserve System may operate like a typical bureaucracy. Specifically, because the Fed must return excess revenues to the Treasury, it has an incentive to take a portion of its profits in the form of amenities rather than dollars. Since the success of bureaucratic organizations is often measured by the relative size of staffs, we expect the empirical importance of our hypothesis to be revealed in terms of the number of officers and employees in the Federal Reserve System, although the Fed's propensity to enlarge its purchases of amenities could take the form of more sumptuous offices, larger salaries, or other perquisites.(9)

A. Regression Model

We estimated the parameters of the following money supply equation to test the predictions of our hypothesis about amenities and profits:

$$\text{BASE} = b_0 + b_1\,\text{SYSEMP} + b_2\,\text{CD} + b_3\,\text{INT} + b_4\,\text{RGNP} + b_5\,\text{TREND} + b_6\,\text{TREND}^2 + e.$$

The variables are defined as follows: BASE is nominal monetary base; SYSEMP is the number of Federal Reserve System employees; CD is the actual currency-deposit ratio; INT is the interest rate on prime commercial paper of four- to six-months' maturity; RGNP is real Gross National Product; TREND is a linear time trend; and e is the regression error term.

The principal prediction of our hypothesis is that the sign on SYSEMP will be positive. As we noted earlier, the Fed produces money and sells it to commercial banks and a small group of securities dealers in exchange for income-earning assets. Although the definition of money is a much-debated concept, there are two principal types in the U.S. economy; currency sold by the Fed (Federal Reserve notes) and money produced by commercial banks in the form of demand deposits. The stock of nominal money, referred to as M_1, is the sum of currency in the hands of the public and the dollar value of demand deposits outstanding.(10)

The portion of the money supply produced by the Fed consists of currency in the hands of the public and bank reserves. Fed money is referred to as the 'monetary base' or 'high-powered money.' In its simplest formulation the relation between M_1 and the monetary base is an identity that depends on two ratios. These are the currency-deposit ratio which gives the proportion in which the public holds the components of M_1, and the reserve-deposit ratio which measures the amount of currency held by banks against their outstanding demand deposit liabilities.

For given values of the two deposit ratios, increases in the stock of high-powered money raise M_1. Expansionary policies such as open market purchases of securities both raise the monetary base and increase the Fed's profits. Since higher profits can be used by the Fed to purchase more amenities, the sign on SYSEMP is predicted to be positive, ceteris paribus.

Our regression equation in other respects is a traditional money supply function. Under the typical assumption that the Fed actively pursues a stabilization or control function, the monetary authority will use macroeconomic data to guide it in deciding whether to expand or contract the money supply by changing the stock of high-powered money. Three monetary indicators suggested in the literature are the actual currency-deposit ratio, interest rates, and the level of real income.

The sign on CD is predicted to be positive. Other things equal, the Fed responds to increases in the public's holdings of currency relative to demand deposits by expanding the monetary base. It does so because increases in the currency-deposit ratio lead to reductions in bank reserves. Since reserves are the basis on which bank money is supplied, the lower level of reserves causes a contraction in M_1. This effect can be offset by increasing the supply of high-powered money. Thus, if the Fed uses a counter-cyclical feedback rule in which a higher currency-deposit ratio signals the need for expansionary policies, the sign on CD will be positive.

Until quite recently, the Fed used interest rates as a monetary control target. Ceteris paribus, higher interest rates led the monetary authority to expand the base in order to increase the supply of available credit. Similarly, a contractionary policy was called for whenever the rate of interest reached relatively low levels. Other things equal, the regression coefficients on INT should therefore be positive.

Increases in the level of real income will lead to expansions in the monetary base if the Fed supplies the amount of real balances desired by the public. Other things equal, an increase in income raises the demand for money because at higher income levels individuals hold larger money balances to finance a greater number of market transactions. Moreover, raising the stock of high-powered money when income increases will counteract the tendency for prices to fall. The sign on RGNP should therefore be positive.

Finally, a time trend is included to account for secular growth in Fed employment. We might expect the number of Federal Reserve System employees to rise over time as part of the increase in the size of government as a whole. Such tendencies, which are exogenous to the profits-amenities relation, will be captured in the coefficient on TREND, whose sign is likely to be positive. Squaring the trend variable allows for nonlinear growth over time.

B. The Data

We estimated the regression model using data from the Federal Reserve System's *Annual Report* and from other sources. (The basic data are shown in Table 1.) We define system employment to include the officers and employees of the district and branch banks as well as those of the Board of

Table 1
Federal Reserve Employment, Monetary Aggregates, GNP, and Commercial Paper Rate

Year	Paid Civ. Empl. of Federal Govt.	Empl. of Board of Governors	Empl. of Fed Res. Banks	Currency ($bil.)	Demand Deposits ($bil.)	Bank Reserves ($bil.)	Monetary Base ($bil.)	GNP ($bil.)	Prime Commercial-Paper rate (Percent)
1915	395429	59	442	1.93	10.55	0.45	2.38	40.0	4.01
1916	399381	61	920	2.17	12.53	0.88	3.05	48.3	3.84
1917	438500	77	2985	2.17	14.91	1.58	3.75	60.4	5.07
1918	834500	227	7706a	2.76	16.20	1.81	4.57	76.4	6.02
1919	794271	319c	9459b	4.02	17.77	2.02	6.04	84.0	5.37
1920	655265	255c	12285d	4.48	19.25	1.86	6.34	91.5	7.50
1921	561142	249e	12745	4.04	17.47	1.88	5.92	69.6	6.62
1922	543507	211c	12256f	3.69	17.98	1.97	5.66	74.1	4.52
1923	536900	209	11996g	3.96	18.98	1.96	5.92	85.1	5.07
1924	543484	197	10761g	3.96	19.71	2.31	6.27	84.7	3.98
1925	553045	181	10126g	3.96	21.70	2.26	6.22	93.1	4.02
1926	548713	203	10280g	4.00	22.18	2.28	6.28	97.0	4.34
1927	547127	201	10108	3.98	22.12	2.53	6.51	94.9	4.11
1928	560772	196	9989h	3.89	22.49	2.44	6.33	97.0	4.85
1929	579559	234	9986h	3.90	22.74	2.41	6.31	103.1	5.85
1930	601319	209	9609i	3.73	22.03	2.52	6.25	90.4	3.59
1931	609746	197	9340j	4.16	19.98	2.13	6.29	75.8	2.64
1932	605496	203	10319k	4.92	16.19	2.56	7.48	58.0	2.73
1933	603587	261	12042l	5.09	14.82	2.87	7.96	55.6	1.73
1934	698649	320	11706	4.63	17.23	4.41	9.04	65.1	1.02
1935	780582	334	11551	4.80	21.08	6.39	11.19	72.2	0.75
1936	867432	323	10390	5.23	24.32	7.11	12.34	82.5	0.75
1937	895993	401	10385	5.59	25.32	7.58	13.17	90.4	0.94

Table 1 (continued)

1938	882226	416	10919	5.55	24.97	10.09	15.64	84.7	0.81
1939	953891	426m	11355	6.04	28.11	11.47	17.51	90.9	0.59
1940	1042420	435m	11640	6.76	32.89	14.07	20.83	100.0	0.56
1941	1437682	455	14083	8.40	38.12	12.81	21.21	125.0	0.53
1942	2296384	422	19972	11.54	43.82	13.15	24.69	158.5	0.66
1943	3299414	459	24741	16.35	55.89	12.75	29.10	192.1	0.69
1944	3332356	448	24442	21.22	64.12	14.17	35.39	210.6	0.73
1945	3816310	455	24442	25.33	73.90	16.03	41.36	212.4	0.75
1946	2696529	480	21430	26.48	79.98	16.52	43.00	209.8	0.81
1947	2111001	504	19364	26.58	85.22	17.26	43.84	233.1	1.03
1948	2071009	527	19081	26.07	86.24	19.99	46.06	259.5	1.44
1949	2102109	548	17967	25.50	85.67	16.29	41.79	258.3	1.49
1950	1960708	578	17993	25.05	89.08	17.39	42.44	286.5	1.45
1951	2482666	586	19832	25.53	93.67	20.31	45.84	330.8	2.16
1952	2600612	568	20011	26.70	98.52	21.18	47.88	348.0	2.33
1953	2558416	581	20272	27.78	100.64	19.92	47.70	366.8	2.52
1954	2407676	558	19334	27.52	102.75	19.28	46.80	366.8	1.58
1955	2397309	559	19134	27.63	106.79	19.24	46.87	400.0	2.18
1956	2398736	586	19307	27.98	108.05	19.54	47.52	421.7	3.31
1957	2417565	580	19817	28.26	108.48	19.42	47.68	444.0	3.81
1958	2382491	603	19307	28.37	109.98	18.90	47.27	449.7	2.46
1959	2382807	600	19500	28.90	114.38	18.93	47.83	487.9	3.97
1960	2398704	596	19931	28.99	112.62	19.28	48.27	506.5	3.85
1961	2435804	599	20023	29.10	114.82	20.12	49.22	524.6	2.97
1962	2514197	601	20380	30.09	116.91	20.04	50.13	565.0	3.26
1963	2527960	615	20269	31.55	119.74	20.75	52.30	596.7	3.55
1964	2500503	632	19468	33.49	123.74	21.61	55.10	637.7	3.97
1965	2527915	648	18687	35.26	128.54	22.72	57.98	691.1	4.38
1966	2759019	665	19131	37.48	133.58	23.83	61.31	756.0	5.55
1967	3002461	753	18996	39.37	138.38	25.26	64.63	799.6	5.10
1968	3055212	796	19607	41.97	148.47	27.22	69.19	873.4	5.90

Table 1 (continued)
Federal Reserve Employment, Monetary Aggregates, GNP, and Commercial Paper Rate

Year	Paid Civ. Empl. of Federal Govt.	Empl. of Board of Governors	Empl. of Fed Res. Banks	Currency ($bil.)	Demand Deposits ($bil.)	Bank Reserves ($bil.)	Mone-tary Base ($bil.)	GNP ($bil.)	Prime Commercial-Paper rate (Percent)
1969	3076414	902	20755	44.82	156.94	28.03	72.85	944.0	7.83
1970	2921909	1047	22079	47.69	162.30	29.27	76.96	992.7	7.72
1971	2862894	1169	22480	52.60	176.80	31.33	83.93	1077.6	5.11
1972	2811779	1208	24254	56.90	193.60	31.35	88.25	1185.9	4.73
1973	2765664	1276	26655	61.60	202.50	35.07	96.67	1326.4	8.15
1974	2893119	1363	27637	67.80	207.40	36.94	104.74	1434.2	9.84
1975	2896944	1445	26515	73.80	214.10	34.99	108.79	1549.2	6.32
1976	2883134	1470	25272	80.60	224.40	35.14	115.74	1718.0	5.34
1977	2841152	1477	24114	88.60	239.70	36.47	125.07	1918.0	5.61
1978	2872851	1477	23373	97.40	253.90	41.57	138.97	2156.1	7.99
1979	2875872	1451	23416	106.10	262.80	43.97	150.07	2413.9	10.91
1980	2875866	1525	24208	116.10	267.40	40.10	156.20	2626.1	12.29
1981	2895712	1504	23696	123.10	236.80	42.10	165.11	2922.2	14.76

Sources: Paid civilian employees of the federal government, 1915-64, from U.S. Department of Commerce, *Historical Statistics*. The years 1965-81 were taken from U.S. Department of Commerce, *Statistical Abstract*, various years. Employees of Federal Reserve System are listed in Board of Governors of the Federal Reserve System, *Annual Report*, various years. Currency in the hands of the public, demand deposits, and bank reserves, 1915-70, are from *Historical Statistics*; data for 1971-81 are from the *Economic Report of the President*. Gross National Product, 1915-39, is given in *Histroical Statistics*; data for the years 1940-81 are contained in the *Economic Report of the President*. The implicit *GNP* price deflator was spliced to change the base year from 1958 to 1972. The interest rate on prime commerical paper of four- to six-months maturity was taken from *Historical Statistics* for the years 1915-70, and from the *Economic Report of the President* for 1971-81.

a Includes 6 part-time employees.

b Includes 111 detailed currency counters.

Table 1 (continued)

c As of December.

d Includes 34 detailed employees and 2 part-time employees.

e Includes 19 detailed employees, as of December.

f Includes 3 detailed employees and 1 part-time employee.

g Includes 2 detailed employees.

h Includes 9 part-time employees.

i Includes 10 part-time employees.

j Exlcudes 15 part-time employees paid on an horly basis.

k Excludes 14 part-time employees paid on an hourly basis.

l Excludes 14 part-time employees and 4 temporary employees paid on an hourly basis, and 3 special temporary employees paid on a monthly basis.

m Estimated.

Governors. The observations are on an annual basis and cover the period from 1915 through 1981. Although the Federal Reserve Act was passed in late 1913, the Fed did not officially open its doors for business until the fall of 1914; 1915 was the first full year of operation for the central bank.

All variables, except for the interest rate and time trend, were transformed by taking the natural logarithm of the observations. Initial estimates using ordinary least squares indicated significant autocorrelation in the residuals. The equation was therefore re-estimated using generalized squares.(11) We also allowed for feedback effects on monetary policy by using the values of the currency-deposit ratio and interest rate lagged one year.

C. The Results

The regression results are given in Table 2. The estimated coefficients in column 1 provide broad confirmation of the profits-amenities hypothesis. An increase in the stock of high-powered money is strongly associated with an increase in the number of employees on the Fed's payroll. The coefficient is statistically different from zero at the 1 percent level. Moreover, the contemporaneous currency-deposit ratio has the expected sign and is equally significant. An increase in real income also leads to expansions in the monetary base; the coefficient reaches significance at the 10 percent level.

The insignificant coefficient on the interest rate variable conflicts with our a priori expectations. It is possible that this result obtains because we have used nominal rather than real interest rates, or because money demand effects dominate the postulated supply relationship. In addition to its role as a monetary target, the rate of interest represents the opportunity cost of holding money. Because individuals must forego the income from interest-bearing assets by holding money, other things equal, they reduce their money balances as interest rates rise.

In column 3, the contemporaneous currency-deposit ratio is replaced by the value of the same variable lagged one year. This specification would be appropriate if the Fed uses a feedback rule in which this year's monetary base is affected by last year's currency-deposit ratio. Lagged interest rates are deleted from column 4. The overall regression results seem to be unaffected by this substitution.(12)

The models in Table 2 explain 94 percent or more of the variation in the monetary base. Since we have run the regressions in logs, the coefficients can be directly interpreted as elasticities. The coefficient on the employment variable, LNSEMP, is about 1.4, indicating that a 1 percent increase in Fed employment results in more than a one-tenth of 1 percent rise in the monetary base. Over the 1915-81 period, the mean nominal stock of high-powered money was $44.7 billion, and there were on average 17,328 workers on the Fed payroll. Thus, each additional 173 Fed employees added roughly $62.6 million to the monetary base. Put another way, every time the Fed hired one more worker, the stock of high-powered money rose by about $362,000. Assuming these funds were used to purchase securities yielding a 10 percent return, the $362,000 would generate a thirty-year annuity of $20,745. This appears to be about the order of magnitude required to support the career of an average Fed employee.(13)

Table 2
Regression Results

Constant	– 1.0233	– 1.0863	– 1.5327	– 1.2860
LNSEMP	0.1308	0.1503	0.1523	0.1497
	(2.66)***	(3.63)***	(3.03)***	(3.22)***
LNCD	0.3357	0.2703		
	(3.14)***	(2.73)***		
LNCD(– 1)			0.3437	0.2774
			(2.94)***	(2.54)**
INT(– 1)	– 0.0068		– 0.0052	
	(– 0.75)		(– 0.54)	
LNRGNP	0.3108	0.2615	0.3757	0.3079
	(1.95)*	(1.79)*	(2.19)**	(1.96)*
TREND	0.0569	0.0596	0.0537	0.0567
	(6.13)***	(6.38)***	(5.71)***	(6.12)***
$TREND^2$	– 0.0002	– 0.0002	– 0.0002	– 0.0002
	(1.80)*	(– 2.07)**	– (1.74)*	(– 2.02)**
$\hat{\rho}$	0.7657	0.8234	0.7329	0.7939
R^2	0.952	0.940	0.956	0.943

Notes: *Dependent Variable: Natural Logarithm of Nominal Monetary Base, 1915-81.* t-values are given in parentheses; $\hat{\rho}$ is the estimated autocorrelation coefficient. Asterisks denote significance at the 1 percent (***), 5 percent (**), and 10 percent (*) levels.

III. ADDITIONAL EMPIRICAL FINDINGS

A. Relative Fed Growth

We considered whether the growth of the Fed relative to the federal government as a whole would explain variations in the monetary base. Such a formulation would be appropriate if the central bank's behavior is driven in part by a desire for prestige, which Acheson and Chant define as '. . . the position of the bureau in the social hierarchy of government bureaus' (chapter 7, p. 131). To test this proposition, we replaced LNSEMP by the natural logarithm of the ratio of Fed employment to the total number of paid civilian workers in the federal government, LNSYSPCT, and obtained the following results:

(1) LNBASE =

$$\underset{(2.42)^{**}}{-\,0.4534} + \underset{(3.36)^{***}}{0.1094\text{LNSYSPCT}} + \underset{(3.13)^{***}}{0.3824\text{LNCD}} +$$

$$\underset{(7.37)^{***}}{0.5003\text{LNRGNP}} + 0.0657\text{TREND} - \underset{(-3.80)^{***}}{0.0004\text{TREND}^2}$$

$$\hat{p} = 0.7908;\ R^2 = 0.944.$$

The coefficient on the Fed employment ratio is positive and significantly different from zero at the 5 percent level. This lower significance level is undoubtedly due to the tendency of increases in total government employment to swamp increases in the number of workers on the central bank's payroll. However, the overall results are similar to those obtained when the absolute number of Fed employees is used as an explanatory variable.

The result in equation (1) suggests that increases in the base are used to finance increases in the Fed's relative bureaucratic standing. That is, the employment ratio coefficient can be interpreted as showing that the Fed has been more successful in enlarging its employee staff over time than the federal government as a whole.

B. Fed Growth and the Velocity of Money

We investigated whether the positive and significant coefficient on the employment variable could be explained by spurious correlation arising because LNSEMP was picking up changes in the velocity of money. Velocity measures the number of times each \$1 turns over in financing a given level of nominal transactions. If more Fed employees are required, for example, to clear a larger volume of checks during times when velocity is relatively high, the estimated base-amenities relationship would be misleading.

Using the logarithm of contemporaneous velocity, LNV, as an

explanatory variable in the regression equation, we obtained the following results:

(2) LNBASE =

$$0.2980 + 0.2384\text{LNSEMP} + 0.1510\text{LNCD} - 0.6505\text{LNV} +$$
$$(5.19)^{***} \quad (1.41) \quad (-3.74)^{***}$$

$$0.0386\text{TREND} + 0.0003\text{TREND}^2$$
$$(3.72)^{***} \quad (1.58)$$

$$\hat{\rho} = 0.7052;\ R^2 = 0.967.$$

The estimates are quantitatively similar to those obtained in the other specifications. The negative sign on LNV is consistent with a countercyclical feedback rule of the following form – other things equal, a rise in velocity lowers the public's demand for money because a higher turnover rate implies that each $1 finances a higher proportion of transactions. Contractions in the monetary base will counteract the tendency for prices to rise as velocity increases.

Table 3
Test of Causality

	Lags						
Constant	−2	−1	0	+1	+2	$\hat{\rho}$	R^2
	Monetary Base Regressed on Past and Future Fed Employment						
0.0493	0.0606	0.1343	0.0102	0.0492	−0.1258	0.4295	0.226
	(1.02)	(1.89)*	(0.14)	(0.41)	(−1.04)		
0.0481	0.0782	0.1245	−0.0029			0.4284	0.211
	(1.39)	(1.81)*	(−0.04)				
	Fed Employment on Past and Future Monetary Base						
−0.0601	0.1942	0.3236	0.3093	0.8119	0.0027	0.2619	0.307
	(0.80)	(1.27)	(1.21)	(3.13)***	(0.01)		
−0.0359	0.3248	0.3362	0.5209			0.2042	0.192
	(1.26)	(1.20)	(1.93)*				

Notes: See Table 2.

The results obtained here as well as those in equation (1) suggest that Fed employment has not risen merely because more people are required to supervise larger money stocks. On the contrary, the bureaucratic aspects of Fed behavior appear to be powerful enough to overcome the substantial scale economics in fiat money production.(14)

C. Test of Causality

A third important issue is whether an increase in Fed employment leads to expansions in the monetary base or, alternatively, changes in the stock of high-powered money result in changes in the number of employees. To answer this question, we performed the test of causality suggested by C. W. J. Granger and later formalized by Christopher Sims.

After detrending the data by taking first differences of the logged observations, Sims' test involves estimating two-sided distributed lag regressions. For the hypothesis that there is no feedback from current changes in the monetary base to future Fed employment, one regresses the current monetary base on past, contemporaneous, and future employment figures. For the reverse hypothesis that there is no feedback from current employment levels to future base changes, this year's change in employment is regressed on past and future money.

The results are reported in Table 3. For each dependent variable, one regression includes two future and two past values of the right-hand side variable; the other regression omits the leading lags. In the first row, the small and insignificant coefficients on future changes in employment do not lead one to reject the null hypothesis that money does not cause employment in the sense of Granger. Moreover, comparing the overall results with those in row 2, the relevant F-statistic implies that the coefficients on the future values of employment are zero.(15)

In contrast, the results in rows 3 and 4 are consistent with the hypothesis that employment causes money. The coefficient on the one-year-ahead money value is significantly different from zero and is absolutely larger than the coefficients on the lagged money variables. Moreover, the calculated F is 4.65, which exceeds the critical value at the 5 percent level.

We conclude that the appropriate regression specification is one in which the monetary base is the dependent variable. That is, employment belongs in the money supply equation; the base does not belong in an input demand function. This result provides further support for the notion that bureaucratic incentives drive the money supply process and contradict the alternative view that increases in the base result in more employee hiring for the purpose of handling larger numbers of accounting entires.(16)

D. Implications

In Section I, we noted that Fed employment contains both 'real' and 'fake' components, the latter representing that portion of the payroll not justified by cost-minimizing money production. The theory also predicted that the postulated budget constraint would lead the Fed to over-purchase amenities (and therefore have a flatter expansion path) relative to a for-profit central bank. The empirical discussion has focused on the strong employment effect in the data without showing that the Fed's profit-amenities choices are different from those of the for-profit benchmark.

We have reported three pieces of evidence which are consistent with our theory. First, the positive base-employment relationship was not weakened by including velocity (transactions per dollar) as an explanatory variable. This result indicated that Fed employment rose by more than the amount required to perform the additional accounting work arising from increased velocity. Second, the causality tests implied that Fed employment properly appears in the money supply function, and not vice versa. People cause money; money does not cause people. Third, we found that growth of central bank employment relative to the federal government as a whole was associated with increases in the base. It is difficult to explain any of these results on the basis of hypotheses other than bureaucratic expansionism, given the very large scale economies in fiat money production.

As a fourth element of support for the bureaucratic hypothesis, consider the plot of the Fed's actual 'expansion' path in Figure 2. The amount of real current profits appears on the vertical axis; contemporaneous real expenditures are on the horizontal axis. The data include the central bank's current income from all sources, the bulk of which arises from open market operations, and all current expenses, that is, both real and fake costs. In a given year, the sum of the two figures represents the Fed's gross income.

At low values of the two variables, the expansion path is virtually horizontal, indicating that during the early years of its existence the Fed expensed a large proportion of its income. Until the end of the 1930's the Fed turned back roughly one-third to one-half of its annual securities portfolio income to the Treasury. In later years, the expansion path moves slowly upward and to the right, showing a strong amenities bias that is consistent with our theory. The Fed's actual expansion path appears remarkably similar to ray 3 in Figure 1,

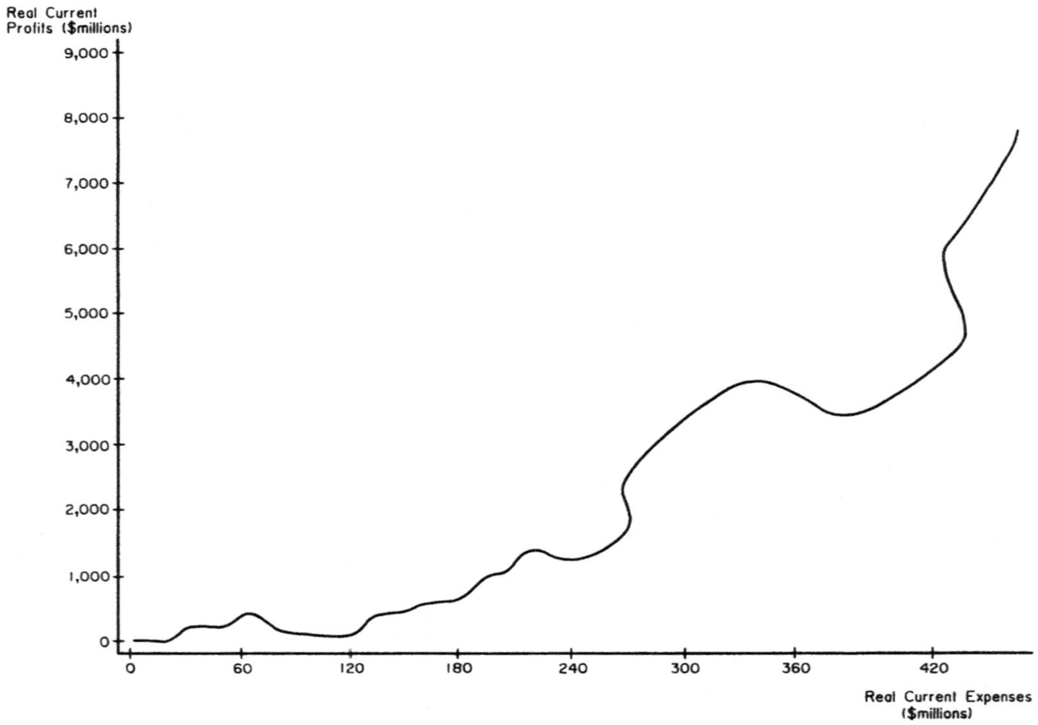

Figure 2. The Fed's Actual "Expansion" Path.

and is clearly not the type of path one would expect with, for example, substantial economies of scale in fiat money production.

IV. CONCLUDING REMARKS

In this paper we have presented evidence of a positive and statistically significant relationship between changes in the size of the Fed and changes in the nominal stock of high-powered money. This result suggests that the Federal Reserve System may function like a typical bureaucracy. That is, the Fed seems to adjust to the requirement that it return its profits to the Treasury by augmenting the number of employees on its payroll.

The employment effect that we have identified in the data is not a substitute for more traditional money supply theories, but serves as an additional determinant of the stock of high-powered money in the economy. In particular, our findings provide an explanation for what Friedman refers to as the Fed's '. . . extraordinary record of bureaucratic inertia, of mistakes what have not been corrected despite their widespread recognition' (chapter 2, p. 21). In the words of Acheson and Chant, 'frequently such policy failures are judged as aberrations or are ascribed to ignorance or bad judgment' (chapter 7, p. 132). Our results suggest, however, that the employment effect may partially explain why the Fed has apparently been more willing to engage in expansionary than in contractionary monetary policies. As we noted earlier, contractionary open market operations reduce the Fed's profits and therefore diminish the funds available for hiring. That such a tendency exists is a consequence of having a monopoly supplier of money whose profits are confiscated by the Treasury. Competition would certainly mitigate the incentive for money producers to overinvest in amenities. However, the current monetary system may provide benefits which balance the costs associated with the use of money stock expansions to finance central bank employment. Our paper does not address such issues.

NOTES

1. Gerald Dwyer has recently produced evidence, however, that '. . . there is no immediately apparent connection between the federal government's deficits and debt purchases by the Federal Reserve' (p. 327).
2. See Boris Pesek and Thomas Saving, pp. 102-04.
3. Federal Reserve notes are not a true liability in the sense that they do not represent a call on the real assets of the Federal Reserve System.
4. Pesek and Saving observe that 'even a moron who gets the right to print government current

(Federal Reserve notes) and sell it for income-earning assets . . . is bound to show a profit' (p. 407).

5. See any *Annual Report* of the Board of Governors.
6. We adopt here George Stigler's (1966, p. 73) formulation of the pioneering work of Armen Alchian and Reuben Kessel.
7. The diagram is not intended to show the actual relative magnitudes of foregone profits and operating expenses. During 1981, the twelve Federal Reserve Banks earned \$15.51 billion in income, \$14.55 billion or 94 percent of which was attributable to the Fed's portfolio of U.S. government securities. After paying their operating expenses, contributing \$63.16 million to defray the expenditures of the Board of Governors, and making other accounting adjustments, the banks turned over \$14.02 billion in profits to the government's general revenue account as 'interest on Federal Reserve notes.' For the entire 1915-81 period, the Fed retained on average 14 percent of its income, contributing \$98.79 billion to the Treasury out of \$115.10 billion in total revenues.
8. On this point, see Stigler (1976).
9. Gordon Tullock informs us that the 'old' Federal Reserve Board Building was for many years the building in Washington with the highest cost per square foot.
10. The Fed supplies the nominal base; the real stock of money is determined by the public.
11. A. C. Harvey (pp. 189-92) discusses the relative small-sample efficiency of generalized least squares to the Cochrane-Orcutt method when the model contains a trending explanatory variable.
12. We estimated an alternative specification which involved including the natural logarithm of the implicit price deflator as an explanatory variable. The price variable would be appropriate if the Fed uses a feedback rule in which higher prices lead to contractionary policies, and vice versa. The estimated coefficient on this parameter was not significantly different from zero, however. In addition, results qualitatively similar to those in Table 2 were obtained when percentage changes in the variables were used.
13. Employment at the Board of Governors is highly correlated with employment in the district and branch banks ($r^2 = 0.804$, which is significantly different from zero at the 1 percent level). The regression results are therefore unaffected by our choice of System employment as the input measure.
14. The results are also consistent with Friedman's (chapter 2, p. 26) contention of bond market 'churning.' He observes that in 1980 the Fed's \$800 billion of open market purchases led to a net change of only \$4.5 billion in the bank's securities portfolio. Such an 'excessive' number of transactions may result from an excessive number of securities traders.
15. Let K denote the number of independent variables in the regression equation, which omits the leading values, and Q the number of right-hand-side arguments for the full expression. If the added variables (Q > K) are not relevant in explaining variations in the dependent variable, then differences in the regression sums of squares would be attributable to sampling error. The test statistic has the following form:

$$\frac{R^2_Q - R^2_K}{1 - R^2_Q} \; \frac{n - Q}{Q - K} \sim F_{Q} - K, n - q$$

where n is the number of observations. For the first regression pair, R^2 rises trivially when the leading employment values are added. The two variables do not therefore contribute significantly to the equation's explanatory value.

16. We also estimated all regression specifications augmented by a dummy variable that took on

the value of unity for the years 1934-81, and zero otherwise. The dummy variable was employed to account for a possible effect connected with repeal in 1933 of the requirement that the Fed pay half of its yearly net earnings to the Treasury. Prior to this change, which Toma describes as a quid pro quo for creation of the Federal Deposit Insurance Corporation, the Board of Governors was funded through the normal congressional budgetary process. The member banks paid their own way, however, and because the turnover requirement was expressed in terms of net earnings, it is not entirely clear a priori how this constraint might have affected the base-amenities relation. However, the results invariably showed a positive and significant coefficient on the dummy variable with no change in either the magnitude or significance of other coefficients. This suggests that removal of the half-yearly-net-earnings turnover requirement led to greater monetary expansionism, without affecting the Fed's amenities bias. If anything, the bias was strengthened in the sense that the coefficient on the Fed employment ratio in equation (1) was significant at the 1 percent level when the dummy variable was included.

REFERENCES

Acheson, Keith and John F. Chant, 'Bureaucratic Theory and the Choice of Central Bank Goals,' chapter 7 in this volume.

Alchian, Armen A. and Reuben A. Kessel, 'Competition, Monopoly and the Pursuit of Pecuniary Gain,' in *Aspects of Labor Economics*, Universities-National Bureau of Economic Research Conference Series, 14, Arno Press: New York, 1962, 157-75.

Chant, John F. and Keith Acheson, 'The Choice of Monetary Instruments and the Theory of Bureaucracy,' chapter 6 in this volume.

Chant, John F. and Keith Acheson, 'Mythology and Central Banking,' *Kyklos*, 2, 1973, 26, 362-79.

Dwyer, Gerald P., Jr., 'Inflation and Government Deficits,' *Economic Inquiry*, July 1982, 20, 315-29.

Freidman, Milton, 'Monetary Policy: Theory and Practice,' chapter 2 in this volume.

Granger, C. W. J., 'Investigating Causal Relations by Econometric Models and Cross-Spectral Methods,' *Econometrica*, July 1969, 37, 424-38.

Harvey, A. C., *The Econometric Analysis of Times Series*, John Wiley & Sons: New York, 1981.

Pesek, Boris P. and Thomas R. Saving, *The Foundations of Money and Banking*, Macmillian: New York, 1968.

Sims, Christopher A., 'Money, Income and Causality,' *American Economic Review*, September 1972, 62, 540-52.

Stigler, George J., *The Theory of Price*, 3rd ed., Macmillan: New York, 1966.

Stigler, George J., 'The Xistence of X-Efficiency,' *American Economic Review*, March 1976, 66, 213-6.

Toma, Mark, 'Inflationary Bias of the Federal Reserve System: A Bureaucratic Perspective,' chapter 3 in this volume.

Board of Governors of the Federal Reserve System, *Annual Report*, Board of Governors: Washington, various years.

U.S. Council of Economic Advisers, *Economic Report of the President*, USGPO: Washington, 1982.

U.S. Department of Commerce, Bureau of the Census, *Historical Statistics of the United*

States, Colonial Times to 1970, 2 vols., USGPO; Washington, 1975.
U.S. Department of Commerce, Bureau of the Census, *Statistical Abstract of the United States*, USGPO; Washington, various years.

Chapter 5

THE STRUCTURE AND USE OF INPUTS BY THE FEDERAL RESERVE
Reconsidered: The Monetary Constitution, Human Capital, and Property Rights

Wm. Stewart Mounts, Jr. and Clifford Sowell

Recently William Shughart and Robert Tollison (S-T), found a (chapter 4 in this volume) significant, albeit small, and causal relationship between the size of the Federal Reserve, measured by the number of system employees, and the annual growth of the monetary base. Elsewhere, Mark Toma (chapter 3 in this volume) found a positive relationship between Fed operating expenses and the level of earnings turned over to the Treasury. Both studies used a bureaucratic framework of central bank behavior as the theoretical foundation for empirical analysis. This perspective stresses the notion that bureau behavior is the result of interacting individuals (bureaucrats) pursuing self-interest within a system of institutional incentives and constraints.

Our point of departure is not controversial but is necessary for proper time series analysis of monetary aggregates and is based on the simple idea that the behavior of policymakers will change when the constraints they face change (see Sargent, 1981). Of particular importance is Toma's discussion of the incentive structure within which the Fed has operated since its inception. In this interpretation, the 'monetary constitution' or 'revenue setting' has undergone two essential changes. The first occurred in 1933 with the creation of the FDIC and the repeal of the original fifty percent franchise tax on annual Fed earnings. At this time, the disposition of total earnings was shifted to the discretion of the Fed hierarchy and with the creation of the Federal Open Market Committee (FOMC) in the Banking Act of 1935, the revenue raising function of the system was also centralized. In 1947, the

Toma, E.F. and Toma, M. (eds.) Central Bankers, Bureaucratic Incentives, and Monetary Policy

ISBN 90 247 3366 9

Board of Governors, fearing legislative sanction, voluntarily returned to the Treasury the remaining portion of its earnings after expenses. This practice continues today.

Clearly, changes in the revenue setting constitute changes in the institutional constraints in which monetary policy is made. In this paper we modify the S-T bureaucratic model to refine the measurement and impact of the institutional constraints contained in the changing relationship between the Federal Reserve and the Treasury as outlined by Toma. The S-T treatment implicitly assumed a stable institutional setting thereby partially misspecifying the effect of bureaucratic incentives on the supply of high-powered money.

In addition, we expand S-T by including human capital variables and other bureaucratic factors that affect monetary policy through the self-interested behavior of members of the Board of Governors in the context of the monetary constitution. Within this extension we develop measures of governors' pre-Board experiences, Board service experience (Fed tenure), and Milton Friedman's (chapter 2 in this volume) concept of 'bureaucratic inertia'.

In general, the findings suggest that changes in the institutional setting inherent in the various periods of the monetary constitution are significant determinants of the supply of high-powered money. Furthermore, support for Friedman is found in that inertia in monetary policy is sufficient, on net, to overcome any learning by experience that may have occurred over time. Also, the division of labor within the central bank and the resulting property rights are found to have significant roles in the bureaucratic model of Fed behavior. All findings are consistent across alternative econometric specifications which account for various adjustment (feedback) rules possibly employed by the monetary authority.

Section I details the extensions and modifications of the S-T model. Also, data construction and measurable variables are discussed. Section II reviews the results within the various econometric forms. A summary and conclusion are found in Section III.

I.

A model of Treasury/Fed linkage must be developed in order to place the changing monetary constitution in a model of the supply of high-powered money. Shughart and Tollison, arguing that the Fed structure contributes to explaining growth in the monetary base, used a model of regulated monopoly to show the incentive the Fed has to pad its own expenses (seen in the number of System employees) when the Treasury serves as residual claimant to excess earnings. This model assumes a tradeoff between amenities and profits and argues that monitoring or profit regulation reduces the relative price of amenities. Thus, more amenities are consumed relative to the level consumed by an unregulated monopolist.

The use of this model of regulation is somewhat misleading however. It implicitly assumes that the Fed could act like an unregulated monopolist if the Treasury was not the residual claimant. As stated above, Toma argues that the monetary constitution has had three distinct periods (1914-1933, 1933-1947, 1947-present). Of central importance is the period 1933-1947 when the Fed was essentially free to spend or retain all excess earnings. Over this period the Fed was, in a sense, an unregulated monopolist. In the S-T view, the removal of profit regulation or monitoring would increase the relative price of amenities thereby reducing their consumption. However, it is not clear where the Fed could legally spend its earnings when unregulated. Could it acquire ownership of productive private capital?

An alternative view is that the Treasury and Congress, in serving as residual claimants to excess earnings, monitor in some fashion the consumption of amenities because they are aware of the tradeoff between profits and amenities. In this perspective the Fed can only spend money on itself. Accordingly, removing the Treasury as claimant reduces monitoring, thereby lowering (rather than raising) the relative price of amenities, encouraging their consumption beyond that which was implicitly allowed under alternative arrangements in the monetary constitution.

Under either interpretation, a change in the monetary constitution causes a change in the bureaucratic incentive system faced by the Board of Governors. This results in changes in Fed size (the variable selected for measuring bureaucratic effects) which then affects the growth of high-powered money. Whether the 1933-1947 period promoted (our view) or discouraged (S-T view) the growth of the base is an empirical question which can be clarified by adding a variable to the S-T equations. A variable is created which is the interaction of System employment and a dummy variable equaling one during 1933-1947 and zero otherwise.(1) A positive coefficient would support our thesis while maintaining the basic S-T monetary base-amenities argument.(2)

While the above modification may link more clearly the issues in Toma and S-T, it does not account for the characteristics of the individuals comprising the Board of Governors. If it is the case that bureau behavior may be studied by examining the actions of self-interested bureaucrats within given constraints, then human capital theory would lead one to believe that the characteristics of bureaucrats should be significant determinants of bureau behavior. For example, Friedman argues that the absence of a 'bottom line' or external accountability promotes bureaucratic inertia which keeps the Federal Reserve from adapting new procedures that would enhance monetary control.(3) It is reasonable to expect governors to develop vested interests in the current methods by which the Fed conducts monetary policy. Over time individual Board members accumulate human capital which has been developed within the context set by the procedures of the Board of Governors and the Fed in general. Changes in procedures offer potential capital losses to this Fed-specific stock and, therefore, would be resisted. In addition, being the monopoly producer of high-powered money gives an individual an amplified feeling of importance, and changes in procedure may threaten stature (losses in psychic income).

This, however, is an incomplete view of inertia. A more complete explanation involves not only the development of Fed-specific human capital, but also the effects of pre-Fed experience on behavior. Governor's stock of human capital developed prior to Fed service reflects different conditioning to monitoring. In general, organizational incentive systems, by constraining behavior, establish the institutional environment in which individual human capital is developed. There is no a priori reason, however, to believe that all organizations monitor individual behavior similarly (see Eugene Fama and Michael Jensen, 1983 (a) and (b)). Rent-seeking literature suggests that government organizations (bureaucracies) have monitoring mechanisms which are more costly and less efficient in altering individual behavior relative to monitoring in private firms. Accordingly, individuals in bureaucracies develop human capital (learned behavior) which has been relatively less constrained by a bottom line compared with individuals whose human capital was subject to more complete private market review. Having been less exposed to a bottom line, bureaucrats have learned to be less responsive or receptive to learning from experience.

This discussion, combined with previous works on the Board of Governors (see Mounts, Sowell and Lindley, 1985), suggest two human capital variables which would be expected to influence monetary policy. One would be a variable which measures human capital developed in pre-Board public sector experience and therefore represents bureaucratic inertia. The second would be a variable measuring capital developed through service on the Board and therefore reflecting learning by experience.

To capture bureaucratic inertia in monetary policy, we use a variable measuring the proportion of a given Board of Governors with any prior public sector experience. By examining biographical references on each governor, sources of significant experience prior to Board membership can be determined and classified as private sector only, public sector only (bureaucratic), or mixed. Prior public sector experience serves as a proxy for a given Board's previous lack of experience with a meaningful bottom line, i.e., receptiveness to forms of external monitoring.

Annual average tenure per governor by year is used to measure the second human capital variable, learning by experience or Board service experience.(4) If it is assumed that a particular growth rate in the monetary base is the desired target for monetary policy, then human capital theory suggests that the Board of Governors would become a better money manager (given a set of monitoring devices) over time. Alternatively, with time, unanticipated growth in the base should approach zero. Thus, increases in average tenure should produce slower overall growth in the base, and learning from experience should promote monetary control.

The prior public experience and average tenure variables are expected to have opposite effects on base growth. The magnitude of the two variables must be compared in order to ascertain whether bureaucratic inertia or learning by experience has a stronger effect on Board behavior.

II.

A. Results Within the S-T Framework

Table 1 lists the S-T results (from generalized least squares) with the inclusion of the interactive dummy indicating changes in the monetary constitution (MONCON), the natural logarithm of average tenure (LNATEN), and bureaucratic inertia (PROPUB).(5) All signs, coefficients, and significance levels for the original S-T variables are confirmed with these additions.

The effect of a changing monetary constitution is positive and significant, offering support to the alternative view presented above. While the coefficient on MONCON is absolutely small, the sign suggests that Treasury monitoring (in its role as residual claimant) serves to raise the relative price of amenities. Also, the coefficient on System employment (LNSEMP) has increased relative to the original S-T coefficient (with exception in the second equation). This implies that omitting an explicit treatment of the changing relative price structure inherent in the monetary constitution (conditioned with LNATEN and PROPUB) results in an understatement of the effect of Fed size on the growth of the base.

Table 1
Regression Results (S-T)

CONSTANT	−1.7262	−1.7838	−2.6119	−1.6253
LNSEMP	0.1496 (2.7656)*	0.1379 (2.6730)*	0.1870 (3.2702)*	0.1702 (3.4342)*
LNCD	0.4310 (3.8848)*	0.4281 (3.9913)*		
LNCD (−1)			0.4810 (3.6619)*	0.3178 (2.6625)*
INT (-1)	−0.0079 (−0.7626)		−0.0058 (0.4997)	
LNRGNP	0.4446 (2.8464)*	0.4664 (2.9243)*	0.5856 (3.2824)*	0.3622 (2.1823)**
TREND	0.0529 (6.1285)*	0.0561 (7.4195)*	0.0505 (5.6605)*	0.0567 (6.8499)*
TREND2	−0.0002 (−1.9949)**	−0.0003 (−3.1499)*	−0.0003 (−2.2253)**	−0.0003 (2.4175)*
LNATEN	−0.0512 (−1.4821)***	−0.0541 (−1.5882)***	−0.0892 (−2.2824)**	−0.0591 (−1.7867)**
PROPUB	0.1447 (1.5918)***	0.1263 (1.4452)***	0.1445 (1.4437)***	0.0854 (1.0193)
MONCON	0.0153 (2.8113)*	0.0159 (2.9699)*	0.0103 (1.7054)**	0.0108 (1.9282)**
R^2	0.9629	0.9622	0.9683	0.9453
N	66	66	66	66
SEE	0.0783	0.0778	0.0865	0.0749
F	1.0406	0.6911	0.2942	0.0994

Notes: In all regressions the dependent variable is the natural logarithm of the nominal monetary base, 1916-1981. The first value in each row is the estimated GLS coefficient and the second is the t value. *, **, *** indicate significance at the one percent, five percent, and ten percent levels, respectively. The S-T independent variables are defined as follows (natural logarithms LN): LNSEMP, Fed system employment; LNCD, currency-deposit ratio; LNCDC(−1), lagged currency-deposit ratio; INT(−1), lagged interest rate (non log form); LNRGNP, real GNP, TREND, and $TREND^2$. SEE, standard error of the estimate.

The two micro bureaucratic variables (LNATEN and PROPUB) have the anticipated signs, the appropriate relative magnitudes and are significant (with the significance of PROPUB an exception in the fourth equation). Furthermore, an F-test does not permit the rejection of the null hypothesis that the estimated effect of learning from experience equals the effect of bureaucratic inertia.(6) Apparently inertia offsets learning.

B. An Alternative Specification

The introduction of LNATEN and PROPUB into the S-T model explicitly places microeconomic concepts in a role of explaining variations in macroeconomic variables. An alternative test is provided in order to strengthen the basic argument presented in Section I. Learning from experience and inertia are undoubtedly dynamic processes and, therefore, should be tested in an explicitly dynamic form in order to complement the S-T static supply formulations. In addition, the role of bureaucratic incentives in the changing Treasury/Fed linkage (the monetary constitution) would gain further support if tested in an alternative setting.

Assume that the policy feedback rule is given by a simple partial adjustment model:

$$M_t = M_{t-1} + \lambda (M_t^* - M_{t-1}) + e_t \tag{1}$$

where M_t^* reflects the desired monetary base from the perspective of the Board. Given the arguments and evidence from S-T and the current extension, M_t^* will reflect overall stabilization objectives as well as bureaucratic goals and incentives. Thus, it is assumed that M_t^* is given by an exact relation in these dual objectives:

$$M_t^* = a_0 + a_1\,LNRGNP_t + a_2\,INT_t + a_3\,LNCD_t + a_4LNSEMP_t + a_5\,LNATEN_t + a_6\,PROPUB_t + a_7\,MONCON_t. \tag{2}$$

In the absence of aggregate supply shocks reflected via e_t, Board behavior reflects a mix of objectives. For simplicity it is assumed that the rate of adjustment to the long run value of the monetary base occurs at a rate of λ per year for both stabilization and bureaucratic objectives.

The adjustment costs reflected in λ arise from the mix of objectives embodied in Board behavior. A major source of these costs is the time required to recognize the need for policy change, to arrive at a consensus, and

Table 2
Partial Adjustment Model

	1	2	3	4	5	6	7	8
CONSTANT	.2497		.0979		−1.1265		.9811	
LNMB(−1)	.8088		.8366		.7632		.7910	
	(21.8319)*		(24.7277)*		(19.0331)*		(20.4560)*	
LNSEMP	.0757	−.3959	−.1017	−.6224				
	(-1.7936)**		(−2.6090)*					
LNBD					.0487	.2056	.0457	.2187
					(1.3378)***		(1.4714)***	
LNCD	.2255	1.1794	.2246	1.3745	.1991	.8408	1.4714	.8598
	(3.9484)*		(3.9842)*		(3.5805)*		(3.2624)*	
INT	−.0107	−.0559	−0.0094	−.0575	−.0121	−.0511	−.0108	−.0517
	(−2.0226)**		(1.8129)**		(−2.1978)**		(−1.9910)	
LNRGNP	.3179	1.6626	.3004	1.8384	.3104	1.3108	.2803	1.3411
	(5.6567)*		(5.5075)*		(5.4890)*		(5.0067)*	
LNATEN	−.0318	−.1663	−.0283	−.1732	−.0377	−.1592	−.0363	−.1737
	(−1.8481)**		(−1.7148)**		(−2.3264)**		(−2.2200)**	
PROPUB	.1285	.6721			.1681	.7099		
	(2.8785)				(4.0382)*			

Table 2 (continued)

INERTIA		.0939 (3.1245)*	.5747				.1189 (3.8443)*	.5689
MONCON	.0089 (3.9798)*	.0465	.0074 (3.3097)*	.0453	.0137 (3.7502)*	.0578	.0107 (2.8187)**	.0512
PC	.0465 (3.3186)*	.2432	.0461 (3.3188)*	.2821	.0374 (2.5606)*	.1579	.0330 (2.2317)**	.1579
R^2	.9985		.9986		.9985		.9985	
N	65		65		65		65	
λ	.1912		.1634		.2368		.2090	
h	.0080		−.3285		.1580		.1234	
F	5.3956		4.5749		9.8670		6.2699	
SEE	.0447		.0443		.0451		.0459	

Note:*, **, *** significant at the one, five and ten percent level respectively. The dependent variable is the natural log of the monetary base, 1916-1981.

to act to bring about policy objectives. A second source arises from the bureaucratic behavior of the Board. Based on the findings listed in Table 1, changes in the monetary constitution, tenure (learning from experience) and inertia affect the rate at which M_t* is reached.

In order to implement the model two stage least squares (TSLS) is used to account for potential simultaneity in terms of the demand for high-powered money.(7) The inverted demand relation assumes that nominal interest rates depend on the current monetary base, current and lagged real GNP, the price level and the lagged inflation rate. The latter term may be viewed as the current expected rate of inflation (Richard Parks, 1978). Also, in order to account for shocks which affect both aggregate supply as well as the monetary base, a dummy variable (PC) is included to account for periods of government intervention in product and factor markets.(8)

Finally, an alternative measure of bureaucratic inertia (INERTIA) is introduced into this specification. This variable is the interaction of PROPUB with the lagged difference of LNATEN. Besides measuring prior public sector experience, the inclusion of the rate of change in average tenure introduces the effects of external monitoring (Board turnover) into the model and enhances the measurement of the dynamic structure inherent in the inertia process.(9) Specifically, it is assumed to measure the vested interest in current Board procedures and the role of the appointment process. It is lagged to allow for a carry over of past policies into a current Board's decisionmaking.

The TSLS results for this specification are found in columns 1-4 of Table 2.(10) Long run elasticities are listed to the right of their respective coefficients.

As indicated, either measure of inertia in monetary policy is significant and larger in magnitude than the estimated effect of average tenure.(11) Thus, in this dynamic specification, the Fed continues to appear to be unable to learn from experience.

Table 2 also shows the effect of Fed size on the monetary base to be negative and significant even though MONCON remains positive and significant. While this seems to be contrary to the theoretical arguments presented here, in S-T, and in Toma, it is premature to argue that the bureaucratic view is an econometric anomaly and ambiguous at best without considering the division of labor within the Federal Reserve System. A division of labor implies the existence of rules or property rights. In general, the literature has long recognized the importance and role of property rights in the constrained optimizing behavior of economic agents.

The Fed may be viewed as performing two general functions: (1) conducting monetary policy and (2) monitoring and regulating banking activities in general. Furthermore, these functions are divided clearly between the Board and the District Banks, respectively.(12) Thus, the Board technically 'earns' the excess revenue by conducting monetary policy and may act as if it 'owns' the excess by appropriating it for its own use.(13) This view is strongly supported by the characteristics of the 1933-1947 period of the monetary constitution.

If it is correct to measure the monetary base-amenities relation through a size variable then, within this property rights perspective, the effects would be specified correctly through Board employment as opposed to System employment.(14) In addition, inertia and learning in monetary policy are Board concepts and, hence, would also be more accurately measured by including a measure of Board employment in the model.

Columns 5-8 of Table 2 list the TSLS results with the natural logarithm of Board employment (LNBD) replacing that of System employment and Board employment interacting with the years 1933-1947 (MONCON). With the interaction of LNBD, MONCON remains positive and significant. Its persistent high degree of significance across the various econometric forms suggests that institutional constraints and incentives relating to the monetary constitution are important in the bureaucratic explanation of Fed behavior and can be seen affecting the growth of the monetary base.(15)

The positive sign and single tail significance of LNBD appear to support the property right/bureaucratic view of Fed behavior. In addition, inertia (both forms), is highly significant and clearly dominates the effect of experience. Based on the F statistic the null hypothesis can be rejected in favor of the alternative that inertia produces net positive effects on the growth of the monetary base. The long run elasticities of the bureaucratic variables indicate their relative importance in the long run supply of the monetary base. The magnitude of inertia (either form) only ranks behind the long run elasticity of real GNP and the currency-deposit ratio.

III.

The purpose of this paper was to extend and modify the recent work of Shughart and Tollison. Central to the foundation of our analysis is the notion that the behavior of bureaucrats, and therefore, the behavior of the bureaus, change as the incentives and constraints they face change. The findings of this research do nothing to contradict this view. Quite the contrary, we offer support for an explicit treatment of the nexus of bureaucratic and human capital factors that govern the dynamics of policy making.

Specifically, we introduced variables measuring (1) changes in the monetary constitution and (2) the human capital characteristics of the Board of Governors. The findings support the idea that changes in the institutional incentives and bureaucratic structure in which the Fed has operated have had significant effects on the supply of high-powered money. Also, estimated coefficients and related tests do not reject Friedman's claim that institutional inertia is more than sufficient to offset learning from experience. In addition, the division of labor within the Fed and the implied property rights were found to have significant roles in the bureaucratic model.

NOTES

1. Shughart and Tollison (chapter 4 in this volume, note 16) mention the use of a dummy variable which equals one from 1934-1981 and zero otherwise. Their discussion implies an appreciation or Toma's interpretation of the monetary constitution. However, this dummy ignores the events of 1947. The S-T variable is probably reflecting the Banking Act of 1935 and not the monetary constitution.
2. Under either model, income effects promote Fed size. However, S-T implicitly argue that the substitution effect caused by the changing monetary constitution have negative effects on size where we claim positive effects. Therefore, in the S-T view the changing monetary constitution has ambiguous net effects on Fed size.
3. Bureaucratic inertia is defined as the general propensity of a bureaucracy to resist change and to ignore or discount learning from experience.
4. Biographical data were collected from various *Who's Who*, *International Who's Who*, *New York Times Obituaries*, and *Federal Reserve Bulletins*. See Mounts, Sowell and Lindley (1985) for further discussion of data. Boards of Governors were constructed from 'Membership of the Board of Governors of the Federal Reserve System, 1913-1980,' *Federal Reserve Bulletin*, June 1980, 490-491. A reconstruction of actual Boards through time permits the measurement of cumulative Fed experience represented in any one Board at any point in time. All other data were taken from the Shughart and Tollison article, Table 1, 297-298.
5. The four equations allow for alternative feedback rules through interest rates and/or the currency-deposit ratio. The original S-T variables are defined at the bottom of Table 1.
6. The F statistic at the bottom of all tables refers to the test of the equality restriction between the coefficients on tenure and inertia. For Table 1, the critical $F(1,55)$ is 4.02 or 7.12 at the five or one percent levels of significance, respectively.
7. All variables are estimated in natural log form if appropriate. Other exogenous variables included in the first stage are the currency-deposit ratio, a price control dummy, and the bureaucratic variables.
8. The spirit of this variable is based on the recent work of Robert J. Gordon (1983). This is, in part, a price and wage control dummy equaling one during 1918-1920 (World War I), 1933-1937 (NIRA and Wagner Act), 1943-1947 (World War II), 1950-1952 (Korean War), 1972-1974 (Nixon years), and zero otherwise.
9. Low or negative rates of change in average tenure would indicate little collective Fed experience by the Board. Resignations, retirements, or new appointments for expired terms would all reduce average Board tenure. These factors suggest some degree of outside monitor-

ing. In addition, newly appointed governors may have some sense of accountability to those individuals who promoted their appointment. This is also a form of external monitoring.

10. The null hypothesis of no autocorrelation could not be rejected. The appropriate test statistic in an autoregressive model is the h listed in Table 2 (See J. Johnson, 318).
11. The alternative inertia term was tested in the original S-T models in place of PROPUB. While the sign was positive the variable was usually not significant. This is not surprising. One would not anticipate a relatively dynamic variable to do very much in a static specification.
12. One may take exception to this by noting that the FOMC conducts open market operations. However, the majority of the FOMC is the Board and four of the five District Bank presidents are rotated off annually thus limiting their persuasive influence. In addition, this division of labor was formalized in the Banking Act of 1935 which, in part, centralized Fed power in the Board of Governors.
13. District Banks collect funds for their use from the sale of services, through the discount window, and by drawing on an account at the New York Fed Bank. This draw is on the excess revenues generated by the Board's open market operations. However, a District Bank's draw is limited by its assets as a percent of System assets. A District Bank's assets are determined by the paid in capital of member banks. Thus, a District Bank's draw is limited by the size of the district. Therefore, they are not like 'owners' of the excess. Their access to it is indirect and constrained.
14. Shughart and Tollison were led by measures of correlation in their selection of System employment.
15. The period 1933-1947 covers the years of World War II when excessive monetary expansion was desired. However, the effect of war is controlled by the wage and price control dummy (PC).

REFERENCES

Fama, Eugene F. and Michael D. Jensen, 'Agency Problems and Residual Claims,' *Journal of Law and Economics*, June 1983a, 26, 327-349.

-----, 'Separation of Ownership and Control,' *Journal of Law and Economics*, June 1983b, 26, 301-325.

Friedman, Milton, 'Monetary Policy: Theory and Practice,' chapter 2 in this volume.

-----, and Friedman, Rose, *Tyranny of the Status Quo*, Harcourt Brace Jovanovich: New York, 1983.

Gordon, Robert J., 'A Century of Evidence on Wage and Price Stickiness in the United States, United Kingdom, and Japan,' in J. Tobin (Ed.), *Macroeconomics, Prices and Quantities*, Brookings Institute: Washington, DC, 1983, 85-121.

Johnston, J., *Econometric Methods*, (3rd ed.), McGraw-Hill: New York, 1984.

Mounts, Wm. Stewart, Jr., Clifford Sowell, and James T. Lindley, 'Rent- Seeking Over Time: The Continuity of Capture,' *Public Choice*, 1985, 46, 87-94.

Parks, Richard A., 'Inflation and Relative Price Variability,' *Journal of Political Economy*, February 1978, 86, 79-95.

Sargent, Thomas J., 'Interpreting Economic Time Series,' *Journal of Political Economy*, April 1982, 89, 213-249.

Shughart, William F. and Robert D. Tollison, 'Preliminary Evidence on the Use of Inputs by the Federal Reserve System,' chapter 4 in this volume.

Tobin, James (Ed.), *Macroeconomics, Prices and Quantities*, Brookings Institute: Washington, DC, 1983.

Toma, Mark, 'Inflationary Bias of the Federal Reserve System: A Bureaucratic Perspective,' chapter 3 in this volume.

II. THE ORGANIZATION OF CENTRAL BANK BUREAUS AND THE PROBLEMS OF CONTROL

Chapter 6

THE CHOICE OF MONETARY INSTRUMENTS AND THE THEORY OF BUREAUCRACY(1)

By John F. Chant and Keith Acheson

Increasingly economists have reached agreement on the requirements for effective monetary control. In theory, control of the price level can be achieved through control of one nominal magnitude and an interest rate.(2) In practice, the requirements as Harry G. Johnson argues, are identical: 'the central bank can control the price level if it fixes the yield on its liabilities and controls the quantity thereof through open market operations' (pp. 977-78). Acceptance of this view ranges over a wide spectrum of economists from Milton Friedman (1960, pp. 50-51), an adviser to the Republican party, to Warren L. Smith, a member of the Council of Economic Advisers under the Johnson administration. Smith for example states:

> I would favor placing complete reliance on open market operations, under ordinary circumstances, as the means of conducting general monetary policy... It is difficult to see that adjustments in reserve requirements and the discount rate give the authorities any ability to change the structure of interest rates and the total credit supply that could not equally well be accomplished by sufficiently flexible use of Federal Reserve open markets and Treasury debt management operations. (p. 281)

As Johnson observes, '... In the actual practice of central banking, however, reliance is placed on additional instruments and techniques of control over the commercial banks. From the point of view of the theory of monetary control, these additional controls are unnecessary' (pp. 977-78).

In Canada monetary policy includes not only additional general instruments such as variable secondary reserve requirements and changes in the

Toma, E.F. and Toma, M. (eds.) Central Bankers, Bureaucratic Incentives, and Monetary Policy

ISBN 90 247 3366 9

Bank Rate but also a labyrinth of institutional arrangements such as purchase and resale agreements, management of government deposit balances, interest rate agreements between the Bank of Canada and chartered banks and numerous other instances of moral suasion. If open market operations are sufficient for central bank control of monetary policy, why do central banks maintain and use a battery of instruments? Moreover, why do covert instruments such as moral suasion often receive a substantial emphasis in the actual operation of monetary policy whereas they are discussed as an afterthought in most textbook accounts of monetary policy? The purpose of this paper is to show that some answers to these questions can be found by studying the central bank's behavior within the context of a theory of bureaucracy.(3)

The theory of bureaucracy applied in this paper assumes that a bureau is concerned with prestige and self-preservation. Prestige reflects the public's and other groups' concern with the goals associated with the bureau, the bureau's degree of responsibility for such goals and the public's and other groups' opinion about actual performance relative to expected performance. Self-preservation requires that the bureau be able to minimize conflict with groups that have the power to alter its status and to have a range of possible defensive actions available if conflict does arise. Imposing a preference ordering that stresses prestige and survival on the alternatives available to a central bank throws considerable light on the actual operation of monetary policy. This approach places in a rational framework many aspects of central banking that would otherwise appear irrational. In this study, the theory is applied to the choice of tools by the Bank of Canada.

To prevent any misinterpretation of the study, a number of aspects of our method must be discussed at the onset. First, this approach should not be interpreted to imply that the fact that a central bank is a bureau, is the sole determinant of its actions. In fact other explanations can also account for some of the phenomena being explained. Yet many other aspects of the Bank of Canada's behaviour remain unexplained by the traditional explanations offered for its actions. The test of the value of analyzing the Bank as a bureau is the ability to explain phenomena which lack convincing explanation in the current theories of central banking. A second issue arising from the present approach is the degree of realism of the assumptions about the central bank's concern with prestige and self-preservation. In other words, does the degree to which officials of central banks take these goals into account in determining their actions influence the acceptability of our hypotheses? Here the analogy with the theory of profit maximization appears relevant, for the main issue there was not realism of the assumptions but 'the conformity to experience of the implications of the marginal analysis' (Friedman, p. 15). Central bank actions then are studied throughout this paper on an 'as if' basis. The usefulness of any results clearly will not be to illuminate the underlying motives of the central bank, but to provide a framework in which predictions of the actions of central banks can be made. The most valuable insights from the present line of development will concern the probable reactions of central banks to alternative institutional arrangements in formulating their monetary policy.

I.

In making decisions about its mode of operation, a central bank generally faces a large number of alternative paths of action, the choice among which would be expected to be subject to the influence of its desire for prestige and self-preservation. The aspect of this decision most likely to be influenced by these attitudes is the choice among open and covert methods of operation. Open methods of operation are those which provide full information to the public concerning the actions of the central bank in the conduct of monetary policy. In contrast, covert methods do not provide full information on the central bank's operations and may even obscure the action taken. Maintenance of autonomy and self-preservation of the bureau are forces which would seem to lead officials of the bureau to prefer covert to overt methods. By use of covert methods, combined with a skillfully created mythology, the management of any bureau can increase its immunity to critical investigation. In the absence of information on the bureau's operation, the potential critic is disarmed and becomes a reduced threat to the bureau's autonomy and existence. Moreover covert methods provide the management with the possibility of magnifying its successes and minimizing apparent failures.

A further appeal to central banks of the use of covert instruments is the broad range of initiatives implicit in their use. Through open methods of control, central banks are quite limited in their powers to determine the allocation of credit by financial institutions, even those under its direct control. With use of a covert instrument such as moral suasion, central banks are able to discourage financial institutions from particular types of lending and even influence the behaviour of institutions over which it does not have any direct authority. To the extent a central bank desires this wider range of authority, a covert approach has distinct advantages relative to other more direct methods. By relying on moral suasion, the central bank is able to keep its powers ill defined. In some cases, its powers may become apparent after the fact, if at all. If the central bank were to seek direct instruments explicitly incorporated within the legal framework within which it operates, the prospect is raised of public discussion of the merits of the extension of central bank powers into this sphere and even of explicit prohibition of certain actions by the central bank.

A central bank can influence the overall covertness of its monetary policy in two ways. First, the instruments of policy available to the central bank differ from one another considerably with respect to their degree of visibility. These differences permit the Bank to rely on those instruments which are most covert. For example, moral suasion need not leave any direct evidence for outside observers whereas use of open market operations will generally be apparent to some other participants in financial markets and then eventually to other observers through scrutiny of the central bank's statements and statistical records. Even more evident would be changes in the Bank Rate or changes in legal reserve requirements which require a formal announcement of the policy change by the central bank. Secondly, a central bank can also influence the degree of openness by judicious combination of a number of different instruments. Sole reliance on any given instrument leaves a central bank vulnerable because only one signal is provided of the Bank's actions. On the other hand, combination of several instruments used in different degrees and even in different directions at the same time makes interpretation of the central bank's actions much more difficult and provides a degree of covertness unobtainable by exclusive reliance on any instrument. Thus if our hypothesis that central banks are concerned with being covert is correct, central banks would be expected to maintain a number of instruments of policy in order to reduce the scope for effective criticism of their actions.

Section II of this paper provides an analysis of the actual use of moral suasion by the Bank of Canada. Since moral suasion is the most covert of the instruments available to the Bank of Canada, frequent reliance on this instrument is predictable. The lack of emphasis by the Bank of Canada on this instrument in its publications and in speeches by Bank officials need not reflect accurately the actual operational significance of moral suasion. In section III the expected extension of the Bank's jurisdiction beyond that explicit in its charter through moral suasion and semi-clandestine arrangements is confirmed.

If maintaining the option of covert action is attractive to a central bank as we hypothesize, a central bank would attempt to create and protect a policy environment that makes such behaviour possible. Since moral suasion, the most covert instrument available to the Bank of Canada, loses its effectiveness with a fragmented financial system, it is predictable that the Bank would not champion the cause of reducing concentration in the banking system. Similarly, an international financial system which allowed wide discretionary options for the monetary authority combined with the necessity of maintaining secrecy about such operations would be attractive to a central bank. Documentation that these predicted attitudes are held by the Bank of Canada appears in section IV.

The next section documents the active use by the Bank of Canada of switching government deposits in pursuing its monetary objectives. The extent and direction of such switching is not consistent with the Bank of Canada's explanation of the purpose of these operations, but it is consistent with the prediction that a number of instruments would be employed to accomplish purposes that technically could be achieved by one.

II.

The term moral suasion, as the Bank of Canada notes, is used to refer 'to a wide range of possible initiatives by the central bank designed to enlist the co-operation of commercial banks of other financial organizations in pursuit of some objective of financial policy.'(4) The Bank admits the imprecision of the term and points out the wide range of actions covered from 'general exchange of views' to 'efforts by the central bank to achieve, through suggestion, discussion and persuasion, specific changes . . . in policies or practices of private financial institutions.'(5)

In discussing moral suasion a distinction should be drawn between formal and informal moral suasion. Formal moral suasion describes instances where the central bank obtains commitments from the commercial banks or other financial institutions to refrain from activities judged to be in conflict with policies of the central bank. Informal moral suasion is much harder to characterize and takes a less open form. Causal discussions occur continually between the central bank and participants in financial markets. Since the behaviour of the central bank can have a considerable impact on the fortunes of financial concerns, these conversations are interpreted carefully and the Bank finds it easy to spread information through this channel. D. H. Fullerton has described the verbal exchange that occurs during the frequent meetings of jobbers and officials of the Bank:

> In this way the market may be influenced by a hint by a Bank official that 'he is concerned about the downward trend of the U.S. bond market' or 'dealer inventory is surprisingly high' or 'business is picking up faster than he has thought,' all of which gives the impression that the Bank has a somewhat bearish view on bond prices. Since the Bank often has the power to make its own forecasts come true, the dealer usually listens attentively. (p. 110)

One reason for the potential effectiveness of informal moral suasion on the chartered banks is the present method of calculating their reserves which forces them to anticipate the ease with which the central bank is going to make required reserves available (Gordon and Read, pp. 479-80). Hints from the central bank could not fail to have an impact on the chartered banks' behaviour. From the central bank's point of view the impact on expectations of its present objective actions can be reinforced by use of informal moral suasion.

Although not generally recognized, informal moral suasion may also provide the Bank with information concerning plans of financial institutions about their dealings in security markets. J.S.G. Wilson, in his review of the development of the Canadian money market, has observed:

> Although it [the Bank] has no foreknowledge of the other bids, since all are sealed, it will have had access to a wide range of relevant information. Much of this is given to the Bank by the [money market] dealers themselves. Apart from the regular weekly return, they are not compelled to report either their positions or the transactions they are putting through, though the Bank may sometimes telephone them and ask them. However, they do in fact furnish quite a lot of unsolicited information, presumably out of the desire to be 'co-operative'. (p. 292)

Even though disclosure of their intentions to the central bank may reduce the returns to the money market dealers, this desire to be 'co-operative' is certainly understandable, given the money market dealers' dependence on the Bank of Canada for lines of credit.

The degree to which the Bank of Canada uses moral suasion to avoid public scrutiny, is difficult to determine because of the intangible nature of the instrument. Evidence, some direct and other indirect, is available from a number of sources. For example, in 1963 Governor Rasminsky outlined the use of formal moral suasion over the period 1946 to 1956 in answer to a question of a member of the Royal Commission on Banking and Finance.(6) Moreover instances of moral suasion are sometimes cited in the Bank's *Annual Reports*. Although the Bank has repeatedly stressed the quantitative nature of monetary policy and its preference for general instruments,(7) it does not appear to have been reluctant to use moral suasion to influence bank lending policy in a wide variety of ways. As shown in Table 1, the Bank either obtained new agreements or altered existing agreements with chartered banks in no less than twelve of the twenty-four years from 1946 to 1969. Moreover this measure to an extent understates the degree of reliance because many of the agreements extended beyond the year in which they were made.

In the cases cited by the Governor in 1963, the Bank appeared to have been open to admitting use of moral suasion. In each case, the use of moral suasion had been reported in the subsequent *Annual Report*. Despite this willingness to discuss past reported uses of moral suasion the Governor at times has been less willing to discuss more recent instances or moral suasion, as illustrated by the following exchange:

> Commissioner Brown: Have you had any experience with the use of moral suasion?
> Mr. Rasminsky: Yes.
> Commissioner Brown: Has it been –
> Mr. Rasminsky: I have been satisfied with the results, yes.
> Commissioner Brown: I gather that you prefer not to –
> Mr. Rasminsky: I think that the experience is not recent – I mean, it is obviously an experience within the last eighteen months, Mr. Brown, and if you don't mind I would prefer not to discuss the details.(8)

It is significant that the nature of this use of moral suasion, in contrast to those explicitly cited by the Governor, has not been disclosed subsequently in the Bank's *Annual Report*.

Less formal uses of moral suasion pose even greater problems for analysis of monetary policy. Some forms, such as the exchanges referred to by Fullerton, undoubtedly occur continually. Yet between the informal conversations and the formal 'agreements,' considerable scope exists for the central bank to make it's views known about proper and improper behaviour by financial institutions.

One example where the central bank's views appear to have influenced behaviour is in money market dealer holdings of bankers' acceptances. Under the existing arrangements both bankers' acceptances and Treasury Bills are eligible security for day-to-day loans from the chartered banks to the dealers. As far as money market dealers are concerned, bankers' acceptances and Treasury Bills are close substitutes since bankers' acceptances are indirect liabilities of the chartered banks, and as a result are subject to negligible probability of default. From the introduction of the bankers' acceptance onward, the yield on acceptances has continually exceeded the yield on Treasury Bills by amounts ranging from 0.10 per cent to 1.20 per cent. Despite this yield differential money market dealers do not appear to have substituted acceptances for Treasury Bills as security against their day-to-day loans as to increase their profits. Moreover, at times, parts of lines of

Table 1

Use of Moral Suasion by the Bank of Canada: 1946-69

Year	*Purpose*
1946	Limit on Government security holdings of chartered banks to 90% of Canadian personal savings deposits.
1948	Limit on term loans.
1951	Limit on total loans. Limit on term loans.
1955	Limit on term loans in amount exceeding $250,000. Minimum liquid asset ratio.
1956	Limit on lending to consumer finance companies. Special consideration to small borrowers.
1957	Encouragement to mortgage loans. Restrictions on term lending.
1958	Term loan agreement revised to $2,000,000 ceiling.
1959	Term loan agreement revised to $1,000,000 ceiling.
1965	Accommodation to finance companies. Request to discourage U.S. subsidiaries from switching to Canadian sources of funds because of U.S. balance-of-payment guidelines.
1967	Agreement on maximum interest on term deposits. Request to refrain from extending credit for the purchase of gold.
1968	Request to discourage use of bank credit to make abnormal transfers of funds or to replace funds normally obtained from parent companies by U.S. subsidiaries. Request to restrict the outflow of funds through certain currency deposit transactions.
1969	Ceiling on 'swap' deposits accepted by chartered banks. Special regard for borrowers in less prosperous areas of the country. Special attention to loan applications from small businesses without alternative sources of credit.

Source: Bank of Canada, *Annual Report*, various issues.

credit have remained unused despite a profitable margin between the yield on bankers' acceptances and the day-to-day loan rate. One explanation of this behaviour by money market dealers is application of pressure by the central bank on the money market dealers to limit the use of lines of credit primarily to Treasury Bill holdings. This surmise is given some credence by other information. We have been told that the Bank of Canada has discouraged at least one money market dealer from excessive use of his line of credit to finance holdings of bankers' acceptances. This concern of the Bank of Canada apparently culminated in late 1968 in a directive to money market dealers instructing them to restrict their holdings of bankers' acceptances after February 1969 to a level of no more than 15 per cent of their line of credit.

In order to make any financial institution act against its own profits over a prolonged period, a central bank must have some sanction for non-compliance. Money market dealers are dependent on the Bank of Canada for determining their eligibility for day-to-day loans from chartered banks. These lines of credit yield appreciable profits for those dealers who qualify. For example, a line of credit of $20 million on a day-to-day basis would have yielded an annual profit of $100,000 if invested in 90-day Treasury Bills, or even more if invested in bankers' acceptances at the average rates prevailing in 1968.(9) A money market dealer can receive day-to-day loans only if he has a line of credit at the Bank of Canada. Moreover, the volume of day-to-day loans of any dealer is limited by the amount of his unused line of credit from the Bank. If the criteria by which the eligibility and the size of the dealer's line of credit are determined were fully known, and if qualification were automatic, the Bank's administration of these lines would not strengthen its ability to enforce compliance with its desires. The arrangements, however, are not of this sort. In fact, both the Bank and the Minister of Finance have refused to divulge to the public the name of the jobbers, the size of their lines of credit, the terms for qualifying as a jobber and the criteria for determining the size of the line of credit for a jobber.(10) In reply to a recent question concerning the identity of money market dealers, the Minister of Finance replied, '. . . because of the banker-client relationship that is involved and because of the number of changes from time to time the Bank has not made a practice of publishing the name of such jobbers.'(11) Thus in its power to determine eligibility for day-to-day loans without any apparent accountability, the Bank of Canada has an effective sanction against uncooperative money market dealers.(12) Whether, in fact, the Bank has explicitly invoked this threat cannot be determined.

III.

Evidence derived from examination of the Bank of Canada's actions is consistent with an appreciation by the Bank of the advantages of moral suasion for extending its powers. In a number of instances the Bank appears to have had a preference for adoption of new techniques by indirect means rather than through the amendment of its legislative powers. For example, although it has now been over fifteen years since the Bank of Canada started 'lending' to money market dealers, the repurchase agreement by which the Bank makes these loans has remained unchanged as 'a devise to circumvent the limitation in the Bank of Canada Act on the Bank's lending to other bodies than governments and banks' (Fullerton, p. 110).

Similarly in 1955 the Bank obtained agreement from the chartered banks to hold liquid assets equal to 15 percent of their deposit liabilities. The Bank of Canada felt it necessary to introduce this requirement less than one year after a Bank Act revision. In 1957, Donald Fleming, the Minister of Finance asked the Bank of Canada to lower the minimum liquid asset ratio from 15 percent to 13 percent and, more fundamentally, questioned its authority to impose such a ratio.13 The Bank refused to lower the ratio and defended its right to establish such a ratio. In his reply Governor Coyne wrote:

> You have also asked about the authority for establishing a standard of liquidity. There is no provision in the Bank Act or the Bank of Canada Act bearing on the subject in question but it has always been recognized that the Bank of Canada has general interest in, and, I think, duty to discuss with the chartered banks from time to time, any matters which seem to be of importance in the field of money or relating to the sound operation of the banking system.(14)

The Governor proceeded to argue that the Bank of Canada had merely requested the chartered banks to operate in this way. If, after consultation with the central bank, a chartered bank did not concur with the Bank of Canada's reasoning, it could refuse to adhere to the agreement.(15) Mr. Fleming did not agree that the relations between the central bank and the chartered banks gave the chartered banks freedom to behave in this manner. He also restated his opinion that 'to make the 15 percent liquid asset virtually permanent would be to usurp the legislative function of Parliament.16 Although this event was one of a series that led to conflict with the government and the eventual resignation of Governor Coyne, the powers of the central bank itself were not reduced substantially. Twelve years after the fact the secondary reserve ratio was made legitimate through legislation. The scope for use of moral suasion as a method of avoiding legislative constraints has not, however, been reduced.

Additional evidence on the Bank's appreciation of the use of moral suasion to supplement its formal powers, particularly with reference to the non-bank financial institutions, is suggested by its subsequent actions. In discussing the need to extend the formal range of central bank powers to include the near-banks, Governor Rasminsky stated:

> The fact that a certain group of financial intermediaries, called the near-banks, do not come under the fractional reserve system and are not required, or agree to maintain certain liquid asset ratios, does not, in our judgement, constitute a major impediment to the exercise of monetary policy.(17)

Yet later, the following exchange occurred between the Governor and one of the commissioners:

> Mr. Rasminsky: . . . If it were thought desirable in the public interest that public control of that type [selective credit controls] should be exercised to guard against excessive amounts going to certain types of borrowers and to ensure that adequate amounts go to certain other types of borrowers, I would assume that this would be for Parliament to decide rather than the central bank.
>
> Commissioner Leman: So it is not because you are necessarily convinced it would never be needed, you feel someone else should do it?
>
> Mr. Rasminsky: I am certainly not necessarily convinced it would never be needed; in fact, somewhere in the submission I believe we have indicated there would be circumstances in which such controls or such powers could be useful.
>
> Commissioner Leman: Don't these exceptional circumstances we have talked about arise sufficiently suddenly that the stand-by approach would be necessary rather than having to go to Parliament at the time?
>
> Mr. Rasminsky: If the situation does arise, Mr. Leman, in great force, suddenly, and the situation is one in which the public interest is seriously endangered and this action is needed to counteract it, then I would conceive that to be a situation in which even without statutory power to do so the central bank would, mainly through its relationship with the chartered banking system, take steps to try to bring the situation under control . . . .(18)

Even before Mr. Rasminsky's testimony, the Bank of Canada under another Governor had on occasion attempted to extend its influence to non-bank financial institutions. The affected financial institutions, recognizing their immunity from direct central bank authority, have not always acceded to the pressures from the central bank. For example it was reported that Governor Coyne discussed the possibility of voluntary constraint of consumer loans with finance companies and large department stores but 'agreement with all concerned could not be reached.'(19) Subsequently the Bank of Canada was able to bring less resistible pressures to bear, persuading the chartered banks to freeze lines of credit to finance companies.(20)

Shortly after the Governor's testimony, the Bank of Canada, regarding its responsibilities as extending beyond the chartered banks, took action on the collapse of the Atlantic Acceptance Corporation in 1965. In the *Annual Report* for that year, the Governor stated:

> . . . I consulted with the chartered banks and indicated to them that while I did not wish to influence their judgment as to the credit standing of any customer I hoped that they would not feel unable, for reasons relating to the total amount of their resources, to accommodate credit-worthy finance companies which might find themselves in a difficult liquidity position. This unusual step was taken because in the atmosphere prevailing at the time there was a risk that difficulties in any part of the credit system might have wider repercussions of a disturbing character . . . .(21)

Thus only three years after the Governor's testimony to the Porter Commission that extension of central bank powers to include responsibility for financial institutions other than chartered banks was unnecessary, circumstances had arisen, as envisaged by the Governor, where the central bank felt compelled to act through its relationship with the chartered banks in the area in which it lacked statutory power.

Although the exact circumstances could not have been foreseen, it was apparent from the Governor's testimony that the Bank was aware that events could require its intervention into the affairs of non-bank financial institutions, yet the Bank preferred not to request any extension of its legal powers. This somewhat puzzling attitude can be explained by the theory of bureaucracy. Any consideration of the extension of the Bank's powers to other financial institutions would have brought the Bank into the midst of controversy over the ill-defined division of responsibility for financial markets between the federal and provincial governments. One outcome of such controversy could be increased awareness by the provinces of the scope for indirect intervention by the Bank and consequent explicit constraints on the future behaviour of the Bank. By reliance on the covert instrument of moral suasion to deal with any events that might arise, the Bank was able to escape such scrutiny and maintain its scope for future policy intact.(22)

Recent developments in Canadian balance-of-payments policy provide further examples of the Bank of Canada and other agencies cooperating to avoid the need for legislative sanction by using covert instruments. The frequent use of moral suasion in this area has been buttressed by semiclandestine arrangements with other countries. In fact, a North American monetary area has been evolving without the explicit approval of the electorate of either country. It is known that the Canadian exemption from the balance-of-payments programme of the United States was not achieved at a zero cost since Canada explicitly accepted a ceiling on foreign exchange reserve accumulation in negotiating a release from the interest equalization tax in 1963.(23) Later the ceiling on reserves was lowered as Canada negotiated exemptions from the then voluntary restraint programme of the United States.(24) Finally, in 1968 Canada was exempted from 'all the United States balance-of-payments measures affecting capital flows that are administered by the Department of Commerce or the Federal Reserve System.(25) The ceiling on foreign exchange reserves was removed shortly after this complete exemption but no quid pro quo was announced.(26)

In addition to accepting the reserve ceiling, Canada has taken a number of other steps that have reduced pressure on the balance of payments of the United States. In 1968, the Canadian government agreed to invest its entire holdings (above those necessary for working balances) of United States dollars in special non-marketable issues of the United States Treasury so as to improve the American balance-of-payments position as measured by the liquidity balance approach. In that year, the Canadian government borrowed funds in European capital markets in order to rebuild its foreign exchange reserves.(27) By investing these funds in the special issues of the U.S. Treasury it was performing an act of intermediation which improved the reported balance of payments of the United States. It is doubtful that this intermediation was itself profitable to Canada.

Canada has also been cooperating by holding an increasing amount of U.S. dollars in its international reserves although it has not disclosed a commitment to do so. From January of 1968 to March of 1970, Canada's holding of U.S. dollars increased from 1,151.9 million (a figure which included dollars borrowed by activating the swap arrangements with the United States) to 2,056.4 million while the U.S. dollar value of Canadian holdings fell from 1,024.8 to 879.1 million. By shifting the composition of its reserve structure Canada has either changed its preferences between reserve assets, has been responding to changes in imputed returns, or has been holding more dollars than it would like to as part of the payment for exemption.

A broader area in which explicit legislative approval has been avoided has been the active participation by the Bank of Canada in a credit network with other central banks. Although public attention has been concentrated on the SDR arrangements, much of the effective liquidity creation in the present international system has been covert. The extension of credit from one central bank to another through swap arrangements and special rescue missions has increased dramatically over the past decade. The terms and conditions of such loans have been kept secret and have not received the public scrutiny that much smaller development loans have received.

IV.

A virtual requirement for effective use of moral suasion over a prolonged period is the existence of only a small number of financial institutions to be influenced by the central bank. With large numbers of financial institutions the low cost of non-compliance for any single financial institution will reduce the impact of moral suasion. If the hypothesis that central banks prefer the covert instrument of moral suasion is correct, then any bank can also be expected to encourage, or at least not actively discourage, concentration of any part of the financial sector that is vulnerable to the use of moral suasion. This argument has been made with respect to the Bank of England by Harry G. Johnson who refers to '. . . a situation of oligopolistic competition in British banking . . . which has been tolerated and even encouraged by the monetary authorities since it lends itself readily to control by persuasion and directive . . .' (Johnson, p. 975). While in Canada the regulation of competition in banking and finance is in general outside the powers of the Bank of Canada, the Bank has at times had the chance to influence the degree of competition in financial markets.

The most important area where the Bank of Canada has had the opportunity to affect the degree of competition is in the position of the chartered banks relative to other financial institutions. In discussing the scope of banking legislation and the extent of reserve holdings at the central bank, the Royal Commission on Banking and Finance in 1964 argued that the nature of the liabilities offered by a financial institution should determine applicability of banking legislation.(28) As a result, coverage of banking legislation, including access to credit from the Bank of Canada, would extend to any financial institutions that issue deposit liabilities. While it could be argued that the Bank of Canada cannot act in the absence of legislation, it could make these changes with little difficulty through informal means if it wished. The 'lender of last resort' privileges could be extended on a voluntary basis to all such financial institutions. Any difficulties arising from absence of specific lending powers with respect to these institutions could be avoided by arrangements similar to those used to provide the Bank with lending powers to money market dealers through repurchase agreements. To date the Bank of Canada has not reacted to implement these recommendations of the Porter Commission, nor has it objected to their absence from the relevant federal legislation. This reluctance to act could be explained by either inhibitions against interference with provincial jurisdiction or a desire to maintain concentration. Any attempt by the Bank of Canada to extend its formal control over other financial institutions would bring it into the midst of controversy between the Federal Government and the provinces over responsibility for financial institutions. Still, since this problem of interference with provincial jurisdiction did not prevent the Bank from lending to provincially incorporated money market jobbers through repurchase agreements, the combination of silence and inaction is at least consistent with an expected desire to preserve the efficacy of moral suasion as a covert instrument through preservation of concentration in financial markets.

The central bank's scope for moral suasion is also determined by the existing international monetary system. The present system is attractive because it gives scope for pursuing balance-of-payments goals by covert methods. In addition, it has a built-in rationale for secrecy. The recent practice of focusing balance-of-payments policy on the capital account seems to be a rational choice for central banks since it allows the authorities to employ moral suasion on financial institutions and to intervene in the forward exchange market rather than using more visible tools. Central bankers justify the secrecy that surrounds balance-of-payments policies by referring to the fear of triggering destabilizing speculation. The obfuscation of true reserve positions and the masking of intervention in the forward exchange market are rationalized by the need to avoid adding fuel to speculative fires. While it may blunt speculation, secrecy also allows the central bank to control the outward flow of information about its balance-of-payments policy. In addition, the lack of clear criteria for expected behaviour by deficit and surplus countries make it very difficult for the public to assess balance-of-payments policies. Central banks have not been willing to formally adopt a schedule of adjustment responsibilities such as those proposed by James Tobin (pp. 201-11).

V.

Up to this point, our discussion has emphasized the covert nature of particular instruments. A bureau also has the opportunity to increase the overall covertness of its policy by using a multiplicity of instruments to obscure the thrust of its policy.

The Bank of Canada's use of transfers of government deposits between itself and the chartered banks as a monetary instrument appears to have a clearer rationale in terms of bureaucratic behaviour than in relation to monetary control. As far as the authors are aware, it has never been argued that the central bank is able to achieve anything through transfer of government deposits that cannot be achieved through open market operations. While one advantage of transfer of government deposits is greater covertness relative to open market operations,(29) probably the most important advantage to the central bank from this instrument is its contribution to the multiplicity of instruments available to the Bank. Through this additional instrument various possibilities are open to the Bank which would not otherwise be available. If the Bank wishes to reduce the reserve base of the banking system but for some reason, such as public criticism, is disinclined to use open market operations to the required degree, it can reinforce its open market operations with changes in government balances. Alternatively, potential critics can be confounded by offsetting changes in the Bank's portfolio and the Government's deposits. Thus the potential critic not only must examine the Bank's open market operations but also must determine the changes in Government balances to ascertain the net effect (MacIntosh, pp. 37-38).

For a long time it was widely believed that shifting of government deposits was rarely used to change monetary conditions. The Bank of Canada stated in its brief to the Royal Commission on Banking and Finance: 'In order to assist in the day-to-day management of chartered bank cash reserves the level of the Government's balance at the central bank may be varied within a moderate range but does not go outside this range frequently or for long.'(30) While this statement suggests that management of Government cash is used, at least occasionally, as an active as contrasted to an accommodating instrument, elsewhere in their brief the Bank de-emphasized this aspect stating: 'In the main, transfers of Government funds between the Bank of Canada and the chartered banks . . . are undertaken to prevent the uneven flow of Government receipts and expenditures from affecting the level of cash reserves rather than for the purpose of changing the level of cash reserves.'(31)

Some indications of the actual extent of active use of transfer of Government deposits can be obtained by examining their use during 1969. Changes in Government balances at the Bank of Canada in any week will be regarded as accommodating by any of the following criteria:

i) the change in Government balances is less than $20 million,

ii) the change in Government balances does not fully offset other changes in reserves,

iii) the net change in reserves is less than $10 million.

By these criteria changes in Government balances were used actively in sixteen weeks. In five of these weeks the transfer augmented other changes in reserves and in the other eleven weeks the transfers dominated the other changes by more than $10 million.

From the evidence, it appears that transfer of Government deposits was relied on to effect large changes in reserves. For example, in five of the twelve weeks in which reserve changes exceeded $75 million, Government balances were used actively. It must be noted, however, that these changes were generally temporary. Seven of the weeks when Government deposits were used actively were parts of sequences when transfer of Government deposits to the Bank was reversed within one or two weeks of the initial change.

The effects achieved by the multiplicity of instruments can also be attained by alternative means. For example, by taking steps in 1954 to create new money market institutions, the Bank of Canada has been able to obscure the paths of adjustment to monetary policy. In our opinion the introduction of purchase and resale agreements for certain dealers and the accompanying development of day-to-day loans did not basically alter the process of monetary adjustment.(32) The creation of an institutional labyrinth has augmented the effect of the multiplicity of instruments in reducing the number of outsiders who are aware of what is happening and thereby mitigating potential outside criticism.

VI.

This paper has examined the hypothesis that the Bank of Canada has been influenced in choosing its means of operation by the contribution of alternative possibilities to its prestige and autonomy. In this context, decisions to emphasize covert instruments, to acquiesce in preserving a concentrated banking system and to maintain an excessive battery of tools appear rational. It is not clear that these decisions have furthered social welfare and it is our opinion that many of them have not done so. However, decisions that may appear irrational when judged by society's preferences can be consistent with rational behaviour when the perspective is altered by focusing on the central bank's preferences.

Social losses may occur when the two preference functions differ. Policy reforms should be directed towards minimizing these costs by altering either the preference function of the central bank or the set of options that are available to the central bank. The latter is a more promising approach since the former would be equivalent to attacking problems of monopoly, or oligopoly by persuading the managers not to maximize profits, sales, or whatever was leading to socially undesirable behavior. On the other hand, the government might be able to alter the bureau's behaviour by changing decision making in the bureau and thereby restructuring its aggregate utility function.

In establishing a bureau, attention should be concentrated on possibly reducing scope for choice between alternatives with characteristics that are valued by society but have a cost to the bureau or vice versa. For instance, visibility is a positive social attribute but a negative one from the point of view of the bureau. Society is interested in making bureaus accountable for their behaviour. A necessary condition for judging whether policy has been conducted responsibly is a specific knowledge of what that policy in fact has been. Bureaus have a predictable but contrary desire not to leave a clear record of their actions and instead prefer to have the power to select a favourable account of their actions. In addition, the technically redundant instruments or by making the process of interaction between monetary policy and the economy more superficially confusing than it needs to be.

Since the bureau's and society's attitudes to visibility differ, more careful consideration should be given to limiting the scope for covert behaviour by the Bank of Canada than has occurred to date. Explicit steps that would reduce divergences between monetary policy as conceived by the legislators and such policy as carried out by the Bank of Canada would include a general prohibition of moral suasion. Moral suasion would only be employed where the legislature had specifically approved its use for the purpose in advance. Where there is any doubt, the presumption should be that the bureau does not have the power to act in a particular area and explicit permission of the government should be sought before action is initiated. If there are instruments available that have equivalent technical properties, those that are most covert should be excluded. For example, Government deposits could be kept either exclusively at private financial intermediaries or exclusively at the Bank of Canada so that the switching of such deposits would no longer be possible. Because of the difficulties of arriving at a just formula for distribution between private institutions and difficulties in creating an alternative tendering system, keeping government deposits at the Bank of Canada may be preferable. However such a policy would require compensatory open market operations.

Legislators and society in general should be aware that the theory of bureaucracy suggests the central bank will not be inclined to actively promote either increased competition in the banking system or certain reforms to the international monetary system since such changes reduce the ability to take discretionary and covert initiatives. In the past, in our opinion, too much weight has been placed on the central bank's submissions on these issues, perhaps as a result of the misguided feeling that if reforms were socially desirable the central bank would be in the vanguard of those prescribing change. Increased financial competition and an international system without a built-in justification for covert action might have benefits for society but both have costs to the monetary bureau. Under the present arrangements, the initiative for reform must come from Parliament in such areas. However, if moral suasion were not possible the rationale for central bank opposition might disappear.

Economists who have previously discussed the organization of the central bank have concentrated their attention on the relative independence from governmental control of this bureau. Many of these commentators have strongly advocated that the central bank be reorganized as a government department. Despite agreement with many of the reasons for this proposal, we feel the improvement in performance attributable to that change by itself might be of marginal importance. If the Bank of Canada were made a department but retained the right to use covert instruments and its other existing privileges, problems similar to those at present could be predicted to reappear. A government department is after all a bureau. The Bank of England, for instance, has been more closely integrated with the Treasury than the Bank of Canada has been with the Department of Finance but the scope for employing covert instruments and other tactics of obfuscation has been as great. To the extent that performance can be compared we know of no evidence that suggests that one has had a better record than the other. Meaningful reform must involve changing the set of options available to the central bank as well as altering its legal responsibilities to the government.

The theory of bureaucracy adds a further dimension to the choice between rules and discretionary monetary arrangements. Advocates of rules have rested their case on the existence of long and variable lags. They believe that discretionary policy may replace rules at some future date when knowledge of the interaction of money and the state of the economy is better understood (Friedman, 1960, p. 98). The theory of bureaucracy would predict that rules could be better than discretionary arrangements for another reason. Since rules do not allow any scope for alternative choices by the bureau the central bank has no opportunity to choose and the possibility of secretive behaviour by a bureau may allow it to act outside the law. With particular reference to the Bank of Canada the availability of covert instruments permits it to extend its activities into sensitive areas without having the explicit power to do so and permits it to choose whether to accept responsibility for the outcomes. The Bank can further obscure its actions by using a number of alternatives which are preferable to it but are inferior from a social point of view. Rules ought not to be compared to the best possible results under a discretionary regime if such results could not be realized because of bureaucratic decision making.

Consideration of the fact that a central bank is a bureau could lead to salutary reforms that would improve the implementation of monetary policy. Since the government and its departments are groups with similar appreciation of covert means, pressure from outside the governmental apparatus is needed for reforms of this nature to be initiated.

NOTES

1. The research for this paper was financed by a grant from the Institute of Public Administration of Canada. The authors thank H. S. Gordon, W. P. Yohe and P. Laverty for their helpful comments. The present paper is an elaboration of parts of a paper presented at the meetings of the Canadian Economic Association in June, 1970.
2. See Harry G. Johnson, p. 977.
3. Our approach parallels and draws upon the work of Breton, Downs, Niskanen, Selznick, Tullock, and Wilson.
4. See Bank of Canada, 1962, p. 37.
5. *Ibid.* (p. 38).
6. See Bank of Canada, 1964, pp. 53-54.
7. For example, the Bank has stated 'in general the approach of the Bank of Canada to monetary control is much closer to the first approach . . . (i.e. influencing credit conditions indirectly through variations in cash reserves),' Bank of Canada, 1962 (p. 28).
8. See Bank of Canada, 1964, p. 54.
9. The figures were chosen to reflect approximately $330 million lines of credit (the maximum outstanding in the past) distributed over some 14 money market dealers. The data are from Bank of Canada *Statistical Summary*, 1968 Supplement, p. 17.
10. *House of Commons Debates*, p. 2067.
11. *Ibid.*
12. The potential sanction in the arrangements has not gone unrecognized. R. M. MacIntosh (p. 39) states: 'The Bank of Canada is in a position to exercise a great deal of arbitrary discre-

tionary authority in the money market . . . If a dealer exceeded his limits, or used his credit to hold the longest term and highest yielding eligible securities, his borrowing privileges could be cut off by the Bank of Canada.'

13. See letter from J. E. Coyne to Donald M. Fleming, November 19, 1957.
14. *Ibid.*
15. *Ibid.*
16. See letter from Donald M. Fleming, Minister of Finance to J. E. Coyne, Governor of Bank of Canada, November 21, 1957.
17. See Bank of Canada, 1964, p. 37.
18. *Ibid.* (pp. 52-53).
19. See Bank of Canada, 1956, p. 34.
20. *Ibid.* (p. 35).
21. See Bank of Canada, 1965, p. 7.
22. It is interesting to note in a speech a year after the Atlantic Acceptance incident, the Governor, rather than arguing the need to extend the formal powers of the central bank to include near banks, declared: 'The central bank cannot, however, disregard any threat to competence in the credit system, whether or not the source of trouble is an institution in the central bank reserve system. It cannot be unconcerned merely because it has no direct powers or responsibility. (Emphasis added) See Bank of Canada, 1966, p. 5.
23. See Bank of Canada, 1965, p. 8.
24. *Ibid.*, (p. 9) and Bank of Canada, 1966 (p. 7).
25. Letter from Secretary of the Treasury to the Minister of Finance, March 7, 1968.
26. Letter from Secretary of the Treasury to the Minister of Finance, December 6, 1968.
27. Letter from Minister of Finance to Secretary of Treasury, December 16, 1968.
28. See Royal Commission on Banking and Finance, p. 396.
29. Transfer of government deposits is more covert than open market operations for two reasons: (i) unlike open market operations, transfer of government deposits does not have a direct security market impact, and (ii) because changes in government deposits occur for reasons other than monetary policy, it is difficult to determine the use of this instrument for monetary control.
30. See Bank of Canada, 1964, pp. 147-48.
31. *Ibid.* (p. 137).
32. In a related paper, we have shown that the development of the money market, after some initial success, has done nothing to increase the proportion of Treasury Bills held outside the chartered banks. In fact, when account is taken of the finance by the chartered banks of money market inventories, non-bank holdings of Treasury Bills have declined as a proportion of the total.

REFERENCES

Breton, Albert, 'A Theory of the Demand for Public Goods,' *Canadian Journal of Economics and Political Science*, 32, November 1966, 455-67.

Downs, Anthony, *Inside Bureaucracy*, Little, Brown Co.: Boston, 1967.

Friedman, Milton, *Essays in Positive Economics*, University of Chicago Press: Chicago, 1953.

-----, *A Program for Monetary Stability*, Fordham University Press: New York, 1960.

Fullerton, D. H., *The Bond Market in Canada*, Carswell Co.: Toronto, 1962.

Gordon, H. S., and L. M. Read, 'The Political Economics of the Bank of Canada,' *Canadian Journal of Economics and Political Science*, 24,
November 1958, 465-82.

Johnson, Harry G., 'Problems of Efficiency in Monetary Management,' *Journal of Political Economy*, 76, September/October 1968, 971-90.

MacIntosh, R. M., 'The Day-to-Day Loan Market in a Year of Easy Money,' *Canadian Banker*, 62, 1955, 22-40.

Niskanen, William A., *Bureaucracy and Representative Government*, Aldine- Atherton: Chicago, 1971.

Rasminsky, Louis, 'The Role of the Central Bank Today,' *Per Jacobsson Memorial Lectures*, November 9, 1966.

Selznick, P., *TVA and the Grass Roots*, University of California Press: Berkeley, 1949.

Canada, *House of Commons Debates*, 28th Parliament, December 17, 1966, p. 2067.

Royal Commission on Banking and Finance, *Report*, Queen's Printer: Ottawa, 1964.

Smith, Warren L., 'The Instruments of General Monetary Control,' *National Banking Review*, 1, September 1963, reprinted in Smith, W. L. and Teigen, R., *Readings in Money, National Income and Stabilization Policy*, Richard D. Irwin, Inc.: Homewood, IL, 1970, pp. 253-292.

Tobin, James, 'Adjustment Responsibilities of Surplus and Deficit,' in W. Fellner, Fritz Machlup, Robert Triffen et al., *Maintaining and Restoring Balance in International Payments*, Princeton University Press: Princeton, 1966, pp. 201-11.

Tullock, Gordon, *The Politics of Bureaucracy*, Public Affairs Press: Washington, DC, 1965.

Wilson, J. S. G., *Monetary Policy and the Development of Money Markets*, George Allen and Unwin Ltd.: London, 1966.

Wilson, James Q., 'The Economy of Patronage,' *Journal of Political Economy*, 59, August 1961, 369-80.

Bank of Canada, *Annual Report*, 1956, 1965, 1966.

-----, *Evidence of the Governor Before the Royal Commission on Banking and Finance*, 1964.

-----, *1968 Supplement to Statistical Summary*.

-----, *Submissions by the Bank of Canada to the Royal Commission on Banking and Finance*, 1962.

Chapter 7

BUREAUCRATIC THEORY AND THE CHOICE OF CENTRAL BANK GOALS:
The Case of the Bank of Canada

*By Keith Acheson and John F. Chant**

Economists have frequently asserted that central bank priorities among economic goals have not been appropriate to the public's desires. For example, one interpretation of the results of Reuber's pioneering study of central bank preferences was that:

> [The Bank of Canada's] reactions reflect the placing of a very heavy implicit weight on price stability compared with higher employment, presumably based on a judgement about the relative economic costs of more unemployment and more price inflation. The evidence examined on the relative economic costs of price inflation and unemployment suggests that the economic costs of inflation are not as high relative to the costs of unemployment as the reactions and statements of the authorities have implied. [Reuber, p. 132](1)

Relatedly, economists have claimed that central banks have placed an undue emphasis on the state of government security markets. The Bank of England, in particular, has been criticized in this vein.(2) Despite the well documented problems in defining social preferences, an implication of such statements is that central bank's preferences differ from the public's priorities. Except for vague statements about the inherent conservatism of

* The research for this paper was financed by a grant from the Institute of Public Administration of Canada. The authors thank G. S. Gordon, W. P. Yohe, and P. Laverty for their helpful comments and Michael Joyce, whose contribution went well beyond his role as research assistant. The comments of Tom Courchene have pressed us toward greater clarity in our arguments. The present paper is an elaboration of parts of a paper presented at the meetings of the Canadian Economic Association in June, 1970.

Toma, E.F. and Toma, M. (eds.) Central Bankers, Bureaucratic Incentives, and Monetary Policy

ISBN 90 247 3366 9

central bankers, economists have not contributed substantially to an understanding of this important phenomenon.

Recently, social scientists have turned their attention to developing theories to explain the behavior of government departments and agencies.(3) The thesis of this paper is that a large part of central bank behavior can best be explained by the simply theory of bureaucracy.(4) In another paper we have used this theory to examine the choice of monetary instruments by the Bank of Canada.(5) The purpose of the present paper is to extend the application of this approach to the ordering of objectives by the bank. Our approach contrasts with both the 'personality' theories of central banking that focus on the character strengths or weaknesses of principal decision-makers in the central bank(6) and the recent work examining the interplay among different individuals in shaping monetary policy decisions in the United States.(7)

We do not intend to imply that the central bank's status as a bureau is the sole determinant of its actions. Rather, we see the alternative approaches as complementary, each furthering our understanding of central bank behavior. Many aspects of the Bank of Canada's behavior still remain unexplained by traditional analyses of its actions. The test of our analysis of the Bank of Canada as a bureau is its ability to explain phenomena which lack convincing explanation within the current theories of central banking.

In many respects the central bank is a particularly suitable object for the study of the behavior of bureaus. Unlike many bureaus which are government departments, central banks are independent of government to some degree. The central bank's position generally means that its senior officials are not nameless civil servants and its reports to the ultimate authority will include a greater proportion of public documents to confidential memoranda as compared to other bureaus.

In the first section of this paper a theory of bureaucracy is developed which identifies those characteristics of goals relevant to the choices of central banks. For many central bank goals, such as price stability and full employment, the characteristics are found to be sufficiently similar to make impossible any unequivocal predictions about the operational emphasis of the central bank.(8) However, significant differences in the relevant characteristics can be identified between the two goals of minimizing the interest expense on the government debt and the development of flexible and efficient money markets. In the final sections of this paper the steps taken by the Bank of Canada ostensibly to develop a viable money market are assessed relative to the predicted weightings of the central bank on this objective, as compared to minimizing the cost of the government debt.

1. THEORETICAL STRUCTURE

Throughout it is assumed that a bureau is concerned with prestige and self-preservation in ranking the alternatives available to it. This emphasis on survival and prestige as important determinants of the behavior of a bureau has characterized other studies of bureaucratic behavior. For example, Selznick has suggested:

> It may be useful to refer to a prestige-survival motif in organizational behavior as a short-hand way of relating behavior to needs. [Selznick, p. 269](9)

Prestige refers to the position of the bureau in the social hierarchy of government bureaus. A number of factors contribute to the evaluation of a bureau by society. If the objectives assigned to a bureau are generally considered to be important ones, it will have a correspondingly high rank among bureaus. Similarly, an exclusive rather than a shared responsibility for a particular objective will enhance the bureau's position. Ceteris paribus, a bureau can be expected to choose options that increase its prestige.

A bureau will also be concerned with enjoying a long life. Members of bureaus can be expected to be interested in survival of the bureau for at least two reasons. First, if the officials feel strongly that the goals of the bureau have a high priority, they will fear that some functions of the bureau will not be performed in the future in absence of the bureau's survival. Secondly, the officials of the bureau will value the survival of the bureau in terms of their individual self-interest.(10)

A bureau's concern with survival will influence its behavior in a number of ways. First, a bureau will attempt to avoid conflict with groups that have the power to influence its status. Such an avoidance of conflict will increase the chances of the bureau's survival in its present form. Second, a bureau will be concerned with maintaining its autonomy. While increased autonomy may increase the possibility of conflict by making responsibility for failure more difficult to avoid, autonomy can also increase security by increasing the bureau's ability to deal with those situations of conflict that do arise. This study is concerned solely with the 'external' interactions of a bureau with its environment; it is not concerned with the internal processes by which decisions are made within the bureau. While changes in both the personnel and the means by which decisions are reached within the bureau undoubtedly influence its behavior to some extent, the effects of these influences are ignored for present purposes. The purpose of the present study is to determine whether the analysis of the central bank as a bureau can contribute to the understanding of its actions. As stated earlier, the success of this approach will be indicated by the ability to explain phenomena which are not explained adequately.

This study assumes that over time a bureau has a stable preference function between prestige and self-preservation. Such a stable preference function is not inconsistent with differing responses under different conditions. The set of choices available to the central bank over time is restricted by a number of factors which include the degrees of freedom allowed under the legislation which created the bureau, the existence and aggressiveness of other bureaus, and the state of knowledge about 'social engineering.' Within the set of available options the bureau will choose a 'best' point, but it will also be concerned with the long-run problem of expanding these options. Since prestige and self-preservation are not necessarily independent of each other, many of the bureau's decisions involve a trade-off.(11)

One important consequence of the explicit recognition of a distinctive ordering of alternatives by the central bank as a bureau is the possibility for differences between the central bank's ordering and that derived from a social welfare function. If such differences exist, the maximizing behavior of the central bank will not lead to the attainment of the social optimum. Thus, attribution of rational behavior to the central bank changes the perspective from which policy failures, with respect to the social goals, are to be judged. Frequently, such policy failures are judged as aberrations or are ascribed to ignorance or bad judgement. One implication of our approach contrasted to others is that, if central banks can be viewed as rational maximizers, the question must be raised whether these policy failures represent rational behavior by the bank in terms of its own preference function, a preference function which does not coincide with that of society.(12) If this is the case, steps to improve policy performance through better forecasting or improved effectiveness of policy instruments may prove futile. With the assumption of rational behavior by the central bank, possible remedies could center on the framework within which the central bank operates and could include both steps to modify the bank's preferences or steps to alter the constraints on its maximizing behavior.

2. DERIVATION OF GENERAL HYPOTHESES

Examination of the characteristics of the possible goals for the central bank in terms of their contribution to prestige and security is an essential antecedent to the analysis of the revealed behavior of the Bank of Canada.

Although every goal has many dimensions and any unequivocal and final ranking of goals would be unlikely, the simple theory of bureaucracy gives some general expectation of the central bank's preferences. We hypothesize that the central bank's choice among goals will depend on the following factors: (1) the degree of identification of goals with the central bank; (2) the visibility of the degree of attainment; and (3) the priority attached to the goal by the authority to which the central bank is responsible.

The degree to which the central bank shares responsibility for any goal, and as a consequence its identification with that goal in the minds of the public, can be expected to influence the operational priority attached to the goal by the central bank. If responsibility for a goal is diffused among many government agencies, any failure in attainment will not direct unfavorable attention solely to the central bank. Moreover, in the case of failure, the central bank will endeavor to minimize its role in the attainment of the goal. In contrast, when responsibility for attainment rests solely with the central bank, failure of attainment will focus attention directly on the bank which will find difficulty in escaping the weights of responsibility for the failure. Thus, the theory of bureaucratic behavior suggests that a central bank will emphasize the attaining of goals according to the share of responsibility it has for each goal.

A second characteristic of goals relevant to the central bank's choice is the degree of visibility. The failure to attain some goals is readily apparent in data generated by the market, such as interest rates, prices, and unemployment statistics. The success or failure in attaining other goals leaves less evident signs. Failure to attain visible goals increases the prospect of critical examination, while failure to attain less visible goals does not. The quest by the central bank for survival and autonomy could thus be expected to lead the central bank to direct its operations toward visible goals so as to avoid the greater threat to survival attendant on any failure with respect to these goals.

In forming its own rankings of objectives, the bank will minimize the possibility of conflict by taking into account the preferences of those groups which pose the greatest threat to its autonomy. Among the groups with power to alter the status of the bank and, as a result the groups to which the bank must be responsible, are the government and the general public. While at various times the most relevant threat to the bank can come from either, the degree of effective power of the government is likely to be greater for a number of reasons.(13) First, since a representative of the government attends Bank of Canada policy meetings, the government is better informed than the public about the activities of the bank. In addition, the government can initiate acts or execute orders which directly affect the Bank of Canada.(14) Any disenchantment of the general public with the central bank, on the other hand, will affect the bank only if that disenchantment is mobilized to influence the government. Thus, the public's power over the central bank is more indirect and diffused than the government's.

To summarize, in the remainder of this paper the hypothesis to be examined is that a central bank's operational emphasis with respect to policy goals can be expected to vary directly with the visibility of the degree of attainment of the goal, the degree that responsibility for attaining the goal is identified with the central bank, and the priority for the goal held by those groups toward which the central bank is responsible.

3. SPECIFIC HYPOTHESIS TO BE TESTED

The major goals of full employment, price stability, and a viable balance of payments appear very similar with respect to the characteristics relevant to the priorities assigned by the central bank. Moreover, differences that can be discerned at any one time are often only transitory and may be reversed at a subsequent time. In terms of visibility, all of these goals are quantifiable and are reflected in published statistical series. While absence of either price stability or full employment also directly affects individuals in the economy, in an open economy such as Canada modern media manage to keep the public well informed about exchange rate movements and the state of the balance of payments. We find it difficult to argue that any one of those goals is more closely identified with the central bank than any of the others. While through the late 1960s and early 1970s the Bank of Canada was held responsible by many for the degree of inflation in Canada, only a decade earlier the bank under Governor Coyne was universally condemned for the prevailing unemployment. It is also doubtful that we could substantiate any permanent differences between these goals in the preferences of the higher authorities, though transitory differences could be identified for certain periods depending on the party in power.(15)

Because of our difficulties in substantiating permanent differences among these major goals, the testing of our hypothesis will have to be confined to the apparent emphasis on two of the remaining goals: minimization of government interest expense and the development of flexible and efficient capital markets. Expectations about the operational emphasis of the Bank of Canada on these goals will be tested in relation to the steps taken toward the development of a money market in Canada.

The Bank of Canada does not explicitly justify any of its postwar actions as aimed at minimizing the cost of government debt, even though this objective has characteristics expected to have a high priority with the central bank. It is a quantifiable goal and therefore highly visible. Not only is the cost of servicing government debt visible in terms of the interest expense in the government's budget, continual reminders appear with announcement of the interest rates paid on new government issues reinforced by daily quotations of government bond rates. Moreover, this goal is unequivocally identified with the central bank. The Bank of Canada Act states 'The bank, if and when required by the minister to do so, shall act as an agent for the Government of Canada . . . generally in respect to the management of the public debt in Canada,' [1934, ch. 3 S2, Sec 20(2)].

Finally minimization of interest expense is of immediate concern to the government. Because interest expense is so highly visible and because of its implications for fiscal deficits, any government finds difficulties in disowning, or even minimizing, its responsibility for this goal.(16)

With respect to the development of efficient and flexible financial markets, the Bank of Canada has taken a number of steps that were ostensibly designed to extend the money market in Canada for the purpose of easing the adjustment of financial institutions to shifts in monetary policy. Yet this objective of flexible and efficient financial markets lacks the characteristics expected for a high priority by the Bank of Canada. This goal is not highly visible. By their very nature, the flexibility and efficiency of capital markets are not concrete concepts and are therefore difficult to quantify. Moreover, while many changes made in financial markets are readily apparent to observers interpretation of such changes and their effects frequently requires subtlety and expertise. This goal, in our view, is less identified with the central bank in the minds of the public, though we accept that this view may be debatable. Finally, the goal of flexible and efficient capital markets is not of immediate concern to government.

To summarize, the qualities of minimization of the cost of the government debt lead to the imputation that this goal will be emphasized by a central bank to a greater degree than maintenance of flexible and efficient capital markets. While it would be difficult to argue any major difference between these goals in terms of central bank responsibility, minimization of interest expense is more visible and has a higher ranking in the priorities of higher authorities. It should be noted, however, that a greater operational emphasis need not imply greater emphasis on this goal in terms of the statements of the monetary authority.(17)

IV. THE DEVELOPMENT OF THE MONEY MARKET

While the Bank of Canada provided little information on the explicit purpose of further development of the money market in 1954, there is general agreement among observers that the primary purpose was to broaden security markets so as to increase the scope of effective monetary policy [J.S.G. Wilson, p. 295]. Although observers note that the changes would ease finance of the government debt, this aspect is regarded as a secondary consideration. Our interpretation differs; close examination of the steps taken and subsequent developments pose a number of quandaries when considered in terms of the apparent primary goal of increasing the scope for monetary policy. Many of the steps appear either extraneous or positively detrimental from the viewpoint of development of efficient financial markets. Some of these steps, however, are given a much clearer rationale when evaluated in terms of their supposed secondary purpose, minimization of government interest costs.

Our tests of the expected emphasis on the goal of minimization of interest expense relative to the goal of development of an efficient capital market will focus on the approach taken by the Bank of Canada toward the development of a money market. The major steps were: (1) the establishment of arrangements by which money market jobbers would finance inventories of government securities, and (2) the agreement of the chartered banks to accept a minimum liquid asset ratio. In this section we describe the steps taken by the Bank of Canada, indicating those instances where the changes appear to be at the expense of the efficiency of financial markets. In the following section, the success of the bank's measures will be assessed in relation to various possible goals.

The chartered banks were to play a critical role in the money market by financing the security inventories of money market dealers through day-to-day loans. A difficulty to be faced by the Bank of Canada in developing the money market was to insure indirect holdings of government securities by the banks through day-to-day loans were at least as attractive to the chartered banks as direct holdings of the same securities. One step taken by the Bank of Canada to limit the risk on day-to-day loans was to give lines of credit to selected money market dealers. The chartered banks, by restricting their loans to these dealers to the amount of the dealer's unused line of credit with the central bank, could be assured the dealers could meet their commitments if the loans were called. Still, in proving any return to the money market jobbers on their inventories, the indirect holdings of government securities yield a lower return than direct holdings of the same securities. As a result, as J.S.G. Wilson has pointed out, 'It was important that loans made at a rate that would tend to be lower than the yield on treasury bills should be highly liquid' [Wilson, p. 273]. To compensate for this lower return, the Bank of Canada took steps to insure the greater liquidity of indirect holdings by reducing the liquidity of direct holdings of treasury bills through increasing the time required for payment on its purchases of treasury bills. [J.S.G. Wilson, p. 275] Thus day-to-day loans to money market dealers became a quicker source of potential cash for the banks than treasury bills. Although Wilson argues that day-to-day loans then had the advantage of providing the banks with a highly liquid asset, this liquidity had existed previously in the form of treasury bills. The greater liquidity of day-to-day loans relative to treasury bills was achieved by reducing the liquidity of the latter.(18) This step by the Bank of Canada can be interpreted either as reducing the return (by the jobber's margin) of the bank's most liquid asset (excluding cash) or as reducing the liquidity of treasury bills. Under either interpretation the banks were made worse off by the decreased liquidity of treasury bills.(19)

Changing the relative liquidity of certain assets in this way had a number of implications that have seldom been made explicit. First, one group of financial institutions – the chartered banks – was required, to the degree it desired to hold the most liquid asset with a positive yield, to subsidize the portfolios carried by money market dealers.(20) While the value of this subsidy is relatively small in relation to total bank profits, the cost to the banks in providing this subsidy exceeded the value of the subsidy because the banks also suffered the reduced liquidity of the remainder of their holdings of treasury bills. To an extent this latter cost could have been offset by a higher yield on treasury bills because of reduced willingness by the banks to hold them. As will be seen later, the acceptance of a liquid asset ratio by the banks limited the possibility of such an adjustment.

In addition to altering the distribution of income between banks and the money market dealers, this change also had some effect on economic efficiency. The change in the clearing arrangements imposed a cost on the banks, an extra day's delay before proceeds from treasury bill sales reached their account at the Bank of Canada, which was not a cost to the economy as a whole. Since the costs to the banks of providing services include this cost, which is not a social cost, the output of banking services will be less than optimal.

The development of the money market was also fostered by differences in the access of chartered banks and money market jobbers to the lender of last resort facilities of the Bank of Canada. For the money market dealers, interest was charged only for the term over which accommodation was actually received from the Bank of Canada; for the chartered banks, up to mid-1968, interest was charged for a minimum term of one week even if the period of accommodation were shorter [1968 Annual Report, p. 41]. In 1962, the difference in the terms of access of the banks relative to the money market jobbers was altered. With the return to the fixed bank rate, money market jobbers were permitted to borrow at the minimum of the bank rate or one-fourth of one percent above the three month treasury bill rate [1962 Annual Report, pp. 3-4]. During the 395 weeks from the introduction of this change in June, 1962, to the end of 1969, the bank rate exceeded the three month treasury bill rate by a least one-fourth of one percent in 230 weeks. The money market jobbers, thus, had preferential access to central bank credit during approximately 58 percent of the period. As a result of these steps, the banks were encouraged even more to rely on day-to-day loans to money market dealers for providing the liquid assets through which adjustment to their cash position could be made, enforcing the subsidization of the money market by the chartered banks.

While it might be argued that the introduction of the day-to-day loan permitted the banks to use their cash more efficiently as in the 'Federal Funds' market in the United States, we are not inclined to accept this view. As we have noted earlier, the qualities of the day-to-day loan existed before its introduction in the treasury bill. With the day-to-day loan, movements of reserves from one bank to another could be accomplished through indirect exchanges of day-to-day loans from a money market dealer, who in turn obtained accommodation from banks with excess reserves. Prior to the change, potential for the same adjustment existed in the exchange of treasury bills among banks. Before the introduction of day-to-day loans, this mechanism was not required because the Bank of Canada supported treasury bill prices within narrow margins, permitting adjustment of cash positions by direct transactions with the bank.

A little over a year after the development of the day-to-day loan arrangements, the Bank of Canada obtained agreement from the chartered banks to maintain a minimum 15 percent ratio of liquid assets to deposits on a daily average basis. As in the case of other steps taken by the Bank of Canada, the motive for this step was not entirely clear. Wilson interprets the objective of this step as trying to achieve 'more adequate control over the banks' commercial lending.' He also suggests that the 'method employed may also have been chosen as a means of ensuring that an appropriate amount of activity was maintained in the short-term money market' [J.S.G Wilson, p. 287]. In addition, this change could be interpreted as an attempt to enforce subsidized holdings of government debt by the chartered banks.

As will be seen, the evidence from subsequent experience tends to favor this last interpretation.

If the liquid asset ratio had been intended to control bank lending, it could be expected that the ratio would be adjusted to reflect the appropriate changes in bank lending relative to current conditions. The liquid asset ratio, however, remained unchanged for the twelve years from its introduction until it was given legal status by the Bank Act revision of 1967. Thus, whatever the Bank of Canada's initial intentions, the liquid asset ratio did not serve subsequently as an instrument through which the Bank of Canada actively influenced changes in bank lending appropriate to the prevailing economic conditions.(21)

If the secondary reserve requirement were aimed instead at developing the short-term money market, it is important to distinguish between those changes which broadened the market to alleviate the costs of adjustments for the chartered banks and those changes which instead led to additional holdings of short-term government debt by the chartered banks. To achieve the former objective, any changes must lead to an expansion of non-bank holdings of short-term securities relative to bank holdings of these securities. As will be seen in the following section, despite the expansion of the general public's holdings of treasury bills in the years immediately following the bank's steps to develop a money market, the long-run effect has been only to expand chartered bank holdings of short-term debt without any growth in the general public's holdings.

V. THE DEVELOPMENT OF THE MONEY MARKET AND THE HYPOTHESIS

The development of the money market in terms of its intended objective, the attainment of a broader market for short-term government securities, has received little attention from economists in recent years. Previous studies, all of which were concerned with the period up to 1958, have acknowledged success in meeting this goal. Neufeld, for example, argues '(t)here is no doubt that the machinery of the money market functions reasonably well. The market for treasury bills has broadened substantially' [Neufeld, p. 56].

Wilson, while noting a decline in corporate holdings of treasury bills between 1955 and 1956, observed:

> When the new money market arrangements were first established, it was hoped that there would be a considerable widening of the market for Treasury Bills in Canada and,

Table 1
The Distribution of Holdings of Treasury Bills, 1950-70*

End of:	(1) Bank of Canada	(2) Chartered Banks	(3) General Public	(4) Day-to-Day Loans to Money Market	(5) Net General Public (3)-(4)	(6) Net General Public as a percent of Holdings outside Bank of Canada (2) + (3)
1950	263	129	57			
1951	187	236	28			
1952	283	139	28			
1953	376	245	24			
1954	169	363	208	68	140	25
1955	264	430	494	81	413	45
1956	507	743	285	74	211	21
1957	469	808	289	210	79	8
1958	36	956	415	123	292	21
1959	309	983	755	101	654	40
1960	407	974	549	172	377	28
1961	314	1162	405	215	195	12
1962	458	1137	523	293	240	14
1963	469	1291	430	253	177	10
1964	482	1265	332	253	79	5
1965	612	1368	157	251	-94	-
1966	412	1567	170	278	-108	-
1967	544	1742	157	306	-149	-
1968	459	2145	200	193	7	-
1969	486	2116	268	183	85	4
1970	630	2714	246	310	-64	-

*Source: Bank of Canada, *Statistical Summary Supplement*, various years.

> in fact, that has been achieved. Since the middle of 1954, when the day-to-day loan was introduced, the volume of Treasury Bills outstanding has been increased two-and- one half times. [J.S.G. Wilson, p. 300]

When examination of the performance of the money market is extended to the present, a different judgement appears to be required.

The development of the money market could be judged either in terms of the expansion of (1) holdings of treasury bills by the general public, or (2) combined holdings of the chartered banks and the general public. Obviously the criterion chosen depends on the point of view from which the development is judged. If the development is judged in terms of contributing a broader market for the purposes of monetary policy, the holdings of the general public would appear to be the most appropriate criterion. The size of these holdings relative to bank holdings will determine the degree to which adjustments to the charter banks liquidity positions can be made without involving intervention by the Bank of Canada. The combined holdings of the chartered banks and the general public appear to be a more appropriate measure of success in terms of the goal of minimization of the interest costs of government debt.

As shown in Table 1, 1959 was the peak of the market's development in terms of the net holdings of the general public which had risen to 40 percent of outstanding bills held outside the central bank. As can be seen from column 5 in table 1, the development was not sustained; the public's net holdings declined by 42 percent in the subsequent year. The decline in the public's net holdings continued, with only one interruption, to 1967 when the public's holdings of treasury bills fell short of outstanding day-to-day loans by $149 million. At the end of 1970 the public's holdings, which include inventories held by money market dealers financed by day-to-day loans, were $64 million less than outstanding day-to-day loans. In only two of the last six years have the public's holdings of treasury bills exceeded outstanding day-to-day loans, and then only by insubstantial margins.(22)

It has been suggested that the failure of the money market to expand the public's holdings of treasury bills can be attributed to factors other than the Bank of Canada's desire to minimize the interest expense of the government debt. For example, it could be argued that in the period 1963-1969 Canada's acceptance of a ceiling on international reserves constrained Canadian interest rates from rising because of the threat of reserve increases beyond the agreed ceiling. Still the decline of the money market does not correspond that closely with the reserve ceiling. Net public holdings of treasury bills had fallen from the 1959 peak of 38 percent of holdings outside the Bank of

Canada to 14 percent at the end of 1962, the year before the acceptance of the ceiling. Moreover, the deterioration of net public holdings of treasury bills does not appear to have been reversed to any substantial degree since removal of the reserve ceiling in 1968.(23)

The failure of the money market 'experiment' to maintain a broader market for treasury bills raises a number of questions when judged from its apparent rationale in terms of making monetary policy more effective. First, the Bank of Canada has not made any public expression of concern over the recent trends despite their persistence for four to five years, nor does there appear to have been any major change in the terms by which the money market jobbers qualify for their lines of credit.(24) Yet the apparent rationale for these implicit subsidies from the banks to the jobbers was their contribution to the development of broader outside holdings.

In terms of the goal of minimizing interest costs the money market experiment must be judged a success; chartered bank holdings of treasury bills expanded continually from 1954 to a level almost six times higher and at the end of 1969 accounted for 73 percent of the total Treasury Bill issue compared to only 49 percent in 1954.

The apparent complacency of the Bank of Canada with the failure of the money market to develop outside holdings of short-term government debt does not appear consistent with a desire for greater response to monetary policy through development of broader outside holdings of treasury bills and other short-term securities. Whatever the initial purpose of the development of the money market, lack of concern could be expected if, in fact, the rationale for the continuation of the money market measures were maintenance of the chartered banks' holdings of treasury bills to reduce the costs of debt finance.

6. OTHER EVIDENCE AND THE HYPOTHESIS

In addition to predictions about central bank priorities, the theory of bureaucracy leads to suggestions about the means used by the central bank to attain these goals. If the central bank chooses a goal of immediate concern to one of the groups to which it is responsible but which has a low priority to other groups, public acknowledgement of this choice would not be desirable from the Bank's standpoint. As Selznick has pointed out in a somewhat different context:

> When co-optation is to fulfill the function of an adjustment to organized centers of institutional power within the community, it may be necessary to maintain relationships which, however consequential, are informal and covert. If adjustment to specific nucleuses of power become public, then the legitimacy of the formal authority, as representative of a theoretically undifferentiated community (the 'people' as a whole) may be undermined. It therefore becomes useful and often essential for such co-optation to remain in the shadowland of informal interaction. [1949, pp. 260-61]

Open acknowledgement of this co-optation would tend to increase the prospect of conflict with groups whose priorities differ with the priority chosen. Thus, in addition to the emphasis on minimization of interest on government debt predicted earlier, the theory of bureaucracy predicts that central banks can be expected to pursue this goal through covert, rather than open, methods of operation.

The prediction that the central bank would pursue the goal of minimizing government interest expense by covert methods clarifies features of the Bank of Canada's actions which are anomalous in terms of conventional explanations of the process of monetary control. The bank's frequent use of moral suasion or administrative secrecy is understandable in terms of this goal, for both moral suasion and administrative secrecy can be viewed as means for either inducing money market institutions to hold short government securities themselves or enabling the government to sell its securities easier.(25) While no direct evidence is available to substantiate this argument, it is supported by indirect evidence of several sorts.

The first of this evidence pertains to moral suasion and the portfolio choices of the money market jobbers. These jobbers can finance their holdings of bankers' acceptances, as well as treasury bills and short-term governments, by day-to-day loans from the banks. Since bankers' acceptances are high-quality securities which have consistently borne higher yields than treasury bills, it is difficult to understand why the jobbers have not substituted bankers' acceptances or borrowed to the full extent of their lines of credit in order to invest in acceptances. In a related study concerning the choice of instruments, we cited this behavior as indirect evidence of the use of moral suasion by the central bank. This inference has been confirmed by reports that a directive was issued to money market dealers requesting them to limit their holdings of bankers' acceptances relative to their lines of credit from the Bank of Canada. Such a directive has little sense in terms of the effectiveness of monetary control, for bankers' acceptances are as suitable as treasury bills for chartered banks making adjustments in their liquidity positions. On the other hand, bankers' acceptances do compete with treasury bills in the portfolios of the banks and in the inventories of money market dealers. Limits on dealers' holdings would have two effects on the market for the private security, acceptances, relative to government debt. First, the scope of substitution of bankers' acceptances for treasury bills in inventories on holdings of money market dealers would be directly reduced. Secondly, the limit on holdings of money market dealers would reduce the attractiveness of acceptances for the chartered banks because of uncertainty whether sales by the banks for the purpose of adjusting liquidity positions will be absorbed by the jobbers.

Another instance of moral suasion which appears anomalous in terms of the operation of monetary policy is the reported informal agreement between the Bank of Canada and the chartered banks on maximum interest rates for thirty-day deposits.(26) This agreement requests the chartered banks to act in a manner which is now specifically prohibited.(27) As far as the authors are aware, such a constraint on deposit rates has never been regarded as necessary for effective monetary control. Such a control has been justified as protecting certain financial institutions from the pressures of high interest rates.(28) Still this use of moral suasion is consistent with the central bank attaching a high priority to the minimization of government interest expense. If these deposits are felt to be close substitutes for government securities (including Canada savings bonds which are redeemable on demand), a ceiling on the rates paid on these deposits will reduce the upward pressures on the interest rates paid by the government.

The second type of indirect evidence on the use of covert methods for furthering the goal of minimizing interest expense concerns the degree of secrecy in the jobber-Bank of Canada relationship that is difficult to explain in the conventional framework of the working of monetary policy. Both the bank and the minister of finance have refused to divulge the names of the money market jobbers, the size of their lines of credit, the terms of qualifying as a jobber, and the criteria for determining the size of the lines of credit for a jobber [House of Commons Debates, p. 2067]. If the purpose of the development of these lines of credit were to encourage a broader market for short-term securities, then some open formula for lines of credit depending on past levels of inventory and volume of trade in short-term instruments seems adequate to ensure use of lines of credit for their intended purpose. A central bank might be less eager to use open criteria for eligibility if in addition to having an interest in the volume of trade in short-term instruments the central bank were also concerned with the nature of the short-term instruments held and traded. Open admission of a preference for favored treatment of government liabilities would increase the possibility of subjecting the central bank to critical scrutiny.

In addition to eligibility for lines of credit, there is other evidence that administrative secrecy is motivated by concern with finance of government debt. In other instances, the Bank of Canada has included criteria related to the finance of various types of government debt in qualifications for privileges for which these criteria are not directly relevant. For example, although exact criteria are not discussed, the Bank of Canada states 'The amount of bonds (in new government issues) offered on a firm basis to a primary distributor is based on his ability to distribute such bonds tc investors, as determined by his record of taking up firm offerings in past issues and the character of the distribution achieved,' [Evidence of the Governor . . ., p. 158]. Douglas Fullerton, formerly assistant deputy minister of finance, states in his study of the Canadian bond market that 'It is widely believed that a number of other factors enter into the formula, including the size of the firm, the volume of transactions with the Bank of Canada over a certain period, past sales of Canada Savings Bonds.'(29)

From the Bank of Canada's statement, it would be expected that the criteria used are for the purpose of ensuring the success of the current issue being offered. Yet if Fullerton is correct, it would appear that a concern with the sale of Canada Savings Bonds pervades a range of Bank of Canada policy, including the terms of participation in marketing of newly issued securities. To an extent, participation in the profits of the issue of marketable debt appears to be a lever to extend the market for the Government's nonmarketable debt.(30)

7. CONCLUSION

The theory of bureaucracy used in this paper suggests that a central bank cannot be assumed automatically to pursue its goals with the same priority as society would desire. Some characteristics of goals which are relevant to the central bank as a bureau are not relevant to society's ranking of the goals. Policy reforms to be effective must either give incentives to the managers to allocate their efforts in ways more consistent with social priorities or change the set of options available to the central bank to make the bureau's preference ordering more consistent with social preferences.

A bureau can be expected to emphasize goals valued by those groups having most information about it and most power over it. Covert methods of operation permit groups with power over the central bank to have their interests more heavily weighted by that institution without society in general being aware of the distortion. The incentives of the managers of the central bank could be directed more closely to social priorities by insisting that central banks avoid use of covert instruments of policy and disclose fully as is technically possible the nature of their operations.

The options available to the bureau responsible for monetary policy could be changed in several ways. First, bureaus could be redefined to make each bureau's responsibility encompass the smallest set of relatively self-contained tools and goals. For example, monetary, fiscal, and exchange-rate policy could then be under the control of one authority in charge of achieving internal balance, external balance, and the desired structure of the balance of payments. Today the Department of Finance does have ultimate responsibility for all these policies. The responsibility for monetary policy could be clarified further and reinforced if the central bank were in fact a part of the Department of Finance. This approach would reduce the problems arising from shared responsibility for objectives among several bureaus. No longer would bureaus be able to enhance their prospects for survival by failing to accept full responsibility for a shared objective.

A second approach to limiting the options available to the central bank would be through reducing the goals and instruments assigned to it. Again this alternative would reduce the overlapping of responsibility. Bureaus would be unequivocally identified with particular goals for which they must accept full responsibility. Care would have to be taken to ensure that the assignments would lead decentralized behavior to reach desired objectives and that the goals were mutually compatible.

One method of directing the central bank's efforts toward major goals such as price stability and full employment would be through limiting its responsibility for debt management, either through its delegation to another bureau or through establishing a set of rules for debt management.(31) With either of these steps, present arrangements between the Bank of Canada and the money market dealers would lose their rationale from the bank's perspective. Without responsibility for floating the government debt, the Bank of Canada could dismantle arrangements that seem to have no purpose other than subsidizing government debt. If lines of credit to money market dealers were revoked, reinstatement of previous rules for clearing treasury bills would allow the banks to adjust to a cash drain. Such a reform would simplify the lines of interaction between the monetary authorities and the commercial banks and make monetary actions easier to comprehend.

These proposed reforms are intended only to be indicative of the types of proposals that flow from considering central banks as bureaus. In this study we have concentrated on the bureaucratic behavior of the central bank while ignoring to a large extent the similar behavior of other groups. Since other government departments are bureaus and since the legislature itself may be influenced by similar forces, the probability of reform may be reduced and, in light of the theory of the second best, undesirable.

NOTES

1. See Johnson (1967, p. 209).
2. See Johnson (1972). The Bank of England's preoccupation with stabilizing conditions in the bond market is documented in Karaken (1968) and Bain (1970).
3. For general approaches to the theory of bureaucracy, see for example, Downs (1967), Selznick (1949), Wilson (1961), and Breton (1966).
4. Many of the characteristic traits we refer to have been discussed at various times by Johnson (1968) and (1967, pp. 195-236). Johnson, however, does not develop an explicit framework to explain these traits.
5. The choice among techniques of monetary control is discussed in Chant and Acheson (chapter 6 in this volume).
6. Two examples of the 'personality' theory are Boyle (1967) and Friedman and Schwartz (1971, p. 411).
7. See for example, Yohe (1965, 1966) and Canterbery (1967).
8. Throughout this paper the words 'emphasis' or 'priority' will refer to operational emphasis or operational priority, unless otherwise stated. Operational emphasis refers to the weighting attached to goals by the central bank in the formulation of its policy. The relationship between this operational emphasis and the emphasis given in public statements is itself explainable by the theory of bureaucracy. Cf. Acheson and Chant (1973).
9. See also Downs (1967, ch. 1).
10. See Downs (1967, p. 9).
11. Selznick, commenting on the interrelation of these goals, suggests 'organization survival is intimately connected with the struggle for relative prestige' (1969, p. 269).
12. Oliver E. Williamson makes a similar point in a different context: 'Surely it is significant that the second and third chapters of Genesis record that where discretion exists it is apt to be exercised and that merely to charge someone to be a good and faithful servant is not adequate to secure his performance.' (1964, p. 3)
13. To determine the pressures on the central bank from the government, it is necessary to recognize the bureaucratic features of the government's behavior. Like the central bank, the government will be influenced in its choice of goals by their visibility, the degree to which responsibility is shared, and the value attached to the goals by those to whom it is responsible.
14. See Rasminsky (1961). Here Governor Rasminsky outlines the conditions where he believes the government can issue instructions to the central bank.
15. On a number of occasions it has been suggested to us that a difference could be discerned between price stability and other goals in recent years. In particular, price stability appears to have had a high priority attached to it by the Trudeau government. Still one interpretation of Reuber's work suggests an overemphasis on inflation well before Trudeau came to office. Moreover, given our awareness of the bank's apparent emphasis, we feared the danger of testing a hypothesis against the data from which it derived.
16. Harry Johnson has suggested that in the United States 'there is historical reason to fear that the Treasury might be excessively concerned with minimizing the interest cost of the public debt.' (1967, p. 255)

17. For an application of the theory of this paper to the publicly expressed views of central banks, see Acheson and Chant (1973).
18. The decreased liquidity of treasury bills seems to have been most explicitly recognized by MacIntosh (1954, pp. 68-69).
19. It must be noted that at the same time as these steps were taken, the reserve requirement was changed from 5 percent of total deposits on a daily basis to 8 percent on a monthly average. Despite the raised cash ratio, the change to a monthly average permitted the banks to reduce their actual reserves from the 'traditional' 10 percent gradually to a level close to the 8 percent minimum. See Wilson (1966, pp. 285-86). While the net effect of the reserve change and the decreased liquidity of treasury bills together may have made the chartered banks better off, our point is that part of the change in developing the money market was at the expense of the liquidity of the banks' treasury bill holdings.
20. During 1968, the value of the subsidy, approximated by the difference between the day-to-day loan rate and the current treasury bill rate on the average outstanding value of day-to-day loans, reached $1,500,000. To the extent the rate on purchase and resale agreements is below the average treasury bill rate on holdings, part of the subsidy is also borne by the Bank of Canada. A recent change introduced by the Bank of Canada reduced its contribution to this subsidy; see note 23.
21. Since gaining legal status in March, 1968, the secondary reserve ratio has been raised several times and also has now been lowered for the first time. The circumstances surrounding one of these occasions lends substantial support to our view. In early 1970 the government announced a bond issue of $250 million to provide adequate government balances for future sterilization of foreign exchange inflows. As Courchene states, 'To insure that the banks bought this issue the governor raised the secondary reserve ratio from 8 to 9 percent – enough to immobilize more than the whole of the new bond issue' (1971, p. 50).
22. Day-to-day loans can exceed the public's treasury bill holdings by the money market dealers' holdings of bankers' acceptances and certain short-term government securities.
23. To the extent an increase occurred in the public's net holdings of treasury bills between the end of 1967 to the end of 1968, the increase, as comparison of monthly data shows, had developed before the removal of the reserve ceiling in December. See relevant issues of *Bank of Canada Statistical Summary*.
24. In 1970 the money market arrangements were altered by setting a floor at .75 percent below the bank rate for the rate at which money market dealers can 'borrow' from the Bank of Canada. Prior to the change, the maximum penalty for money market borrowings at the Bank of Canada was approximately .25 percent. The effective penalty will now be greater than under the previous arrangements whenever the treasury bill rate is more than 1 percent below the bank rate. Since the change, the borrowing rate for dealers has usually been at the floor leading to the maximum differential between the dealers' borrowing rate and the bank rate of .75 percent, a level rarely attained during the eight years of the previous arrangements.
25. For greater detail on the bank's choice of instruments, see Chant and Acheson (chapter 6 in this volume).
26. See Bank of Canada (1967). This instance of moral suasion has been described as an 'informal understanding between the central bank and the majority of the chartered banks that the latter will not pay more the 6 3/4 percent for thirty-day deposits – the Canadian version of regulation Q' (Greenshields, Inc., 1969).
27. Economic Council of Canada (1969, p. 154). Such an agreement is permissible only at the request or with the approval of the Minister of Finance (Bank of Canada Act, sec. 138).

28. A statement of this justification, though not necessarily agreement with it, can be found in Tobin (1970, p. 10).
29. Fullerton (1962, p. 103). (Bolding added to original.)
30. A referee for this article has pointed out to us that at the time of offerings of Canadian Savings Bonds, the Bank of Canada normally insures that interest rates do not rise, and as a result concern with the sale of savings bonds at times has severely constrained the bank's monetary policy. This behavior of the bank suggests that concern with the costs of the government debt may even overshadow major policy objectives, at least in the short run.
31. This latter proposal apparently has been made by Alan Meltzer. See the reference in K. Brunner (1966, p. 551).

REFERENCES

Acheson, K. and J. F. Chant, 'The Choice of Monetary Instruments and the Theory of Bureaucracy,' chapter 6 in this volume.

Acheson, K. and J. F. Chant, 'Mythology and Central Banking,' *Kyklos*, 1973, 2.

Bain, A. D., *The Control of Money Supply*, Penguin Books: Hammondsworth, England, 1970.

Bank of Canada, *Annual Report*, 1962.

-----, *Annual Report*, 1967.

-----, *Annual Report*, 1968.

-----, *Evidence of the Governor before the Royal Commission on Banking and Finance.*

Bank of Canada Act, 1934.

Boyle, A., *Montague Norman: A Biography*, Cassel: London, 1967.

Breton, A., 'A Theory of the Demand for Public Goods,' *Canadian Journal of Economics*, 1966, 32, 455-67.

Brunner, K., 'The Report of the Commission on Money and Credit,' *Journal of Political Economy*, 1961, 69, reprinted in R. Thorn, *Monetary Theory and Policy*, Random House: New York, 1966.

Canada, *House of Commons Debates*, 28th, Parliament, 1969.

Canterbery, E. R., 'A New Look at Federal Open Market Voting,' *Western Economic Journal*, 1967, 5, 25-38.

Courchene, T., 'Recent Canadian Monetary Policy: An Appraisal,' *Journal of Money, Credit, and Banking*, 1971, 3, 35-56.

Downs, A., *Inside Bureaucracy*, Little Brown and Co.: Boston, 1967.

Economic Council of Canada, *Interim Report on Competition Policy*, Queens' Printer: Ottawa, 1969.

Friedman, M. and A. Schwartz, *A Monetary History of the United States, 1867-1960.* Princeton University Press: Princeton (National Bureau of Economic Research), 1971.

Fullerton, D., *The Bond Market in Canada*, The Carswell Co.: Toronto, 1962.

Greenshields, Inc., *Canadian Money Market Review*, May 8, 1969.

Johnson, H. G., 'Problems of Efficiency in Monetary Managements,' *Journal of Political Economy*, 1968, 76, 971-90.

-----, 'A Summary Evaluation of the Conference,' in *Bretton Woods Revisited*, University of Toronto Press: Toronto, 1972.

-----, *Essays in Monetary Economics*, Allen and Unwin: London, 1967.

Karaken, J., 'Monetary Policy' in R. Caves (ed.), *Britain's Economic Prospects*, Brookings Institution: Washington, 1968, 68-103.

MacIntosh, R. M., 'Broadening the Money Market,' *The Canadian Banker*, 1954, 61, 63-73.

Neufeld, E. P., *Bank of Canada Operations and Policy*, University of Toronto Press: Toronto, 1958.

Rasminsky, L., *Statement by the Governor of the Bank of Canada*, issued on August 1, 1961.

Reuber, G. L., 'The Objectives of Canadian Monetary Policy 1949-61: Empirical "Trade-Offs" and the Reaction Function of the Authorities,' *Journal of Political Economy*, 1964, 72, 109-32.

Selznick, P., 'Foundations of the Theory of Organizations,' *American Sociological Review*, 1948, 13, reprinted in F. E. Emery (ed.), *Systems Thinking*, Penquin Books: Hammondsworth, England, 1969.

-----, *TVA and the Grass Roots*, University of California Press: Berkeley, 1949.

Tobin, J., 'Deposit Ceilings as a Monetary Control,' *Journal of Money, Credit, and Banking*, 1970, 2, 4-14.

Williamson, O. E., *The Economics of Discretionary Behavior: Managerial Objectives in a Theory of the Firm*, Markham Publishing Co.: Chicago, 1964.

Wilson, J. Q., 'The Economy of Patronage,' *Journal of Political Economy*, 1961, 59, 369-80.

Wilson, J. S. G., *Monetary Policy and the Development of Money Markets*, Allen and Unwin: London, 1966.

Yohe, W. P., 'The Open Market Committee Decision Process and the 1964 Patman Hearings,' *National Banking Review*, 1965, 3, 351-62.

-----, 'A Study of Federal Open Market Committee Voting 1955-64,' *Southern Economic Journal*, 1966, 32, 396-405.

Chapter 8

RESEARCH ACTIVITIES AND BUDGET ALLOCATIONS AMONG FEDERAL RESERVE BANKS

By Eugenia Froedge Toma and Mark Toma

1. INTRODUCTION

Throughout the Federal Reserve System's existence, economists have been interested in the process through which monetary policy decisions are formulated. For the most part, this decision-making process has been investigated from a 'public interest' perspective. Policy decisions are assumed to be a product of a procedure whereby officials gather information on the macro relations between money and different policy goals and then attempt to maximize a social welfare function based on these objectives. This approach stands in contrast to the economic theory of individual behavior and, in particular, to the recent extension of economic theory to the behavior of government bureaucrats.(1) In these cases an explicit utility-maximizing framework has been applied, somewhat successfully, to explain the budgetary outcomes of different bureaus.

Although the Fed does not receive an appropriation from Congress, a theory of the budgetary process still can be applied to the individual Reserve Banks within the System. Each year the Board of Governors allocates funds to the twelve Banks out of the open market operation revenue. This internal 'budgetary' process offers a perfect setting in which to compare the explanatory power of the bureaucratic model of Fed behavior to that of the public interest model. Specifically, we argue that the two theories generate different predictions about the way the System's funds will be distributed among individual Banks. If the Board of Governors behaves like its bureaucratic counterparts in other agencies, then we would expect it to reward or penalize Reserve Banks on the basis of whether the actions of their employees enhanced or reduced the discretionary spending opportunities of

Toma, E.F. and Toma, M. (eds.) Central Bankers, Bureaucratic Incentives, and Monetary Policy
© 1986, Martinus Nijhoff Publishers, Dordrecht,
ISBN 90 247 3366 9

the Board. Sections 2 and 3 theoretically develop the budgetary reward structure implied by the bureaucratic model, while section 4 tests the resulting implications.

2. MONEY CREATION AND BUREAUCRATIC SUPPLY

Before developing a bureaucratic theory of the Fed's internal budgetary process, it will prove useful to discuss the theory of bureaucratic supply in very general terms. To begin, suppose voters possess complete information about the operation of a bureaucratic agency. Under a simple median voter model, the decisive voter will require the bureau to provide precisely the amount of output he desires and to produce it for a budget equal to the least cost of production. Any deviation from this solution would result in the replacement of the bureau's present management team.

The bureau, however, will have an incentive to withhold or obscure information about its production process. By creating a degree of uncertainty regarding the least cost of production, for example, two avenues of discretionary behavior are open to bureaucrats. They may be able to increase output beyond the median voter's desired level,(2) or alternatively, produce the desired level of output but at a higher cost. In this latter case, this larger budget could be 'used up' on expenditures that directly benefit bureaucrats rather than voters. These discretionary expenditures may take various forms such as higher bureaucratic salaries, plusher working environments, and more staff assistants, to name a few.

Additionally, the bureau will have an incentive to generate inaccurate information about how alternative sources of supply might perform. These alternative sources could be another management team, or perhaps, supply by a private firm. To the extent the bureau causes voters to view the performance of possible alternatives less favorably, the perceived demand for its services increases. As before, this tends to enlarge the scope of the bureaucrats' discretionary opportunities.

A similar bureaucratic analysis can be applied to the Federal Reserve System. Although the Fed is engaged in many different types of banking and regulatory activities, the monetary policy good provided by the Fed can be defined most precisely as rates of growth in the monetary base (B/B). Generally speaking, these rates of growth are valued by the public because of the degree of price stability (or instability) associated with them. In the long run, higher rates of base growth lead to higher rates of anticipated inflation which tend to reduce people's real money holdings, and thus, reduce the total benefits of money creation.

As with any other government agency, the discretionary opportunities available to the Fed depend ultimately on the information voters possess.(3) However, the way in which a change in information translates into a change in discretionary options is complicated by the Fed's peculiar financing arrangement. The Fed does not have to go before Congress periodically to request a budget appropriation. Instead, it receives earnings primarily from open market operations. After financing its activities, the Fed turns over to the Treasury any residual earnings. Although the Fed formally has the legal right to determine the amount it retains for itself,(4) this amount will be influenced by Congress's knowledge of the Fed's production process, as well as Congress's predictions about the performance of alternative monetary management arrangements. These alternatives might include another management team, a different money creation operating procedure (e.g., a constant money supply growth rule), or perhaps a completely different institutional structure (e.g., a commodity standard).

Consider the extreme case where the public perceives that some alternative to the Fed could produce price stability at trivial costs. Under these circumstances, the Fed's hands would be tied. Since the benefits the public receives from the present management team's existence (over and above the benefits from the alternative) could not possibly be greater than zero, the Fed must produce the $\dot{B}/B$ that generates price stability or else go out of business.(5) Furthermore, it must do so at very low 'budgetary' costs. If, instead, the Fed retained a significant amount of funds for itself, Congress would be certain to react. The threat of turning to the alternative source of money provision would be enough to induce the present Fed management to 'voluntarily' restrict its spending.

Suppose, more realistically, that the public perceives that the next best money supply alternative would produce a relatively high inflation rate. This implies that, at least for moderately inflationary $\dot{B}/B$ levels, the Fed will have some scope for mismanagement. One way this mismanagement may show up is in the form of retaining a greater amount of open market revenue for financing the Fed's operation. Fed members may use the extra funds to purchase goods and services that provide direct benefits to themselves. As with any bureau, the potential magnitude of this discretionary spending depends not only on the perceived performance of the alternative, but also on the public's information pertaining to the costs of operating the Fed. In the simple case where the public possesses little information on these costs, the Fed's discretionary spending opportunities can be pursued as long as they do not dissipate completely the perceived advantage the Fed has over its alternative.(6) Only when the Fed oversteps this boundary will it face the danger of congressional reaction and possible mandated limits on the revenue it can retain for itself out of its earnings.

The Fed can forestall such a congressional response and thereby increase the funds it retains for itself by somehow widening the perceived gap between the performance of its management team and the performance of the next best alternative.(7) One way for the Fed to accomplish this end is to spread information which emphasizes the unattractive attributes of the alternative. If this information is based upon fact, then the cost of persuading the public of its reliability may be relatively low. But there is no reason to assume that the Fed would restrict itself to only this type of revelation. Even misinformation may serve to increase the demand for the present Fed's services. Similarly, the Fed may enlarge its pool of spendable funds by withholding reliable information which would suggest the superiority of alternative means of money provision.

3. THE INFORMATION CONTROL PROBLEM

In exploring the incentives Fed officials have to distort/withhold information, it is necessary to consider the institutional structure of the Fed in more detail. To this point, we have been treating the Fed as one homogeneous unit. In the real world the Federal Reserve System can be construed as a hierarchical bureaucracy. At the top of the structure is the Board of Governors and at the bottom are the Reserve Bank employees. Presidents from each of the twelve Reserve Banks are in the middle of the hierarchy. As the 'central authority,' one of the Board of Governor's main responsibilities is to allocate the System's pool of spendable funds between the Reserve Banks. The Board obviously must consider relevant differences in each of the Federal Reserve districts in allocating the total funds. For instance, a Reserve Bank that has a greater volume of checks to clear requires a larger budget, all other things constant. Although the Fed engages in an assortment of such non-policy activities, the essence of a central bank is its money creation function. For this reason, each Reserve Bank employs a staff of researchers to explore the relationships between open market operations, the money supply and different measures of economic activity. Of course, Bank budgets may vary simply because of differences in the sheer size of their research programs. But for our purposes, the possibility that the research staffs differ in their propensity to reveal/distort information is of paramount importance.

According to the bureaucratic approach, the Board's primary research objective is to widen the perceived gap between its performance and that of some feasible alternative. In pursuing this objective, the Board confronts a control problem. Once the research program is established, researchers might produce reliable information which entails 'adverse publicity' for the System. Suppose, for example, that by using generally accepted econometric procedures, a researcher finds that there is an exact (causal) relationship between some measure of money supply and inflation. The benefits to a researcher of exposing this information stem from two sources. On the one hand, the researcher may enjoy nonpecuniary 'psychic' benefits in the form of personal satisfaction from discovery of new information. Second, to the extent a researcher is getting closer to the truth as judged by the economics profession in general, the value of his research outside the Federal Reserve System increases. Presumably, universities or private firms are willing to pay more for the services of an individual whose work indicates the acquisition of skills (an increase in human capital) which promote rather than impede the understanding of monetary economics. Thus, any researcher who contemplates possible employment outside the System sometime in the future could anticipate benefits from publishing the connection between money and inflation.

In the absence of any attempt by the Board of Governors to control information, this type of research will have spillover effects on individuals throughout the System. When a researcher in one Federal Reserve Bank uncovers information which casts alternative monetary procedures (e.g., a money growth rule) in a favorable light, the perceived demand for the System's services goes down. Armed with this information, Congress will be somewhat less tolerant of mismanagement. This puts pressure on the Board of Governors to decrease the amount of funds it holds out of earnings for spending purposes. With a smaller pool of spendable funds, each Bank receives a smaller budget and each researcher receives fewer support funds. While the researcher finds that life at the Fed becomes a little less pleasant, the full costs of his decision to reveal the money supply/inflation information are not borne by him alone. His co-workers necessarily share some of the budgetary loss. Predictably, a researcher will have an incentive to reveal certain pieces of information even though the exposure takes the form of a 'public bad' for others in the System; i.e., even though it may lead to a substantial loss of total spendable funds.

This systematic erosion of funds is predicated on the assumption that members at the top of the Federal Reserve hierarchy are passive. However, there are two reasons why the Board would not be expected to adopt this stance. The first reason stems from the very fact that the Board is part of a bureaucracy. Since the System is organized along hierarchical lines, the Board would tend to be resistant to any innovations, and especially resistant to those originating from the lower levels of the bureaucracy (Tullock, 1965: 68-72). Second, it is important to note that the Board's own spending opportunities depend upon the common pool of spendable funds. In an attempt to protect this pool, the Board will take an active interest in discouraging certain types of research. This does not imply that it wants to eradicate every instance of information exposure. For one thing, monitoring employee behavior is costly. But even in the absence of monitoring costs, the Board generally will attempt to eliminate only that research whose value to the original researcher is less than the total costs it imposes on the System in the form of reduced spendable funds.(8)

The Board of Governors has at its disposal both a direct and an indirect means of controlling information exposure. Given that the problem involves the generation of too much adverse publicity by the different research departments, the System could take steps to directly screen any material before it comes out of the Reserve Banks in published form. By exercising some censorship powers, the Board of Governors can prevent the publication of articles that represent a high degree of demand-decreasing exposure. One drawback to this method is it high visibility.(9) All other things constant, one would expect the Board to prefer a monitoring technique whose purpose was not so easily understood by the general public.

The Board could accomplish the same end indirectly by manipulating the funds it distributes to the different Reserve Banks. Funds could be distributed in a way that confronts the individual researcher with the budgetary loss he imposes on others through his research activity. For instance, rather than a simple splitting of funds among Reserve Banks, a Bank's budget could be tied inversely to its degree of information exposure. Under this alternative scheme, the hierarchical structure of the System becomes crucial. The Banks' Presidents serve as the link between the Board's interests and the researchers' activities. When the Board is dissatisfied with a research department's provision of information, it can send a signal to that Bank President via a budget reduction. The President, in turn, is in a position to impose costs on the appropriate researchers. By reducing their support funds, he can induce them to restrain their provision of adverse information. Through its ultimate control over Bank budgets, the Board is able to initiate a chain of events culminating in a change in research activity in the desired direction.

Even with this bureaucratic allocation scheme, pockets of information exposure would continue to exist and to be observed at different points throughout the Reserve Banking System. As suggested earlier, the location of these pockets is not entirely unpredictable. To the extent information exposure entails a plan to seek employment outside the Fed sometime in the future, then demand-decreasing research will tend to be undertaken by those researchers relatively close to the margin of leaving and, significantly, will be tolerated by those Bank Presidents similarly situated; i.e., those earning low bureaucratic rents. If Banks differ in their mix of personnel (with different bureaucratic rents), then this should be reflected in different degrees of information exposure by the respective research departments. The next section simply takes these pockets of differential exposure as given. By noting how budgetary rewards vary according to the degree of information exposure in particular Banks, we can test the thesis about the existence of a bureaucratic allocation scheme.

4. EMPIRICAL ANALYSIS

To test for the existence of a bureaucratic allocation scheme, it is necessary to outline explicitly the contents of the opposing public interest theory. Our version of the public interest model is based on the assumption that members of the Board of Governors are motivated to provide accurate information on how the present management team performs relative to the viable alternatives. The Board realizes, however, that no individual, or group of individuals, has costless access to this 'truth.' Instead, it can be discovered only through an exploratory process involving trial and error procedures. Such a process is unlikely to be facilitated by allowing one point of view to monopolize the Fed's research program. Progress in this direction requires a competition of ideas which a Board, reflecting the public interest, can promote best by encouraging a variety of research agendas to be undertaken by the different Banks. This leads to an implication which contrasts sharply to the earlier developed implication of the bureaucratic model. The public interested Fed would not impede new or different lines of inquiry regarding monetary policy, even if the research generated information that decreased the demand for the Fed's services. A finding that the Board, in fact, practices some such form of information control would provide support for the bureaucratic thesis.

One particular means of information control is direct prohibition of research involving adverse publicity for the Federal Reserve System. As explained in the theoretical discussion, the Fed would be hesitant to make extensive use of this technique. It is interesting to note, nevertheless, that the Board does conduct a pre-publication review of the articles produced by the research staffs of the different Reserve Banks. As reported in a 1979 *Business Week* article, this review process was institutionalized by Arthur Burns who 'insisted that all regional bank articles sent to Washington – a pro forma courtesy until his tenure – be scrutinized before they were published' ('The politicization . . .', 1979: 115). While the Board's 'recommendations' can be overruled by the individual Banks, the review procedure increases the cost of publishing those pieces of information which ultimately reduce the System's pool of spendable funds.(10)

These recommendations are made more potent by the fact that the Board allocates funds to the Reserve Banks. As a first step in determining whether the Board uses the budgetary process as a control device, the research activities of the different Banks must be examined. Suppose, for example, we identified a period in a Bank's history when the nature of its research activities changed in a substantial fashion. The Bank in this case begins publishing information which suggests the Fed has greater control over the inflation rate than previously thought. Based on the predictions of the bureaucratic model, the Board of Governors would respond to these circumstances by reducing the budget allocated to that Bank in the adverse publicity period, ceteris paribus. In contrast, the public interest model predicts no such budgetary penalty. Perhaps the Bank in question might even be rewarded for this innovative line of research.

By examining the research publications of the individual Banks within the Federal Reserve System, we were able to identify two Reserve Banks whose research agendas exhibited structural changes. At different points in time, dramatic changes occurred in the research output of both the Minneapolis and St. Louis Feds. Looking briefly at the publication history of the St. Louis *Review* reveals a great deal regarding that Bank's research activities. Throughout most of the fifties, for example, articles focused on general economic conditions in the St. Louis district and included data on farm output and general financial statistics. Around 1959-60, the *Review* began to take on a somewhat more scholarly appearance and started to regularly publish articles which highlighted movements in the money supply, GNP, and income velocity. As an example of the type of research taking place, an article in the July, 1961 *Review* suggested that a recent rise in prices might be attributable to imperfect means of measuring price changes. The policy implication was that better indices must be developed. Although articles reporting money supply's behavior were becoming more commonplace, in publications as late as 1966 the focus was largely statistical in nature. More analytical approaches generally pointed to the fact that both money supply and GNP continued to grow.

In the mid-1960s, however, the seeds were being planted for a structural change in the research agenda at the St. Louis Fed. Homer Jones, a graduate of the University of Chicago who had been director of the St. Louis Research Department since 1958, was in the process of hiring a team of researchers interested in academically exploring the effects of changes in the quantity of money.(11) Jones's attempt to restructure the St. Louis research program was supported by the new President, Darryl Francis, who was appointed in 1966.

In response to the efforts of Jones and Francis, publications in the *Review* took a noticeably different course beginning in 1968.(12) In July, 1968, a guest article by Karl Brunner appeared. As a preface to the article, the *Review* editor explained the debate, then prevalent in academic circles, regarding the monetarist viewpoint. Brunner's article, 'The Role of Money and Monetary Policy,' clearly states the monetarist side of the debate. In November of the same year. Leonall C. Anderson and Jerry L. Jordan's now famous publication appeared. Their work, 'Monetary and Fiscal Actions: A Test of their Relative Importance in Economic Stabilization' served as a direct challenge to orthodox macroeconomic policy. Onc implication of these and subsequent articles was that rates of growth in nominal GNP are linked directly to growth rates of monetary aggregates. Furthermore, since the Federal Reserve System possesses the power to direct monetary policy via money supply changes, the ultimate responsibility for price instability belongs in the hands of the Fed. Continued research along these lines clearly has earned the St. Louis Bank the reputation of being the 'monetarist Fed.'

A review of the history of the publications of another Bank, the Federal Reserve Bank of Minneapolis, proves equally revealing. Like the St. Louis Bank, early publications of the Minneapolis Fed focused on economic conditions of the region. Any effort to explain inflation generally entailed an encyclopedic catalogue of factors. As late as 1973 an article in Minneapolis's regular publication, *Monthly Statistical Report*, listed an assortment of different 1972/73 inflation factors, e.g., 'drastic decline in anchovy catch,''commodity speculation' and 'low points in cattle, hog cycles.' The list mentioned neither the Fed nor money supply as possible factors.

At about this time, however, significant changes were occurring in the research department at Minneapolis. Neil Wallace and Thomas J. Sargent from the University of Minnesota joined the staff as research advisors in 1970 and 1971, respectively. The influence of their work on Minneapolis's research activities became public in October, 1974, when the Bank sponsored a conference on *Rational Expectations and Macroeconomic Policy.* Sargent and Wallace's conference paper, 'Rational Expectations and the Theory of Economic Policy' was published later by the Minneapolis Fed in *Studies in Monetary Economics Series*, No. 2 (June, 1975).

1974 also marked a change in Minneapolis's regular publication format, as it began publishing its *Ninth District Quarterly.* Instead of statistical reports, some articles in this journal addressed monetary policy issues. The *Quarterly* cited the rational expectations literature for the first time in a paper, 'Monetary Policy in Unchartered Waters,' that represented remarks from a speech by Minneapolis Reserve President Bruce Maclaury in September 1975.(13) In the same year, the Bank's research staff conducted a series of seminars on FOMC policymaking and the Bank also held a conference on business cycle research. The rational expectations' theme served as the focal point for both of these research programs. In 1977 the Minneapolis Fed appointed a new President, Mark Willes, and introduced a new periodical, *The Quarterly Review*, which contained an editorial statement declaring 'the new publication will primarily present economic research aimed at improving policymaking by the Federal Reserve System and other governmental authorities.' The first issue contained an article by Neil Wallace titled, 'Why the Fed Should Consider Holding M_0 Constant.' A cursory survey of subsequent issues indicates the Bank's interest in exploring the policy implications of rational expectations.

As these brief historical surveys suggest, there have been rather significant changes in the research programs of the St. Louis and Minneapolis Reserve Banks. While these changes certainly have been evolutionary in character, for each Bank there are readily identifiable turning points. Publication of the 1968 Anderson and Jordan article, more than anything else, served to crystallize the public's perception of the St. Louis Fed as a 'monetarist' Bank. Similarly, a good case can be made for 1974 as the critical year for the Minneapolis Fed. Not only did Minneapolis start publishing a journal that for the first time offered the prospects of serious monetary policy analysis, but also in 1974 the Minneapolis Fed sponsored its first conference on rational expectations. What was common to the new research agendas of both Banks in these periods was an enhanced willingness to publicly criticize (at least indirectly) the policy strategies of the Federal Reserve System. Both Banks, for instance, introduced the possibility that an alternative policy rule, such as a constant money growth rule, could result in greater economic stability than the present system. In so doing, the St. Louis and Minneapolis Banks began revealing information which suggested that the benefits associated with the existence of the present Federal Reserve management team might be lower than previously perceived.

Before examining the effects of the research agenda shifts on the Banks' budget allocations, a final historical observation is in order. Following the appointment of a new President, E. Gerald Corrigan, in 1980, there has been evidence of another shift in research priorities of the Minneapolis Bank. In the 1981 and 1982 Minneapolis *Annual Reports*, for instance, Corrigan cautioned against the deregulatory trend embodied in the Monetary Control Act of 1980. He argues that the Fed must continue to regulate the banking system because of the special nature of banks and the problem in defining and controlling the money supply. This type of publicity tends to increase the demand for the Fed's regulatory services. It seems appropriate, therefore, to distinguish the Corrigan regime from the1974-79 'demand-decreasing' period, even though some rational expectations research continues presently.

A preliminary examination of the budget numbers provides tentative support for the bureaucratic hypothesis that the Board reacts to periods of demand-decreasing information exposure by reducing the budget allocations of the 'uncooperative' Banks. Consider the St. Louis and Systemwide (exclusive of St. Louis and Minneapolis) budget records in the pre-1968. From 1952 to 1967 the annualized real budgetary growth rates at the St. Louis Fed and Systemwide were 3.78% and 3.35% respectively. The average annual growth rate for the System as a whole was somewhat lower (2.40%) during the 1968-80 period. However, expenditures at the St. Louis Fed grew at a markedly lower rate. Over this last thirteen year period the annualized growth rate was only 1.28%. The expenditure shift at the Minneapolis Fed was even more pronounced. In the pre-rational expectations period (1952-74), Minneapolis's average annual growth rate exceeded the Systemwide rate by approximately 1.6 percentage points.(14) This relationship was reversed in the 1974-79 period. During this brief period, real budgets throughout the System declined at an annual rate of 1.10% in comparison to a 3.80% annualized decrease at the Minneapolis Fed.

To test the significance of these budgetary differences, while controlling for other factors, we conducted a time series study of the St. Louis and Minneapolis Banks. Using data for the years 1952-1980, our general equation took the following reduced form:(15)

$$\triangle RB_i = a_0 + a_1 D_i + a_2 \triangle CH_1 + a_3 \& MA_i + a_4 \triangle RW_i + e_i; \quad i = 1 \ldots 28, \qquad (1)$$

where the dependent variable, RB_i, is a Bank's real budget in year i; a_o, a_1, a_2, a_3, and a_4 are estimated coefficients; D_i is a dummy variable representing a structural change in a Bank's research agenda; CH_i is the number of checks cleared by a Bank in year i; MA_i is the total member bank assets in a particular Reserve district in year i; RW_i is the real hourly wage rate in year i for the state in which the Bank is located;(16) and finally, e_i is an independent and identically distributed error term with mean zero and finite variance σ. First differences are used in estimating the equation to overcome problems of multicollinearity in the independent variables.

The dummy variable, D, is given a value of 1 for years of demanding-decreasing information production by a Bank and a value of 0 for all other years. Based on the bureaucratic model, we expect the growth in budget to be less in the demand-decreasing years, ceteris paribus. In this case, the coefficient on D will be negative whereas the public interest model predicts a coefficient either positive or not significantly different from zero. $\triangle$ CH measures the change in the Bank's volume of check clearing output, and MA serves as a proxy for the output pertaining to its regulatory function. With an increase in either, a larger budget would be expected, all other things con-

Table 1
St. Louis and Systemwide Budget Changes as Dependent Variables

Independent variables	St. Louis estimated coefficients and t-statistics (a)	Systemwide estimated coefficients and t-statistics (b)
D	− 969.308*	3793.288
$\triangle$ CH	(1.999)	(0.611)
	25.810*	7.636
$\triangle$ MA	(1.915)	(0.734)
	0.618	− 0.036
$\triangle$ RW	(1.119)	(0.338)
	− 2177.325	98835.430*
Constant	(0.628)	(3.077)
	3.722	− 1221.966
R^2	0.3645	0.4555

*Indicates significant at the 0.05 level.

stant. Because RW serves as a proxy for a change in the least cost of providing a given output, a positive sign is expected on this variable.

Testing the explanatory power of the bureaucratic versus the public interest models was undertaken first with respect to the St. Louis Bank. Based on our previous findings concerning the time of structural change, the dummy variable was assigned a value of 0 for the years 1952-67, and was given a value of 1 for the remaining years, 1968-80. As can be seen in column (1) of Table 1, the results coincide with the predictions of the bureaucratic model. The dummy variable was significant at the 0.05 level with the negative sign as predicted. The dummy coefficient indicates there was a $969 thousand reduction in St. Louis's annual budget growth in the years following the structural change in information exposure that cannot be explained by the other variables in the equation.(17) The variable, CH was positive as expected and significant at the 0.05 level. The other two variables, △MA and △RW, were not statistically significant in this case.

While these results are suggestive, it is possible that the smaller budget increases after 1968 were a reflection of some cost-reducing innovation common to the entire banking industry, but not captured in the regression. To allow for this possibility, we next tested the general equation with data for the entire Federal Reserve System, excluding the St. Louis and Minneapolis Banks. As an example, the dependent variable, △ RB in year one equals the summed budget changes in that year for the other ten Banks in the Federal Reserve System. △ CH and △ MA were calculated in an analogous manner. △ RW represents the change in the real hourly wage rate for the United States. As before, D equals 1 for the years 1968-80 and 0 for 1952-67. The bureaucratic hypothesis will receive further support as long as the coefficient on D is not significantly negative.

Column (b) of Table 1 lists the results of regressing Systemwide budget changes against the independent variables. In contrast to the St. Louis outcome, the dummy variable proves to be insignificant. This indicates there was no structural change in the System as a whole causing budgetary changes to differ in the two time periods. Evidently, the smaller St. Louis budget increases after 1968 are attributable to a unique structural change, such as its new research agenda.

Turning to the Minneapolis case, we tested for a structural change which might affect the Minneapolis Fed's budget allocation by estimating the general equation using Minneapolis data. D equals 1 for the years 1974-79 and 0 for the remaining years.(18) Column (1) of Table 2 reports the results. While particular care should be exercised in interpreting column (a), given the short 1974-79 time span, the results are consistent with the predictions of the bureaucratic model The significant negative sign on the dummy variable indicates there was a systematic decrease in the annual budget changes in the years following the hypothesized structural change. Unlike the St. Louis case, however, an unexplained drop in the dependent variable for the entire System also occurred, as indicated by the coefficient on the D variable in column (b) of Table 2.(19)

Given the inconclusiveness of these Minneapolis results, it seems useful at this point to compare the magnitude of the budget changes occurring in Minneapolis to those of the entire System. A finding that 1974-79 Minneapolis budgets declined relative to the budgets of other Banks, after controlling for other factors, would be consistent with the hypothesis that Minneapolis was being penalized differentially for its information exposure activities. With this objective in mind, we ran an additional first difference equation with the following results:

$$\triangle \frac{MRB}{SRB} = \underset{}{0.0006} - \underset{(1.736)}{0.00014D^*} + \underset{(0.985)}{0.1210} \triangle - \frac{MCH}{SCH} - \underset{(0.329)}{0.1325} \triangle \frac{MMA}{SMA}$$

$$+ \underset{(1.211)}{0.0139} \triangle \frac{MRW}{SRW}$$

$$R^2 = 0.2019$$

The variables are defined as previously except for M-prefix designates the Minneapolis Bank and the S-prefix represents Systemwide variables.(20) The dummy variable assumes a value of 1 if the year is between 1974-79, and 0 otherwise. Note that D has a negative coefficient which is significant at the 0.05 level. This suggests there was a drop in the ratio of Minneapolis to Systemwide budgets that could not be explained completely by the ordinary output and cost factors. As in the St. Louis case, these results provide support for the bureaucratic model as a predictor of budgetary distribution patterns.

Table 2
Minneapolis and Systemwide Budget Changes as Dependent Variables

Independent variables	Minneapolis estimated coefficients and t-statistics (a)	Systemwide estimated coefficients and t-statistics (b)
D	−884.429*	−15992.270*
△ CH	(3.128) 9.341	(3.596) 19.637*
△ MA	(1.691) 0.311	(3.235) 0.066
△ RW	(1.227) 2521.865	(0.731) 66985.569*
Constant	(0.894) 56.691	(2.488) 1740.627
R^2	0.4247	0.6458

*Indicates significant at the 0.05 level.

5. CONCLUSION

While this paper focused primarily on the Federal Reserve System, it offers some insights into the operation of government bureaus in general. At this general level, the paper examined the internal functioning of an agency which consists of several subdivisions. We explored one factor that enters into a bureau's decision on how to distribute its budgetary funds to the various subdepartments. In his role as budget allocator, the head of a bureau confronts a problem that is analogous to the tragedy of the commons problem. Agency employees can undertake actions which deplete the common pool of spendable funds at an imperceptible cost to themselves. By manipulating the budget shares to each subdepartment in a way that penalizes the budget-depleting activity, the agency head can inhibit the erosion of the total budget implied by the independent adjustment outcome.

The propensity of heads to employ such a budget allocation scheme depends on their motivation. In the past, economists have postulated a nebulous public interest motivation in constructing theories of Federal Reserve official behavior. Under this postulate, the Board of Governors and other employees at the Fed have no special desire to protect the System's pool of spendable funds. Hence, the Board has no incentive to employ the innovative budget allocation scheme. We purposely have departed from this traditional approach and developed a bureaucratic model of the Fed. The pursuit of new discretionary opportunities provides the Fed, through the Board, with the incentive to discover and incorporate into the budgetary process the reward/penalty structure that maximizes bureaucratic rents. Our empirical results lend credence to the existence of this bureaucratic budgetary scheme. Apparently, members of the Fed behave much like other individual actors in the economy. They do not simply pursue the 'public good,' no matter what the institutional environment; instead, they respond in a predictable way to changes in their constraints. This is one further indication that if progress is to be made on the broader issue of understanding Federal Reserve System policy decisions, an explicit utility-maximizing perspective must be adopted.

NOTES

1. In particular, see works by Gordon Tullock (1965), William Niskanen (1971, 1975) and Jean-Luc Migue and Gerard Belanger (1974). There are a few studies that examine central banks from a bureaucratic perspective. For instance, John F. Chant and Keith Acheson (1972, chapters 6 and 7 in this volume) used a bureaucratic approach in analyzing the operation of the central bank in Canada. For more recent works, see Edward J. Kane (chapter 10 in this volume), William Shughart and Robert Tollison (chapter 4 in this volume) and Mark Toma (chapter 3 in this volume).
2. The possibility that output will be extended beyond the level desired by the median voter stems from Niskanen (1971, 1972). This outcome depends on the assumption that bureaus confront review committees that have a high demand for the bureau's output.
3. Chant and Acheson (1972) have outlined the specific behavioral traits adopted by the Bank of Canada to take advantage of the existence of information costs.
4. In 1933 the Fed was given the legal right to retain all earnings. The Fed departed from tradition in 1947 and transferred a portion of its earnings to the Treasury. These transfers have occurred annually since that time.
5. This discussion assumes that price stability is the median voter's preferred outcome.
6. Albert Breton and Ronald Wintrobe (1975) emphasize that the representatives will invest in monitoring devices to acquire information on a bureau's cost of operation. The Fed has the same incentive as any bureau to make this information collection process costly.
7. Although we have emphasized the similarity in outcomes under a regular appropriation financing scheme versus the Fed's actual financing scheme, important differences do exist. In not being subject to the regular budgetary process, the Fed has more scope for mismanagement. This stems from the fact that the cost to Congress of controlling undesirable Fed behavior is greater under the present system. For rather than merely reducing the Fed's budget, Congress must agree to a change in the rules governing Fed financing. Another major difference concerns the fact that the Fed's revenue is tied to bond holdings

with the present financing scheme, which creates a bias toward greater base rates of growth and hence, higher rates of inflation. For a development of the last point, see Mark Toma (chapter 3 in this volume)..

8. Consider a case where an employee engages in research that produces personal benefits of $10 and reduces the System's pool of spendable funds by $5. Although elimination of this activity will save $5 in spendable funds, this amount is less than what is necessary to restore the researcher's 'real wage.' Clearly, the Board loses more than it gains in this type of tradeoff.
9. Another alternative simply would be to fire the researchers who publish articles that represent a high degree of demand-decreasing information exposure. This technique has the same drawbacks as the censorship approach.
10. The review process is not necessarily confined to Federal Reserve in-house publications. *Business Week* ('The Politicization . . .', 1979) reports the circulation of a Fed memo requiring Washington staffers to clear any articles intended for publication outside the System.
11. Homer Jones also was responsible for instituting the St. Louis series of weekly and monthly collection of monetary statistics. For more on the connection between Jones and the St. Louis Bank see (Contributions in Honor of Homer Jones, 1976).
12. Milton Friedman (1976: 435) argues that 'Homer and Darryl Francis converted the St. Louis Bank into by far the most important unit in the System. For the first time since the days of Walter Steward, Winfield Riefler, and Randolph Burgess in the 1920s, monetary research from within the System began to influence academic research and thinking. For the first time, a bank publication *The Review of the Federal Reserve Bank of St. Louis*, began to be cited regularly in academic journals.
13. This paper was published in *Ninth District Quarterly* in April, 1976 (see under Fed. Res. Bank of Minneapolis, 1974-1977).
14. The growth rate for the Minneapolis Fed was 6.3% as compared to 4.73% in the System.
15. 1952 was the earliest year for which all the data could be obtained. Our sample period ended with 1980 because of passage of the Monetary Control Act of 1980. Among other things, the Act broadened the basis upon which the Fed provides its services from only member banks to all depository institutions. This changes the relationship between a Bank's real budget and the independent variables in equation (1). For instance, MA is no longer a proxy for a Bank's non-check clearing services.
16. Some specific information concerning our data collection should be mentioned. First, bank budgets are from (Board of Governors . . . 1952-1980) and measure expenses net of reimbursements and assessments for expenditures of the Board of Governors. Second, the calculation of checks differed slightly between Banks. Minneapolis CH measures total checks handled, whereas Systemwide and St. Louis checks exclude United States government checks and postal money orders. This information was supplied by the Minneapolis and St. Louis Feds as part of their volume of operations data. Third, RW represents the real hourly earnings of production workers in manufacturing for the respective states. The Systemwide RW, introduced later, is the real hourly earnings of production workers in the private nonagricultural sector in the United States. Finally, member bank asset data were published in issues of the *Federal Reserve Bulletin* only though 1977. Data for the remaining years were obtained from FDIC tapes for the System and state data from these tapes were used to estimate asset numbers for the Minneapolis district. The Federal Reserve Bank of St. Louis provided unpublished data concerning assets in that district.
17. The dummy coefficients in the tables were computed on the basis of a real budget measured in thousands of dollars.

18. Since Corrigan became Minneapolis's President in the middle of 1980, it is unclear whether 1979 or 1980 should be used as the terminal point of the dummy period. Results from regressions using 1974-80 as the dummy period were qualitatively similar to the findings reported in the text.
19. This result at least partially may be explained by a productivity improvement program from 1975 to 1978 that reduced staffing throughout the System.
20. Assuming constant costs, $\triangle \frac{MCH}{SCH}$, $\triangle \frac{MNA}{SMA}$, and $\triangle \frac{MRW}{SRW}$ should be correlated positively with the dependent variable.

REFERENCES

Acheson, K., and J. F. Chant, 'Mythology and Central Banking,' *Kyklos*, 1972, 16, 362-379.

Acheson, K., and J. F. Chant, 'The Choice of Monetary Instruments and the Theory of Bureaucracy,' chapter 6 in this volume.

Acheson, K., and J. F. Chant, 'Bureaucratic Theory and the Choice of Central Bank Goals,' chapter 7 in this volume.

Board of Governors of the Federal Reserve System, *Annual Report*, 1952-1980.

Breton, A., and R. Wintrobe, 'The Equilibrium Size of a Budget-Maximizing Bureau: A Note on Niskanen's Theory of Bureaucracy,' *Journal of Political Economy*, February 1975, 83, 195-207.

'Contributions in Honor of Homer Jones, A Symposium,' in *Journal of Monetary Economics*, November 1976, 2, 431-471.

Federal Reserve Bank of St. Louis, *Review*, 1952-1980.

Federal Reserve Bank of Minneapolis, *Monthly Statistical Report, Ninth District Conditions*, 1973.

Federal Reserve Bank of Minneapolis, *Ninth District Quarterly*, 1974-1977.

Federal Reserve Bank of Minneapolis, *The Quarterly Review*, 1977-1980.

Federal Reserve Bank of Minneapolis, *Annual Report*, 1952-1980.

Friedman, M., 'Homer Jones: A Personal Reminiscence,' *Journal of Monetary Economics*, November 1976, 2, 433-436.

Kane, E. J, 'Politics and Fed Policymaking,' chapter 10 in this volume.

Migue, J. L., and G. Belanger, 'Toward a General Theory of Managerial Discretion,' *Public Choice*, Spring 1974, 17, 27-43.

Niskanen, W. A., *Bureaucracy and Representative Government*, Aldine-Atherton Press: Chicago, 1971.

Niskanen, W. A., 'Bureaucrats and Politicians,' *Journal of Law and Economics*, December 1975, 617-643.

'The Politicization of Research at the Fed.,' *Business Week*, July 16, 106-115.

Shughart, W. F., and R. D. Tollison, 'Preliminary Evidence on the use of Inputs by the Federal Reserve System,' chapter 4 in this volume.

Toma, M., 'Inflationary Bias of the Federal Reserve System: A Bureaucratic Perspective,' chapter 3 in this volume.

Tullock, G., *The Politics of Bureaucracy*, Public Affairs Press: Washington, DC, 1965.

Chapter 9

BANKING SECTOR INFLUENCE ON THE RELATIONSHIP OF CONGRESS TO THE FEDERAL RESERVE SYSTEM

*By Neil T. Skaggs and Cheryl L. Wasserkrug**

Numerous studies of central bank behavior adopt the view that the central bank is a bureaucratic organization, distinct from the legislature and administration, as a starting point. For example, Chant and Acheson (1973) assume that the central bank is concerned with the maintenance and generation over time of an opportunity set that allows the bureau discretionary options. This basis leads them to conclude that a 'rational' bureau will obscure its actions, either refusing to provide its sponsoring organization (in Niskanen's terminology) with information on its activities, or creating a mythology which serves the same purpose.

Other studies focus on the central bank's activities vis-a-vis outside parties, treating the monetary authority as little more than an extension of the nation's elected representatives. Breton and Wintrobe (1978), using this format, conclude that the operating procedure employed by the Bank of Canada displays bureaucratic characteristics.

This paper seeks to construct and apply a more general theory of central bank behavior. Utilizing a simple utility maximization model, similar to the model informally used by Chant and Acheson, we develop hypotheses about how a bureaucratic central bank, distinct from its sponsoring organization, may utilize its monetary operations to influence non-governmental agents, thereby protecting its scope for discretionary action.

* The authors wish to thank Sam Witsam, Kevin Heid and Tark Choong Sup for their help in computing and data collection and Jack Chizmar for his advice on econometrics. Department of Economics, Illinois State University, IL 61761.

Toma, E.F. and Toma, M. (eds.) Central Bankers, Bureaucratic Incentives, and Monetary Policy

ISBN 90 247 3366 9

Section 1 sets out the model of a bureau used. Section 2 discusses the environmental circumstances within which the Federal Reserve operates. The two general hypotheses drawn from the model are given empirical content. Section 3 discusses a framework within which one of these hypotheses may be examined, extending the simple model to enable interaction between the Federal Reserve and parts of its environment. In Section 4 we empirically examine one part of the system discussed in Section 3. The conclusions drawn from the model conclude the paper.

.SECTION 1

The approach taken here is simple. We assume that the Federal Reserve has an objective function, which may be thought of as the composite utility function of the Board of Governors, which is maximized subject to a cost function. (We shall actually concentrate on the cost-minimization dual of this formulation.) Alchian (1965, p. 39) has observed that

> The utility maximizing theory is applicable and useful if, and only if, (1) we can identify some of its components (besides direct pecuniary wealth) and if (2) we can identify circumstances that involve differences in the cost of each of the various types of managerial non-pecuniary 'goods'. By satisfying these two conditions, we can deduce the relative extent of such activities in each of those circumstances.

Rather than specifying a multitude of possible arguments which might appear in the Fed's objective function, we will assume that, in addition to the traditional policy goals of Federal Reserve officials, primarily macroeconomic in nature, 'discretion' is valued by these authorities. Discretion is defined as the ability to make decisions without rigid direction from outside the organization.(1)

The inclusion of discretion as an argument in the objective function may be justified by noting that the absence of discretion restricts the officials in their choice of activities. Removing discretion is tantamount to raising to infinity the price of any good not acceptable to the bureau's sponsoring organization. This has the effect of shifting the bureau's 'budget constraint' inward, moving the bureau's officials to a lower indifference surface.

All activities in which the Fed may choose to engage have costs. However, the cost of an activity is unknown ex ante. The monetary authorities must form expectations of the cost of each activity. The expected cost of an activity is the subjective probability that the activity will bring a loss of discretion, multiplied times the present value of the future stream of discretionary activities which might be foregone.

There is, of course, no way to attach absolute (dollar) values to the subjectively-determined costs envisaged by bureau officials. However, reasoned conjectures about relative levels of cost, and about changes in cost levels, may be made. Two relevant points should be noted: (1) knowledge of relative costs is sufficient to predict (some) bureau behavior; and (2) institutional detail must be used if the relative costs of a bureau's activities are to be understood. What is costly cannot be known in a general a priori sense; it can only be discovered by examining the environment surrounding the bureau in question.

The level of cost attached to an activity is not independent of the manner in which the bureau pursues the activity. This is analogous to the theory of the firm: The level of cost is directly related to the choice of production technique. The relevance of this point will become clear below.

There would seem to be two primary methods of lowering the expected cost of an activity: (1) by providing no information (or incorrect information) about bureau activities, or otherwise obfuscating bureau actions; and/or (2) by developing a constituency powerful enough to protect the bureau from retribution from its sponsoring organization. The second method may entail the forfeiture of some discretion or the usage of a particular production technique in the effort to cultivate the constituency. However, a strong constituency can provide protection of a sort mere obfuscation cannot. Officials of the sponsoring organization can obtain more information about bureau activities if they are so moved and are willing to pay the price. An effectively-cultivated constituency could prevent the sponsors from being so moved.

In general we may suppose that both methods of cost-minimization are employed by bureaus. The question then immediately arises, How does a bureau develop a constituency? In the absence of coercion, one may suppose that a constituency, which is really just a lobbying group for the bureau, will develop wherever a beneficial quid pro quo relationship exists. This leads us to a discussion of the environment surrounding the Federal Reserve System.

SECTION 2

In an indirect fashion all Americans are part of the Federal Reserve's environment. Monetary policy affects nearly everyone at some point. But construing the Fed's environment in this manner is not an approach likely to bear fruit in an attempt to explain System behavior. Instead, we will define the Federal Reserve's environment much more narrowly. It is composed of those institutions which come into direct contact with the Fed as the Fed carries out its policy functions. On this definition, the Federal Reserve's environment consists of four entities: the Congress, the President, the Treasury, and the financial sector.(2)

The Federal Reserve's 'sponsoring organization' is Congress. It is to Congress that the Fed is finally beholden for its authority to carry out its policy functions. It is to Congress that the System must report on its activities. And it is Congress which, by a simple majority, can change the 'rules of the game' to require the Fed to do whatever it bids.

A cursory examination of history shows that Congress has rarely amended the Federal Reserve Act, however. There are several possible explanations for this. It is obviously true that, in an institution composed of as many people as Congress, arriving at a consensus in favor of changing the Federal Reserve Act in a particular manner is not easy. Another possibility is that the Congress is effectively lobbied by a constituency which favors the maintenance of the status quo. This possibility will be examined in Section 3.

The connection between the President and the Federal Reserve is both less and more direct than the connection between the Fed and Congress. The formal ties which link Congress and the Fed simply do not exist between the President and the Fed. Informal ties do exist, however. The President occupies a position unique in American politics. He reaps the benefits of popular occurrences and suffers the condemnation for unpopular events in a way no individual congressman or senator does. The President is likely to gain more and to lose more from Federal Reserve policies than is any legislator. This makes the Fed's policies of utmost interest to him, particularly during periods of economic duress. During troubled times, when the public demands that something be done, the President is in less of a position to do nothing than is Congress, where remedies may be proposed by legislators who are secure in the knowledge that the proposals will never navigate successfully the turbulent streams of legislative enactment. During such periods, the President has greater incentive to attempt to influence Fed behaviour than do legislators.

The President also has the ability to bring intense pressure on the Federal Reserve, even though he has no formal control over the System. By bringing public attention to bear on the Fed, the President is in a position to make the Fed a scapegoat for a multitude of economic ills. Needless to say, presidential charges of unaccountability could affect the System's subjective probability of loss of discretion.

The Treasury comes in contact with the Federal Reserve through its financing efforts. With regard to influencing the Fed, Treasury officials lack the formal power of legislators and the political necessity of the President. The Federal Reserve can affect the ease of Treasury operations enough to cause interest in the Fed's mode of operation on the part of Treasury officials, however.

Federal Reserve accommodation of Treasury financing makes the process of selling securities by subscription much easier. In the absence of an accommodation agreement, a Federal Reserve operating strategy which moderates interest rate movements provides most of the same benefits. If we assume that there is a negative payoff to Treasury officials for either offering a yield significantly above the market level ('a waste of public funds') or for the failure of a bond issue, then interest rate stability is of concern to them.

Finally we come to the financial sector, defined to include a much broader range of institutions than just commercial banks. By 'the financial sector' we mean those institutions and market participants whose business activities and profitability are directly affected by the flow of credit consequent upon Fed activities. This can be seen to include nearly all organizations which might be classified as financial institutions.

Federal Reserve policy operations are carried out via the financial sector. There are two facets of Fed policy which are relevant to the financial sector, viz., type of policy (contractionary, expansionary, etc.) and mode of operation (interest rate strategy, monetary aggregates strategy, etc.) Market participants may gain from specific types of each.

Other things equal, an accommodative monetary policy is preferred to a restrictive policy by the financial sector, just as such a policy is preferred by other sectors. Plentiful credit makes business easier; we need not comment further on this point. That the financial sector should prefer a particular type of operating strategy is not so immediately obvious. But a case can be made that certain operating strategies yield benefits to financial market participants which other strategies do not.

In a world of perfect information about credit demand and supply, the type of operating strategy pursued by the Fed would be irrelevant to market participants. Knowledge of future credit flows would be sufficient to cause market yields to rationally adjust to market-clearing levels. But in a world of less than perfect information the Fed's mode of operation is not so irrelevant.

Information about the future supply of credit should be easier to obtain than information about credit demands. Given relatively stable multipliers, the amount of high-powered money injected into the economy by the Fed would lead to highly-predictable levels of credit aggregates, given that the Fed provided information on its intentions. To estimate the total demand for credit would prove much more difficult, due to the multitudes of borrowers who tap credit flows each year.

But in practice the Federal Reserve has not provided plentiful information about its intentions. Until quite recently it provided almost no information, subscribing to the 'hidden hand philosophy' of central banking – the most effective policy is a surprise policy. Even today the information provided to Congress at quarterly oversight hearings is scanty (and, some observers feel, totally inadequate(3). The reason for this recalcitrance is, in our estimation, that outlined above – by maintaining secrecy about its activities and decision processes, the Fed is able to insulate itself from criticism and the increased probability of loss of discretion.(4,5)

In a world where future credit demand can only be estimated, and the central bank is unlikely to provide information on its policy-formation process unless forced to do so, the mode of operation by which monetary policy is carried out may be used to convey substantial amounts of useful information to market participants.(6) But by providing information through the market, the Federal Reserve may be able to avoid disclosing the more sensitive information concerning the trade-offs Fed officials are willing to make.

What kind of operating strategy provides the most information to market participants? Due to the nature of market information, a strategy which utilizes interest rates as short-term targets and/or indicators provides more day to day information than a strategy which focuses exclusively on aggregates. A consistently-pursued interest rate strategy may provide considerable information about future movements of some monetary aggregate, as has been shown by Skaggs (1981).(7) In the absence of official policy information, such an operating strategy could be most desirable from the viewpoint of market participants. This could help to explain why the Federal Reserve persisted in utilizing such a policy in the face of technical criticism voiced by monetarists and quasi-monetarists throughout the decade of the 1970s.

The remainder of this paper is concerned with investigating the possibility of a quid pro quo relationship between the Federal Reserve System and the financial sector. (We in no way deny the possibility that systematic ties with other parts of the Fed's environment exist.) In the next section we consider how such a relationship might be structured.

SECTION 3

A trading relationship between two parties may be direct or indirect, with both principal parties dealing with a third party. Breton and Wintrobe (1978) have analyzed one direct relationship, between the Bank of Canada and Canadian commercial banks. Since the number of distinct banking corporations operating in Canada is quite small, the Bank of Canada has found that 'moral suasion' is an effective policy tool. When Bank officials call the private bankers together to apply political pressure, they provide a forum where the private bankers may collude with government approval. According to Breton and Wintrobe, the private bankers are willing to trade compliance to the central bank's suasion in return for the opportunity to collude.

The institutional framework of the U.S. banking sector is much different. With literally thousands of individual corporations doing business in the U.S., a direct, simple policy, such as used by the Bank of Canada, is inappropriate (though isolated attempts at moral suasion have been made). Given that information about Fed operating activities is valuable, and that such information can be passed through the operating strategy, it is obvious how the Fed may provide something of value to the financial sector. But how is the far-flung U.S. financial (or even banking) sector to reciprocate? There seems to be no direct quid pro quo arrangement which would prove satisfactory in the United States. However, it is not hard to imagine an indirect trade, whereby the financial system, the Federal Reserve and a third party, namely, the Congress, all benefit.

As noted in Section 2, the Federal Reserve System is a creature of Congress. The System could be drastically altered, indeed eliminated, by a simple majority vote. More likely, the Federal Reserve Act could be amended to require the monetary authorities to divulge more, and more sensitive, information, or to submit to tighter congressional control. In fact, the history of the Federal Reserve System since World War II is replete with congressional attempts to tighten control over the Fed. Throughout the 1950s and '60s most of these attempts were generated by Congressman Wright Patman, chairman of the House Banking Committee for many years.

Patman introduced the first of his many GAO audit bills, calling for an audit of all Board of Governors activities by the General Accounting Office, in 1954. Prior to that he had already had an influence on the Board's internal accounting procedures.(8)

Patman's 1954 bill did not get out of committee. Nor did any of his subsequent audit bills, introduced annually, almost without exception, throughout the '50s and '60s. Not until 1974, after Henry Reuss had replaced Patman as the chairman of the House Banking Committee, was an audit bill passed by the House (it died in the Senate).

The importance of the audit proposals is that they would have given Congress access to the records of the monetary policy deliberations of the Board of Governors and the Federal Open Market Committee. Such information might have proved detrimental to the Fed official's ability to maintain discretionary powers. Evidence of monetary policy decisions being taken to achieve goals not espoused by Congress or due to political reasons not regarded as valid by Congress could easily lead to congressional demands for more direct control of monetary policy.(9)

On an issue of such importance to the Federal Reserve, a constituency prepared to lobby against tighter control of the Fed by Çongress would be providing Fed officials with a valuable service. Since the nature of the political lobbying process is a positive sum game (for the active participants), members of Congress might also be expected to gain from such an indirect trade, or 'iron triangle,' relationship. In Section 4 we investigate a particular vote on a GAO audit measure to see if there is any systematic banking sector influence.

SECTION 4

Our empirical investigation of congressional (actually, House) voting patterns with respect to control of the Fed focuses on the 1974 audit measure, H.R. 10265. The bill was passed virtually unanimously – but only after it was amended to remove the GAO's authority to examine the monetary policy functions of the System. The particular vote we shall analyze is the vote on the Ashley-Stanton Amendment, which limited the scope of GAO audits to financial considerations. By prohibiting the GAO from auditing the records of policy actions, the amendment effectively eliminated the policy control aspects of the legislation.

In estimating an equation relating various independent variables to the three discrete vote possibilities (for, against, abstain) one must eschew the use of ordinary least squares. The following equations were estimated by a maximum likelihood logit procedure. This procedure(10) simultaneously estimates two equations, the first utilizing the logarithm of the probability of a 'yes' vote relative to the probability of a 'no' vote as the dependent variable, the second utilizing the log of the relative probabilities of abstention and 'no' votes.

The independent variables used in our model are:

PARTY – (0 = Republican; 1 = Democrat)
RATE – The legislators' Americans for Democratic Action voting index for 1973-74. (0 = 'conservative'; 100 = 'liberal')(11)
BKDEP – Total commercial bank deposits, by congressional district
SVDEP – Total savings and loan association and mutual saving bank deposits by congressional district
BKPC – Total bank deposits divided by per capita income, by district
SVPC – Total savings deposits divided by per capita income, by district(12)

The two 'political' variables, PARTY and RATE, are intended to capture any partisan efforts on the issue or any philosophical (liberal-conservative) influences. The 'economic' variables are proxies for the political influence the financial community is able to exert in the various districts. We assume that the larger the banking interests are in a district the more likely it is that the legislator from that district is influenced by these interests. The BKPC and SVPC variables attempt to capture relative size effects.

The results of statistical estimation of the model are shown in Table 1.(13) The empirical model suggests that legislators from districts with large banking interests did indeed tend to vote against auditing the Fed's monetary policy functions (i.e., in favor of the restrictive Ashley-Stanton Amendment). The BKDEP coefficient is significantly negative in equations 1a and 3a, while BKPC is negative and significant in 2a. The savings and loan institution variables failed to be significant in any version of the equation, perhaps reflecting the more distant relationship of S & Ls to the Fed. None of the economic variables are significant in the abstention equations.

The political variables indicate the strong support for the Ashley-Stanton amendment by Republicans. To the GOP, at least, this appeared to be something of a partisan issue. Indeed, because Republicans nearly uniformly voted for the amendment, the equations were run for Democrats only to see if the relationship with banking interests proved as strong. Table 2 presents these results, which are in line with the results for the total vote. It is interesting to note the strength – in the 'right' direction – with which savings institution data affects the Democratic equations. Also interesting is the sign attached to RATE in all equations (1 through 7). It indicates that congresmen with more liberal voting records were more likely to vote against the audit (and with the Republicans!) than were their more conservative counterparts. We suspect that this is due to the fact that midwestern and southern populists, who tend to favor such things as audit legislation, tend

Table 1
Total Vote Equations

	Equation 1a	1b	Equation 2a	2b	Equation 3a	3b
Dep. Var.	Y/N	ABS/N	Y/N	ABS/N	Y/N	ABS/N
C	2.775***	1.218***	2.616***	1.135***	2.885***	1.160***
PARTY	1.535***	1.251***	1.518***	1.252***	1.517***	1.275***
RATE	−0.02***	−0.018***	−0.022***	−0.019***	−0.020***	−0.016***
BKDEP	−.0006*	−.00002			−.0012*	−.00003
SVDEP	−.00006	−.0007			.0018	−.0026
BKPC			−1.161*	0.034	2.338	0.097
SVPC			−0.434	−1.212	−8.442	5.403
$-\lambda$	650.54***		653.50***		648.31***	

Definition of variables: Y/N = log of prob (Y)/prob (N); ABS/N = log of prob (ABS)/prob (N), where Y = vote to audit (i.e., against the Ashley-Stanton Amendment), N = vote not to audit, ABS = Abstain.

$-\lambda = -2$ times the log of the likelihood ratio.

*** Significant at .01 level.

** Significant at .05 level.

* Significant at .10 level.

Table 2
Democratic Party Equations

TOTDEP	Equation 4a	4b	Equation 5a	5b	Equation 6a	6b	Equation 7a	7b
Dep. Var.	Y/N	ABS/N	Y/N	ABS/N	Y/N	ABS/N	Y/N	ABS/N
C	1.8342***	0.0671	1.9737***	0.6000	1.7452***	−0.1727	1.7378***	−0.3029
RATE	−0.0233***	−0.0121*	−0.0262***	−0.0138**	0.0224***	−0.0101	−0.0233***	−0.0142**
BKDEP	−.00046	−.00001			−.00014	−.00015		
SVDEP	−.00194**	−.00188*			−.00557	−.00628*		
TOTDEP							−.00074**	−.00009
BKPC			−1.364	−0.074	−1.954	−0.535		
SVPC			−5.709**	−4.645	11.890	14.469		
$-\lambda$	420.94***		427.42***		421.46***		426.25***	

Definition of variables: TOTDEP = BKDEP + SVDEP; otherwise, see Table 1.

to be more conservative than the average congressman. (Wright Patman was an excellent illustration of this.)

SECTION 5

This paper has used a general model of bureaucracy to posit an hypothesis about the relationship between a bureau (the Fed), its constituency (the banking sector), and its sponsor (the Congress). The model used includes models previously specified by Chant and Acheson and Breton and Wintrobe as special cases.

The hypothesis examined was that congressional support for Federal Reserve independence depends on the extent of banking influence over the various legislators. This is one leg of an 'iron triangle' relationship, whereby three parties trade to their mutual benefit. Our empirical estimates of the impact of banking interests on a 1974 Federal Reserve audit measure do not cause us to reject the hypothesis.

An interesting consequence of this result is that the 'control' of the Federal Reserve System by banking interests, long approached from the 'influence of commercial banks on district Reserve banks' point of view14 is shown to exist 'from the top down.' Our model posits a Federal Reserve response to banking interests, without regard to the structure of the various boards of directors of the district Reserve banks. This suggests that efforts to reform the Fed by 'debanking' district boards of directors are misguided, or, at least, will prove to be ineffectual. So long as the Fed operates directly on a particular sector of the economy, Fed decision-makers stand to gain from quid pro quo relationships with that sector. Only removing the Fed's discretionary powers (e.g., a Friedman monetary growth rule) or totally insulating the Fed from congressional pressure will remove the incentive to develop such relationships.

NOTES

1. Perhaps 'independence' would be a better word, since the Fed has claimed 'independence within government' since the mid-1950s. However, independence has wider connotations than 'discretion.' The narrower concept is stressed here.
2. Perhaps this definition is too narrow in the post-1980 world of monetary arrangements. Since the 1980 Depository Institutions Deregulation and Monetary Control Act was passed the Federal Reserve has had much interaction with other federal financial regulatory agencies. However, since the main thrust of this paper (empirically) is the pre-1980 period, these later additions to the Fed's environment are ignored here.

3. See Pierce (1978) and Weintraub (1978).
4. Benjamin M. Friedman (1978) has outlined the economic and political ramifications of full disclosure of Federal Open Market Committee decisions. He concluded that the former would be minimal, but the political ramifications likely would be substantial.
5. Skaggs (1980) has chronicled Federal Reserve efforts to avoid providing information on its activities to the public. See, especially, Chapter 3.
6. This is a more general variant of the theme stressed by Breton and Wintrobe (1978).
7. Utilizing a model of Federal Reserve open market operations developed by B. Friedman (1978), Skaggs (1981) determined that for the period 1974-1979III current and lagged monthly changes in the federal funds rate significantly improved predictions of the change in total bank reserves.
8. U.S., Congress, House, Debate on H.R. 7602, 83rd Cong., 2d sess., June 1954, *Congressional Record* 100, p. 7783.
9. For an enlightening discussion of this possibility, see Borins (1972).
10. The procedure was developed by Grizzle, Starmer and Koch (1969) and has been adapted into the SAS statistical package.
11. These data were found in Barone, Ujifusa and Matthews (1972, 1974, 1976). For some congressmen the ADA rating for 1973-74 was unavailable; the rating for 1971-72 or 1975-76 was then substituted.
12. Since data on bank and savings deposits were not available by congressional district, BKDEP and SVDEP were derived by adding the bank deposits and savings deposits, respectively, of the counties located in each district. When counties were located in more than one district, the bank and savings deposits of the county were allocated to each district by the percentage of the population of the county located in each district.
13. Other variants of the model, including those with interactive independent variables, yielded materially the same results as those in Table 1.
14. See Reagan (1961) and Havrilesky, Yohe and Schirm (1973).

REFERENCES

Alchian, A. A., 'The Basis for Some Recent Advances in the Theory of the Firm,' *Journal of Industrial Economics*, 1965, 14, 30-41.

Barone, M., G. Ujifusa, and D. Matthews, *Almanac of American Politics*, Dutton: New York, 1972, 1974, 1976.

Borins, S. F., 'The Political Economy of "The Fed",' *Public Policy*, 1972, 22, 175-98.

Breton, A., and R. Wintrobe, 'A Theory of "Moral" Suasion,' *Canadian Journal of Economics*, 1978, 11, 210-219.

Chant, J. F., and K. Acheson, 'Mythology and Central Banking,' *Kyklos*, 1973, 26, 362-379.

Friedman, B. M., 'Public Disclosure and Domestic Monetary Policy,' in R. D. Erb (Ed.), *Federal Reserve Policies and Public Disclosure*, American Enterprise Institute: Washington, DC, 1978, 15-40.

Grizzle, J. E., C. F. Starmer, and G. G. Koch, 'Analysis of Categorical Data by Linear Models,' *Biometrics*, 1969, 25, 489-504.

Havrilesky, T. M., W. P. Yohe, and D. C. Schirm, 'The Economic Affiliations of Directors of Federal Reserve District Banks,' *Social Science Quarterly*, 1973, 54, 608-622.

Pierce, J. L., 'The Myth of Congressional Supervision of Monetary Policy,' *Journal of Monetary Economics*, 1978, 4, 363-370.

Reagan, M. D., 'The Political Structure of the Federal Reserve System,' *American Political Science Review*, 1961, 55, 64-76.

Skaggs, N. T., *An Analysis of Federal Reserve Behavior: A Public Choice Approach*, unpublished Ph.D. dissertation, Duke University, 1980.

Skaggs, N. T., *A Theory of the Bureaucratic Value of Federal Reserve Operating Procedures*, unpublished working paper, Illinois State University, 1981.

Weintraub, R. E., 'Congressional Supervision of Monetary Policy,' *Journal of Monetary Economics*, 1978, 4, 341-362.

III. POLITICAL PRESSURES, BUREAUCRATIC INCENTIVES, AND MONETARY POLICY

Chapter 10

POLITICS AND FED POLICYMAKING: THE MORE THINGS CHANGE THE MORE THEY REMAIN THE SAME

*By Edward J. Kane**

1. INTRODUCTION

Economist critiques of FOMC (Federal Open Market Committee) policy choices typically treat the Federal Reserve System as a sovereign decision-maker, whose managers seek singlemindedly to promote the public interest at every turn. From this perspective, choosing strategy and tactics for monetary control becomes a straightforward exercise in applied welfare economics, albeit one with difficult stochastic complications (Wood, 1967; Poole, 1970; Waud, 1975; Andersen and Karnosky, 1977; Higgins, 1978; Lombra and Struble, 1978). With Fed bureaucracy and bureaucrats having no contending interests of their own, the central bank's policy task becomes merely to maximize the expected value of a constrained social welfare function. This 'utopian' objective function is defined over a set of *policy goals* (ideal values for specific dimensions of national economic performance) and is represented as a decreasing function of squared (or absolute) deviations from these goals. Operative constraints consist of information describing both the developing state of the aggregate economy and the ways in which variables directly under the Fed's control (*policy instruments*) link up with

* Everett D. Reese Professor of Banking and Monetary Economics. The author is indebted to Richard C. Aspinwall, Raymond Lombra and Will Mason for comments on earlier treatments of this material. The paper was presented at the November 1978 meetings of The Southern Economic Association.

Toma, E.F. and Toma, M. (eds.) Central Bankers, Bureaucratic Incentives, and Monetary Policy
© 1986, Martinus Nijhoff Publishers, Dordrecht,
ISBN 90 247 3366 9

the goal variables (Wood, 1967; Friedlaender, 1973; Potts and Luckett, 1978). In this view, the Fed's principal problems are informational: how to quantify its goals and restraints.

This utopian conception of Fed intentions and tactics is carefully nurtured in Fed publications and official statements. Fed leaders depict themselves as waiting in anguish for the economics profession finally to develop an adequate model of how monetary policy truly works. By this subtle open-mouth policy, Fed officials distribute some of the guilt from poor policy performance to economists and shape the way that the Fed is portrayed in money-and-banking textbooks and in most professional research. However, this public-relations campaign has had precious little effect on the thinking of ordinary citizens. In the popular mind and in the financial press, the Fed is a politically beleaguered institution whose chief task is to act as the arbiter of nominal interest rates. During times of monetary restraint, this adversary perception subjects the Fed to political pressures from sectors hurt by rising interest rates. These sectors' political action leads elected officials to resist increases in the level of nominal interest rates. This political response system focuses attention on changes in market interest rates and re-inforces the mistaken popular notion that changes in the level of nominal interest rates are reliable indicators of the macroeconomic thrust of current monetary policy.

Monetarism bridges these discordant views, presuming that the Fed's political task is to lead the fight against inflation and that it can do so best by reshaping the focal issues of monetary-policy controversy. Viewed from this perspective, monetarism can be interpreted as a compromise movement whose principal goal is to liberate the Fed from procyclical political pressures by refocusing the Fed's immediate policy targets from sectorally non-neutral interest rates to average rates of growth in monetary aggregates. The monetarist control strategy holds out the hope that the Fed can validate the utopian conception by loudly and steadfastly denying all responsibility for stabilizing nominal interest rates in the short run.

2. THINGS THE FED HAS CHANGED

During the 1970s, two striking changes in the structure of FOMC policymaking moved the Fed in the direction of the monetarist solution. First, in January 1970 (at Chairman Martin's last FOMC meeting), the Committee decided that 'increased stress should be placed on the objective of achieving modest growth in the monetary aggregates'. Two months later, at the second

FOMC meeting chaired by Arthur Burns, this change in emphasis was formally incorporated into the Committee's directive to the System Open Market Account manager. From that date forward, he was told in the short run to maintain 'money-market conditions' (i.e., nominal interest rates) consistent with specific patterns of growth in the major monetary aggregates. Beginning in 1975, two-month target rates of growth for monetary aggregates were published as part of the monthly 'Record of Policy Actions' of the FOMC. Second, in response to a Congressional Resolution passed in March 1975 (and transformed finally into a legal requirement in November 1977), the FOMC began to vote each quarter a set of target annual growth rates for M1, M2, and M3. Called 'tolerance ranges', these annual targets are reported to Congress every quarter, in testimony delivered alternately before the House and Senate banking com-

Table 1
Quarterly Reports of 12-month Target Ranges on Monetary Growth Rates First Requested by House Concurrent Resolution No. 133[a]

Date		Reported 12-month Target Range (in percent)		
		g_{M1}	g_{M2}	g_{M3}
May	1975	5.0 to 7.5	8.5 to 10.5	10.0 to 12.0
Aug.	1975	4.5 to 7.5	7.5 to 10.5	9.0 to 12.0
Nov.	1975	5.0 to 7.5	7.5 to 10.5	9.0 to 12.0
Feb.	1976	4.5 to 7.5	7.5 to 10.5	9.0 to 12.0
May	1976	4.5 to 7.0	7.5 to 10.0	9.0 to 12.0
Aug.	1976	4.5 to 7.0	7.5 to 9.5	9.0 to 11.0
Nov.	1976	4.5 to 6.5	7.5 to 10.0	9.0 to 11.5
Feb.	1977	4.5 to 6.5	7.0 to 10.0	8.5 to 11.5
May	1977	4.5 to 6.5	7.0 to 9.5	8.5 to 11.0
Aug.	1977	4.0 to 6.5	7.0 to 9.5	8.5 to 11.0
Nov.	1977	4.0 to 6.5	6.5 to 9.0	8.0 to 10.5
March	1978b	4.0 to 6.5	6.5 to 9.0	7.5 to 10.0
May	1978	4.0 to 6.5	6.5 to 9.0	7.5 to 10.0
July	1978	4.0 to 6.5	6.5 to 9.0	7.5 to 10.0

[a] Source: 'Record of Policy Actions of the Federal Open Market Committee, in: *Federal Reserve Bulletin* and *Annual Reports of the Board of Governors of the Federal Reserve System*.

[b] Chairman Miller's testimony was delayed until March 13 by difficulties in clearing his appointment through the Senate Banking Committee.

mittees. Table 1 lists the annual targets adopted in the 3 1/2 years this procedure has been in operation. Table 2 compares the targets with actual experience.

It is not easy to interpret the targets. First, the FOMC does not specify precisely what value in each range it would most prefer. Hence, the 'tolerance ranges' may not be symmetric about the FOMC's estimates of the best growth rate for each aggregate. Second, one wonders why three targets are given and how they are weighted relative to each other. Higgins indicates that M1 and M2 are weighted equally, with little or no weight given to M3. He argues that uncertainty about the relations: (1) between each aggregate

Table 2
Growth in Monetary Aggregates Relative to 12-month FOMC Targets, May 1975 to July 1978 (in percent per annum)[a]

Date of Congressional testimony		Observed rate of growth of M1 during designated control period	Excess over midpoint of FOMC tolerance range	Observed rate of growth of M2 during designated control period	Excess over midpoint of FOMC tolerance range	Observed rate of growth of M3 during designated control period	Excess over midpoint of FOMC tolerance range
May	1975	5.3	−0.95	9.7	0.20	12.3	1.30
Aug.	1975	4.4	−1.60	8.8	−0.20	11.3	0.80
Nov.	1975	4.6	−1.65	9.8	0.80	11.9	1.40
Feb.	1976	6.2	0.20	11.4	2.40	13.2	2.70
May	1976	6.5	0.75	10.9	2.15	12.7	2.20
Aug.	1976	7.0	1.25	10.9	2.40	12.5	2.50
Nov.	1976	8.2	2.70	10.9	2.15	12.6	2.35
Feb.	1977	8.0	2.50	9.3	0.80	11.3	1.30
May	1977	7.3	1.80	8.4	0.15	10.1	0.35
Aug.	1977	8.4	3.15	8.4	0.15	9.7	−0.05
Nov.	1977	8.4	3.15	8.5	0.75	9.4	0.15
March	1978	8.8[b]	3.55	8.7[b]	0.95	9.3[b]	0.55
May	1978	10.5[b]	5.25	9.7[b]	1.95	10.2[b]	1.35
July	1978	9.2[b]	3.95	10.3[b]	2.55	11.7[b]	2.95

[a] Source: Rates of growth calculated from the end-date of the preceding quarter to the same date in the following year, using data supplied in October, 1978 by The Research Department of the Federal Reserve Bank of St. Louis.

[b] Arithmetic extrapolation of growth observed from beginning of the control period through September 30, 1978.

and the goal variables and (2) between the aggregates themselves justifies the use of a weighting scheme. Alternatively, one could cite the need to proxy the growth of demand-deposit substitutes and the desirability of setting out enough targets that Fed arrows are bound to score at least one hit. Finally, the FOMC provides only a loose qualitative assertion that the System Open Market Account Manager should adjust his operative interest-rate targets when monetary-aggregates growth falls outside the target range.

In the last eight accounting periods (three of which are still in progress), the growth rate of M1 has exceeded the FOMC tolerance range. For several consecutive earlier accounting periods, the M2 and M3 growth rates surpassed their target ranges, too. Given that the ranges are fairly wide to begin with and change only slightly from one Congressional appearance to the next, the Fed's failure to meet them leads one to doubt whether in any meaningful sense they are targets (or limits of 'tolerance') at all. In the 1970s, the Fed may be paying more attention to monetary aggregates than ever before, but its policy focus remains very much on the short run.

This paper develops two propositions. First, it argues that strong political forces exist that compel the Fed to dampen the size of short-run increases in nominal interest rates. Because such changes threaten to impose heavy burdens on economically vulnerable but politically powerful sectors, Fed officials are compelled to give increasing weight to interest-rate targets whenever accelerating inflation or other forces induce sharp cumulative movements in the level of nominal interest rates. The monetarist long-run control strategy tends to break down at the politically critical moment. The easy-money policies of the first half of 1978 constitute the latest evidence for this political conception. Actual monetary growth rates exceeded targets because: (1) to raise real interest rates, nominal interest rates would have had to rise unusually rapidly, and (2) congressional elections were scheduled in November. Second, the paper advances the hypothesis that, as an institution, the Fed's ultimate political purpose is to serve as an economic-policy scapegoat for incumbent politicians. It goes on to show that this scapegoat hypothesis can explain a number of seeming anomalies in the structure of Fed decisionmaking.

3. THE FED'S INCOMPLETE CONTROL STRATEGY

A strategy for policy control has three basic elements: policy instruments, intermediate policy targets, and policy goals. Policy instruments are variables that the Fed controls absolutely, while policy goals are socially

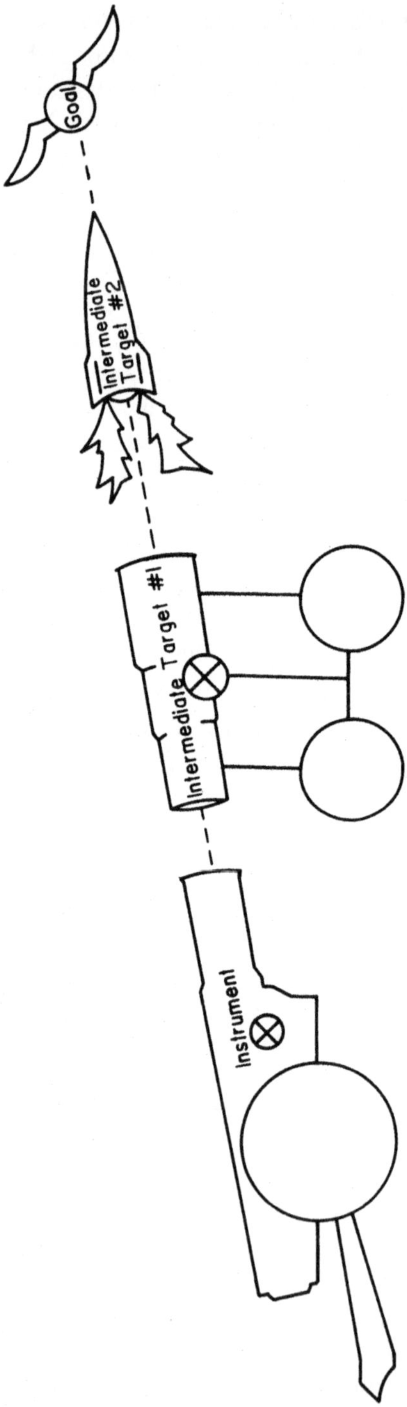

Fig. 1. Aligning instruments with goals in a policymaking framework that uses intermediate targets.

desirable developments that Fed officials want ultimately to promote. Fed goals relate to various dimensions of good macroeconomic performance: low unemployment, price stability, a strong dollar, sustainable economic growth, and an improved distribution of income. Instruments include the Fed's reserve requirements, discount procedures, and open-market portfolio.

As the name *intermediate target* implies, targets stand between instruments and goals. Target variables differ from goals in that hits come easier, if only because misses are easier to monitor and correct. A goal variable is an index of one aspect of macroeconomic welfare, such as the unemployment ratio or the average rate of inflation in consumer prices. Hard information on goal variables becomes available infrequently (once a month or once a quarter) and even then observations lag behind events and remain subject to subsequent revisions in value. Because information on goal variables is dated, sparse, and unreliable, policymakers tend to identify alternative indices that can be tracked closely and that theory and empirical evidence agree should move predictably with goal variables. These proxy variables may be conceived as sighting devices that aid policymakers' to take aim on hard-to-track goals. This conception is illustrated in fig. 1 The policy instrument is portrayed as a cannon that aims proximately at a wheeled intermediate target that in turn pivots to track a heat-seeking missile (intermediate target number two), which itself follows the tiny goal variable (more accurately, the current *flock* of goal variables) as it winds along.

For its policy strategy to be complete, the Fed must not only list its instruments, targets, and goals. It must go on to spell out projected links between its targets and goals over different time spans and to explain the feedback processes that lead it to alter the intermediate targets (Brunner and Meltzer, 1964; Guttentag, 1966). But the Fed steadfastly refuses to take these additional steps. Only the first step in the feedback loop that links the three types of variables is laid out and this only for very-short control periods.

3.1 The Fed's Current Day-to-Day Strategy of Open-Market Operation

In the Fed's current framework its first and close-at-hand target is the federal-funds rate, FFR: the market interest rate on one-day loans of member-bank reserve balances on deposit at Fed Banks. The second more-distant target is the growth rate of the money stock, g_M. Observations on the first target are precise and up-to-the-minute, while observations on the second are only available weekly and, even then, are subject to substantial measurement error, some of which is ultimately reduced by interpolating subsequent benchmark-date survey data.

Taking a monetarist view, Fed officials anticipate that the monetary growth rate will closely track the less frequently observed growth rate of aggregate demand. The targeted range of monetary growth rates, g_M^* is to be changed whenever data show one or more goal variables developing along an unacceptable track. Between readings on the goal variables, the g_M^* range remains a firm target. However, with readings on g_M, themselves infrequent, Fed officials focus in the short run on the FFR. Their plan is to establish a range of federal-funds rates (FFR_{LO}, FFR_{HI}) consistent with the g_M^* target and to supply or absorb reserves *via* open-market operations whenever the FFR threatens to depart from its targeted boundaries. In turn, the FFR boundaries are to be adjusted when data on g_M show substantial shortfalls or over-runs and when the g_M^* target is itself revised.

Interpreted in terms of fig. 1, this Rube Goldberg system of multiple gunsights seems designed for use by hopelessly nearsighted gunnery crews. The Fed high command takes it for granted that the vision of its cannoneers is too weak to track either the goal variables or even the monetary-growth variable chasing along in their wake. Fed open-market operatives, located just off Wall Street in the Federal Reserve Bank of New York, train their guns on interest rates that are determined just a few yards away in the offices of federal-funds brokers. FFR bullseyes are virtually guaranteed, but relative to goals and more-distant targets, the resulting angle of fire can wander far astray. To reduce the chance of this, Fed staff economists act as artillery scouts, collecting and analyzing information about hits and misses both on g_M^* and on the goals and recommending compensatory changes in FFR and g_M targets. But this part of the process is too arcane for an outsider to diagram.

3.2 The Value of Incompleteness

The speed and adequacy of FOMC revisions in targeted trajectories are critical to the success of this chain-of-targets open-market strategy. One reason for the Fed's adopting this strategy in the 1970s was to stop academic economists from poking fun at Fed officials by characterizing the cannoneers (and their field commander, the 'Desk') as suffering perennially in Brunner and Meltzer's famous phrase from 'money-market myopia'. However, until the Fed spells out the link between its policy misses and future angles of fire, charges of myopia of some sort must be left on the docket.

Maisel (1973) has made the point that an incomplete strategy makes it easier month by month for disparate elements within the FOMC to agree on a specific FFR target. The ultimate question is whether leaving these loose ends somehow leads to more satisfactory levels for goal variables. Fed pronouncements glorify the incompleteness of its control strategy as giving officials the 'flexibility' they need to tailor adjustments in Fed instruments at any time to the economy's precise constellation of needs. I believe that in the Federal Reserve lexicon flexibility is a code word for openness to procyclical direct and indirect political influences. In my view, the incompleteness of the Fed's control strategy survives in part because of its role in surmounting internal dissent, but more importantly because it makes it relatively unembarrassing for Fed officials to adapt operative monetary-policy priorities to the ebb and flow of external political pressure. Incompleteness gives the Fed bureaucracy day-to-day freedom to deal politically with Congress and the White House, but by no means should it be presumed that these dealings lead over time to better macroeconomic performance.

Since Congress and the President have chosen not to force the Fed to adopt a complete strategy, it is reasonable to presume that they also find advantages in incompleteness. The advantage that I see is that by leaving the Fed high command a substantial amount of ex ante discretion, elected officials leave themselves scope for blaming the Fed ex post when things go wrong (Kane, 1975). Overseeing a complete strategy would undercut Fed 'independence' and implicate incumbents in monetary policy before the fact. Looking always toward the next election, holders of elective office prefer to position themselves so that they can choose after the fact which policies to claim and disclaim. Currently, it's heads they win and tails the Fed loses. Whenever monetary policies are popular, incumbents can claim that their influence was crucial in their adoption. On the other hand, when monetary policies prove unpopular, they can blame everything on a stubborn Federal Reserve and claim further that things would have been worse if they had not pressed Fed officials at every opportunity.

4. DISCOVERING THE PUBLIC INTEREST

Inherent in the utopian view of the Fed is the presumption that the Fed can somehow evaluate the public interest on its own. In the contemporary United States, it is hard to conceive of *the* public interest except as a delicate balance of conflicting private interests. Though influenced by the ebb and flow of intellectual and journalistic argument, this interest finds legitimate expression only through juridical, legislative and regulatory decisions. In these arenas, to a large extent, Might makes Right. A sector's Might is exercised by influencing the politics of representative democracy and the party process. The effective public interest is determined *via* adversary proceedings. Hence, it shifts with the sectoral distribution of political power.

It is no accident that those sectors most vulnerable to increases in nominal interest rates have made themselves strong politically. The low-interest lobby is led by builders and construction unions and by financial institutions that earn their living by borrowing short to lend long. It is supplemented by securities dealers who interact on many levels with System Open Market Account officials in New York. Because dealer balance sheets are highly levered, dealers continually press Fed personnel to *gradualize* any and all cumulative increases in nominal interest rates. During inflationary episodes these constituencies help Fed officials to decide just how quickly it is 'feasible' to push up nominal interest rates (i.e., how vigorously in the short run to wage the battle against inflation).

These institutions' political muscle constitutes the bulk of their hedge against interest-rate risk in general against inflation risk in particular (Kane, 1976). Acting through and on cabinet departments, specialized agencies, and Congressional committees charged administratively with monitoring their economic welfare, elements of the low-interest constituency exploit an implicit social consensus that no identifiable subset of the population should be forced to bear an inordinate (i.e., certifiably unfair) portion of the burden of stabilizing the national economy. Ironically, their incontestable exposure to interest-rate risk is the source of the low-interest advocates' ability to shape the public's perception of how monetary policy works.

They also exploit pressures that electoral and business cycles place on elected officials (Tufte, 1978). In election years, Congress and the President typically join in trying to rally support for lower interest rates by publicly warning the Federal Reserve that 'excessive' interest rates would (by the definition of 'excessive') cause a recession. Often they do this despite overwhelming evidence that monetary policy is highly expansive, on the theory that higher levels of employment improve incumbents' chances for reelection even when purchased at the cost of higher inflation later. (The alternative hypothesis was tested and rejected in an electoral test conducted in 1976 by Gerald Ford.)

5. A POLITICAL THEORY OF FED DOUBLETALK: THE FED AS SCAPEGOAT

In an election year, perhaps the least-reliable indicator of the state of U.S. monetary policy is what Federal Reserve Chairman tell us about FOMC intentions. Particularly in the late stages of any business-cycle expansion, the occupant of this political hotseat is virtually forced to talk out of both sides of his mouth. To placate the Fed's own constituency in the business and financial community, the Chairman must emphasize how vigorously Fed officials are fighting inflation with high and rising nominal rates of interest. However, to keep Congress and the Administration off their backs, Fed officials must simultaneously fight unemployment by expanding the money stock. Since monetary growth can produce rates of inflation high enough to undo the restrictive effects of high nominal interest rates, the conflicting effects of monetary policy can most easily be explained by focusing public attention on real interest rates.

For me (and recently for the President and staff of the Minneapolis Federal Bank as well), the burning question is why doesn't the Fed – as the nation's chief representative for the constituency against inflation – make a greater effort to educate the public to the dual effects of money-supply changes. Why don't Fed officials refocus the public's perception of how monetary policy works so that they can build a consensus for anticyclical movements in real interest rates? Why aren't they in the forefront of the effort to provide better measures of anticipated inflation?

During the summer of 1978, University of Michigan surveys of consumers' inflation expectations over the next year rose almost two percentage points above the inflation forecasts prepared by the major econometric forecasting services. In the first half of 1978, Fed officials claimed repeatedly that monetary policy was highly restrictive, even though survey-based and ex post real interest rates were falling. By not putting the policy issues in proper perspective, the Fed ill serves its anti-inflation constituency. It helps to take pressure off elected officials by deceiving the public into believing that, even when no one else is, the Fed is waging an effective fight against inflation. That Fed officials would cite changes in nominal interest rates as evidence of anti-inflationary policies indicates that they value the political options that public confusion currently confers on them.

For anyone schooled in the utopian tradition, this cynical hypothesis is hard to swallow. However, as a working hypothesis, it is best tested by asking what it can explain that competing theories cannot. The doubletalk theory is fully consistent with the microeconomics of Federal Reserve bureaucracy. After all, the Fed is a political institution designed for politicians to serve politicians. Its chief officials (i.e., the Board of Governors) are nominated by the President and their appointments cleared with the Senate. They are forced to defend their performance before Congressional committees several times a month and must be prepared to respond expeditiously to letters and telephone calls from individual Congressmen and Senators at a moment's notice.

However good or bad this performance may be, Fed officials are expected to let Congressmen and Senators blame them for whatever financial and economic developments their constituents back home dislike. In exchange for playing economic-policy scapegoat, Fed officials are offered unusually long terms in office and substantial budgetary autonomy.

This duality and ambiguity of function are paralleled in the very language of the Federal Reserve Act, which sets up a uniquely confusing bureaucratic structure that makes the Fed appear both 'independent' of short-run political influence and decentralized in its internal organization. Later legislation – The Employment Act of 1946 and the Humphrey-Hawkins Act of 1978 – enlarges the Fed's statutory mission without providing legislative guidance as to how Fed officials should execute politically sensitive tradeoffs among conflicting goals. The Fed has allowed elected politicians to make it responsible for a series of impossible economic-policy tasks, with the implicit understanding that, when the Fed fails, how loud these politicians and the successors will bark (and whether or not they will also bite) depends on the quality of Fed efforts to get along.

Sherlock Holmes' acid remarks on the undeserved reputation of Scotland Yard detectives would apply as well to Congress' conception of the Federal Reserve System and might well be mounted over the doorway of the FOMC's meeting room:

> 'What you do in this world is a matter of no consequence. The question is, what can you make people believe that you have done?' (*A Study in Scarlet*)

Being programmed to fail repeatedly at its policy assignments, the Fed is led to glorify its lesser accomplishments as the Treasury's fiscal agent and as the banking system's chief correspondent. Its officials learn to talk in a code that makes it hard for hind-sighted critics to scold them effectively. This code masks their openness to political influence and facilitates the formulation of quasi-contradictory explanations both of the mechanics of their policies and of the rationale behind them. To protect itself from criticism and political punishments, the Fed tends systematically to misemploy its unique opportunities for educating the U.S. public about the macroeconomic consequences of alternative economic policies.

6. SUMMARY

Although money-and-banking textbooks oversell the utopian conception of Fed policymaking, the profession has always known better. I do not want to emphasize the vacuous proposition that, when the going gets tough, the Fed acts first and foremost as a political animal. What I do want to emphasize is how many seemingly inexplicable structural and policy phenomena can be developed as consequences of this proposition. On my analysis, the perennial incompleteness of Fed control strategies and most of the Fed's special bureaucratic features (its independence, its acceptance of impossible policy assignments, and its murky lines of internal authority) serve definite political ends. Once the Fed is viewed as a policy scapegoat for elected officials, these developments emerge as intelligible adaptations to recurring political pressures.

Fed officials desire better performance. They make changes in the structure of Fed decisionmaking and in procedures for monitoring the effects of open-market operations with the best of intentions. However, since these changes have no palpable effect on the balance of political forces, they have precious little effect on the short-run compromises Fed leaders find it prudent to make among alternative policy goals.

REFERENCES

Andersen, Leonall C. and Denis S. Karnosky, 'Some Considerations in the Use of Monetary Aggregates for the Implementation of Monetary Policy,' *Federal Reserve Bank of St. Louis Review*, September 1977, 59, 2-7.

Brunner, Karl and Allan H. Meltzer, 'The Federal Reserve's Attachment to the Free Reserve Concept,' U.S. House of Representatives Committee on Banking and Currency, Subcommittee on Domestic Finance, May 7, 1964, U.S. Government Printing Office, Washington, DC.

Doyle, A. Conan, *The Complete Sherlock Holmes*, Garden City Publishing Co.: Garden City, 1938.

Friedlaender, Ann F., 'Macro Policy Goals in the Postwar Period: A Study in Revealed Preference,' *Quarterly Journal of Economics*, February 1973, 87, 25-43.

Guttentag, Jack, 'The Strategy of Open Market Operations,' *Quarterly Journal of Economics*, February 1966, 80, 1-38.

Higgins, Byron, 'Weighting Multiple Monetary Aggregate Targets,' *Economic Review Federal Reserve Bank of Kansas City*, February 1978, 3-13.

Kane, Edward J., 'All for the Best: The Federal Reserve Board's 60th Annual Report,' *American Economic Review*, December 1974, 64, 835-850.

Kane, Edward J., 'New Congressional Restraints and Federal Reserve Independence,' *Challenge*, November/December 1974, 37-44.

Kane, Edward, J., 'Expanded Powers for Thrift Institutions: Superthrifts vs. Superlobbyists,' in *Proceedings of a Conference on Bank Structure and Competition*, Federal Reserve Bank of Chicago: Chicago, 174-178.

Lombra, Raymond, and Frederick Struble, 'Monetary Aggregate Targets and the Volatility of Interest Rates,' Mimeo, September 25, 1978.

Maisel, Sherman J., *Managing the Dollar*, W. W. Norton & Co.: New York, 1973.

Poole, William, 'Optimal Choice of Monetary Policy Instruments in a Simple Stochastic Macro Model,' *Quarterly Journal of Economics*, May 1970, 84, 197-216.

Potts, Glenn T., and Dudley G. Luckett, 'Policy Objectives of the Federal Reserve System,' *Quarterly Journal of Economics*, August 1978, 92, 525-534.

Roberts, Steven M., 'Congressional Oversight of Monetary Policy,' *Journal of Monetary Economics*, 1978, 4, 543-556.

Tufte, Edward R., *Political Control of the Economy*, Princeton University Press: Princeton, 1978.

Waud, Roger N., 'Information Lags and the Interest Rate as a Proximate Monetary Policy Target,' *Oxford Bulletin of Economics and Statistics*, May 1975, 37, 103-113.

Wood, John H., 'A Model of Federal Reserve Behavior,' in George Horwich (ed.), *Monetary Process and Policy: A Symposium*, Irwin: Homewood, IL, 1967, 135-166.

Chapter 11

CENTRAL BANK INDEPENDENCE: AN INTERNATIONAL COMPARISON

By King Banaian, Leroy O. Laney, and Thomas D. Willett

The independence of the Federal Reserve System has once again become a major topic of debate. Over the years, critics of existing institutional arrangements have included both those who fault the Federal Reserve for being too responsive to outside pressures and those who fault it for not being responsive enough. But many observers consider the Fed to exercise more autonomy from the executive and legislative branches of the Government than is the case with central banks in most other countries, and today the criticism is heard principally from those who do not regard institutional independence as a virtue.

This debate raises basic issues about the design of institutions in a democratic society. What government activities should be responsible directly to the electorate and its representatives? In what areas should the direct operation of political forces be constrained by constitutional limitation, an independent regulatory commission, or the checks and balances of the different branches of government?

An autonomous central bank typically has several functions: it usually serves as fiscal agent to the government, as lender of last resort for private financial institutions during emergencies, and as a regulator and supervisor of the financial system. As the principal public sector agency charged with the execution of a country's monetary policy, however, the bank can encounter a number of conflicting objectives. It must weigh economic growth in the near future against control of inflation, the external balance, and long-run economic growth. It is almost always under economic and

Toma, E.F. and Toma, M. (eds.) Central Bankers, Bureaucratic Incentives, and Monetary Policy

ISBN 90 247 3366 9

political pressure to emphasize some goals at the expense of others in the formulation and conduct of monetary policy. The extent to which the central bank accommodates this pressure can depend greatly on its institutional independence.

No judgment is made here on the relative importance of the various goals of monetary policy. The focus, however, is on a highly important goal. How successful has the institution of independent central banking been in countering inflationary tendencies?

The United States has not had postwar experience with monetary policy under institutional arrangements fundamentally different from those now in existence. Nevertheless, some useful information on the matter can be provided by comparison with the experiences of other industrial countries. If distinguishing independent from dependent central banks is possible, this comparison can shed light on the effects of independence in the conduct of monetary policy. This article concludes that the more independent central banks have indeed been associated with less inflationary policies. In addition, central banking arrangements appear to be more important than several other structural factors that have been put forth in explaining differences in inflation across countries.

FEDERAL RESERVE INDEPENDENCE AND A U.S. MOMETARY CONSTITUTION

Arguments for reducing the independence of the Federal Reserve are usually based on a combination of views about the most appropriate structure of democratic institutions and about how alternative institutional arrangements are likely to affect the objectives emphasized by monetary policy. Proposals range from reforms to constrain the discretionary scope of monetary policy through a return to some form of gold or other commodity standard – or at least a constitutionally mandated set of limitations on monetary growth – to the advocacy of making Federal Reserve policy more directly responsive to the Congress or the executive branch of the Government. In general, those who are more concerned with inflation have been inclined toward the former types of reform, while those more concerned with generating short-run reductions in interest rates and unemployment have tended to favor the latter approaches.(1)

A major traditional argument for the independence of the central bank is that those responsible for paying the Government's bills should not also be responsible for printing the country's money. The temptation to engage in inflationary finance is too strong. In recent years this rationale has been supplemented by concern that the direct operation of the political process, with its tendency to focus primarily on the near future, would force extensive monetary accommodation in the short run at the cost of long-run destabilization of the economy.(2) But recently, critics have argued that Fed independence actually has proved conducive to monetary accommodation because it makes determining who is responsible for such accommodation more difficult.(3)

Few argue that any central bank should be divorced completely from government. After all, a central bank is inherently a public sector institution, not only in discharging its responsibilities for monetary policy and financial supervision but also in performing its traditional function as banker to the government. But the extent to which the bank is independent within the public sector can make a great deal of difference in the conduct of monetary policy.

Advocates of closer executive branch control over the Fed contend that a more coordinated national economic policy would result and that such coordination would be desirable.(4) Others have argued that because the Fed is accountable by law not to the President but to the Congress, it is this body that should exercise more direct control over the central bank.(5) It might be countered that the central bank is, in fact, likely to impose more discipline upon itself than would be imposed by the diffuse goals of a legislative body or the short horizon of the President. Nevertheless, some would evidently view direct Fed accountability to either the executive or the legislative branch of the Government as more desirable than current arrangements.(6)

Those who believe that the Federal Reserve has not paid enough recent attention to interest rates and unemployment generally assume that institutional independence has insulated monetary policy from short-term political considerations, allowing greater emphasis on fighting inflation over the long run. But this assumption has been challenged by the view that Fed independence is overstated.(7) The present independence of the Fed may remain at issue, but it can be put in clearer perspective by examining central banking relationships in other countries.

ASSESSING CENTRAL BANK INDEPENDENCE

The concept of central bank independence has practical meaning primarily for institutions in industrialized countries with deeper capital markets. Governments of most less developed countries must rely on their own central banks and foreign capital markets to finance their debt. In more developed countries, private domestic capital markets provide an additional source of government finance, so greater scope for central bank independence is at least possible. Because of these distinctions, comparisons here are limited to central banks of more developed countries. Even among those countries, however, techniques for conducting monetary policy and the depth of financial markets differ greatly.

Measuring central bank independence is not simple because independence can be ensured or undermined through a wide range of channels. Consequently, there is no single institutional characteristic by which to rank central banks from most to least independent. Several sources can provide information on this question, however. Not only can information be gathered on formal, structural relationships specified by statute, but information on informal relations between central banks and government may prove useful as well. Formal indications of independence can be gleaned from the sources of appointment of governors in the bank, their terms of office, and their methods of reaching decisions. Relevant, but sometimes misleading, information may be conveyed by whether the stock of the central bank is owned by the state or the private sector. Formal liaison or interchange of staff with the finance ministry may be indicative of ties to the executive branch of government, just as reporting requirements and other accountability to Parliament or Congress are revealing about the relationship to the legislative branch.

Statements concerning goals in the charter of a central bank may also help reveal its degree of independence. Such goals can range from a statutory duty to foster the general welfare of the country to specific requirements set by law – for example, controlling inflation, promoting full employment or production, or stabilizing the exchange rate.

But all these indicators may be misleading. A central bank that appears not to be constrained by law may be influenced strongly, and not just episodically, by other branches of government. And it is also conceivable that a central bank that seems to be constrained can establish a fair amount of autonomy over time. The relationship between the central bank and other entities of government can be strongly influenced by tradition, a result of gradual evolution rather than any well-articulated or easily observed formal linkage.

How, then, can a line be drawn between dependent and independent central banks? Economists and other observers tend to agree that countries with a traditional sentiment toward controlling the financial power of the national government – such as is generally found in federal unions like

West Germany, Switzerland, and the United States – also have central banks that are the most likely candidates for being classified as independent. Most of the indicators discussed above lend support to this view.

The central banks of most developed economies do not show much independence in the determination of monetary policy. Although central banks are almost always charged with the execution of monetary policy and some scope for disagreement with government exists, they are usually subordinate to the treasury or finance ministry in the formulation of policy.

British monetary policy is subject to the direction of the U.K. Treasury, and Parliament generally holds the government responsible for the actions of the Bank of England. In Japan, too, the Finance Ministry dominates. Both the Finance Ministry and the Economic Planning Agency in Japan are represented on the Policy Board of the central bank, and this board's annual report to the Japanese Diet must be submitted through the Finance Ministry. French and Italian monetary policies are also dictated by the Treasury, even on a very short-term basis. In Canada the central bank had more formal authority before 1967, when an amendment to the Bank of Canada Act gave the Minister of Finance the power to issue directives to the bank. This general pattern of subordination to the Treasury extends to most of the world's other developed countries as well.(8)

THE MORE INDEPENDENT CENTRAL BANKS

Even though its stock is owned by public authorities, the central bank of West Germany has experienced substantial independence in postwar years. The current organization of the Deutsche Bundesbank dates from 1957, when restructuring actually increased the influence of the federal government but still left the central bank one of the most independent in the world. Government authorities can attend meetings of the bank's highest deliberative body, the Central Bank Council. But they have no vote, only the power to delay a decision a maximum of two weeks.

Although the Bundesbank is charged with supporting general economic policy, this is subordinate to its responsibility for safeguarding the value of the currency. The government itself is responsible for fiscal policy, and the central bank deals with monetary policy. While the government is responsible for decisions about the exchange rate regime, subject in practice to central bank approval, the Bundesbank is responsible for discretionary foreign exchange intervention policy. This division has allowed some conflict in the past, but it has not been prolonged. The Bundesbank is not formally answerable to the Parliament, except for submission of an annual report.

The President of the Deutsche Bundesbank and not more than 10 directors are appointed to eight-year terms upon nomination by the federal government. The Central Bank Council is composed of this directorate plus the presidents of 11 'Land' Central Banks, which are somewhat analogous to district Federal Reserve Banks in the United States. The 11 presidents provide regional representation to the decisionmaking body; they are proposed by appropriate local authorities and then nominated by the Parliament for eight-year terms, subject to reappointment. The council, chaired by the Bundesbank President, sets monetary policy by simple majority vote. There is no formal liaison or interchange of staff with the Ministry of Finance.

Probably the only monetary agency that can be ranked with the German central bank in terms of institutional independence is that of Switzerland. Although the Swiss National Bank and the government must consult with each other on policy matters, approval before implementation by the other party is not necessary. The bank is constitutionally independent of the parliamentary body but, as in the German case, submits an annual report. Unlike West Germany, the Swiss Confederation owns no shares in its central bank. Stock is held by the cantons, cantonal banks, and the public. Shares are listed on the Swiss Stock Exchange.

The policy of the Swiss National Bank is made indirectly by the Bank Council, which consists of 40 members, 25 of whom are appointed by the government cabinet to four-year terms. The remaining 15 are elected by bank stockholders. The council selects a smaller board that directly manages monetary policy. The role of the government in the bank is explicitly limited by law to such matters as determining the size of the bank's capital, the denomination of bank notes, and the division of profits among cantons. Formal government participation in monetary policy is quite minor overall.

The U.S. Federal Reserve System is also independent when judged against most other central banks. But the Federal Reserve has a formal responsibility to the legislative branch of the Government that is greater than in the two foregoing cases. It must report in testimony to the Congress twice yearly on the conduct of monetary policy, and it submits an annual report. The Chairman and the six other members of the Board of Governors of the Federal Reserve System are frequently called upon to testify before Congress on monetary policy and various other subjects.

Although the Board does not report formally to the executive branch, there is frequent contact with the Treasury and other Government agencies.

Board members are appointed by the President, subject to Senate approval, to 14-year, nonrenewable terms. (A Board member may serve more than 14 years if a full term follows an incomplete term created by a vacancy.) The Chairman and Vice Chairman of the Board are appointed similarly to four-year renewable terms.

Monetary policy in the United States is actually decided by the 12-member Federal Open Market Committee, on which 5 district Reserve Bank presidents sit. And since these presidents are appointed by the boards of directors of the district Reserve Banks (two-thirds of the directors are elected by district member banks and one-third by the Board of Governors), subject to approval by the Board of Governors, there is at least some formal scope for non-Government-approved representation.

INDEPENDENT BANKS AND INFLATION

How have these more independent central banks measured up with respect to the rates of inflation their societies have experienced? A number of indicators of inflationary performance have been suggested – for example, different price indexes, exchange rates (a reflection of the external value of the currency), and growth rates of monetary aggregates. Price indexes are subject to various biases, especially when compared internationally, while exchange rates are often subject to important non-monetary influences. For money growth rates, simple comparisons across countries can be misleading because of substantial differences in velocity trends. Consequently, it is useful to examine several indicators.

Chart 1 shows clearly that since the early 1950's, national price levels in the world's larger economies have diverged markedly. But overall, prices in West German, Switzerland, and the United States have increased at the slowest rates. (Inflation in Canada over the long haul has been quite close to that of the United States.) And since the advent of more flexible exchange rates in the early 1970's, overall movements in the external values of national moneys have reflected inflation differences also. Chart 2 depicts effective (trade-weighted) exchange rates for the currencies of the eight major countries. The Swiss franc and the German mark have been the strongest currencies, at times challenging the U.S. dollar's role as the world's primary international reserve currency. The U.S. dollar retains that status, however, and dollar inflows in recent years have been reflected in the observed weakness in the Swiss and German trade-weighted rates. (The strength of the Japanese currency over the period has been partly due to the rising interna-

Chart I
Consumers Prices in Major Countries
(1952=100)

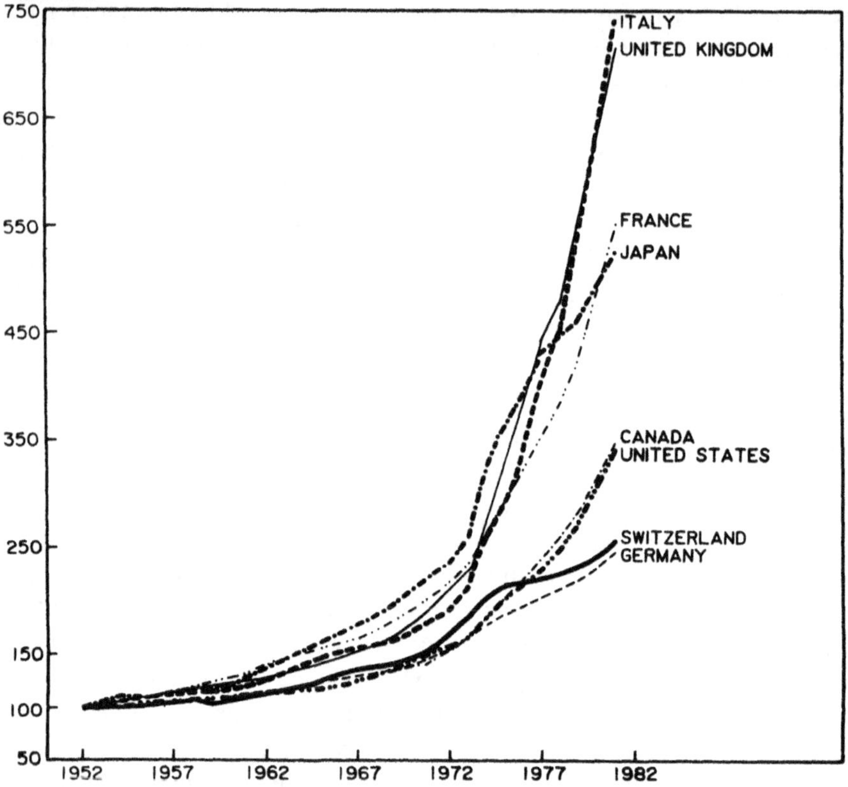

SOURCE: Board of Governors, Federal Reserve System.

tional role of the yen, as well as Japan's economic growth and international trade performance.)

Further comparisons for the eight countries over the past two decades are presented in Table 1. Both measures of the price level, the GDP implicit price deflator and the consumer price index, show lower inflation in the countries with the more independent central banks. The ranking according to inflation is not borne out in the figures for growth rates of the narrow and broader money supplies. However, the inflationary stance on the monetary authority cannot always be judged on the basis of money supply growth alone, although there is often some tendency to do so, as this growth does not account for changes in money demand.

Chart 2
Trade-Weighted Exchange Rates of Major Currencies

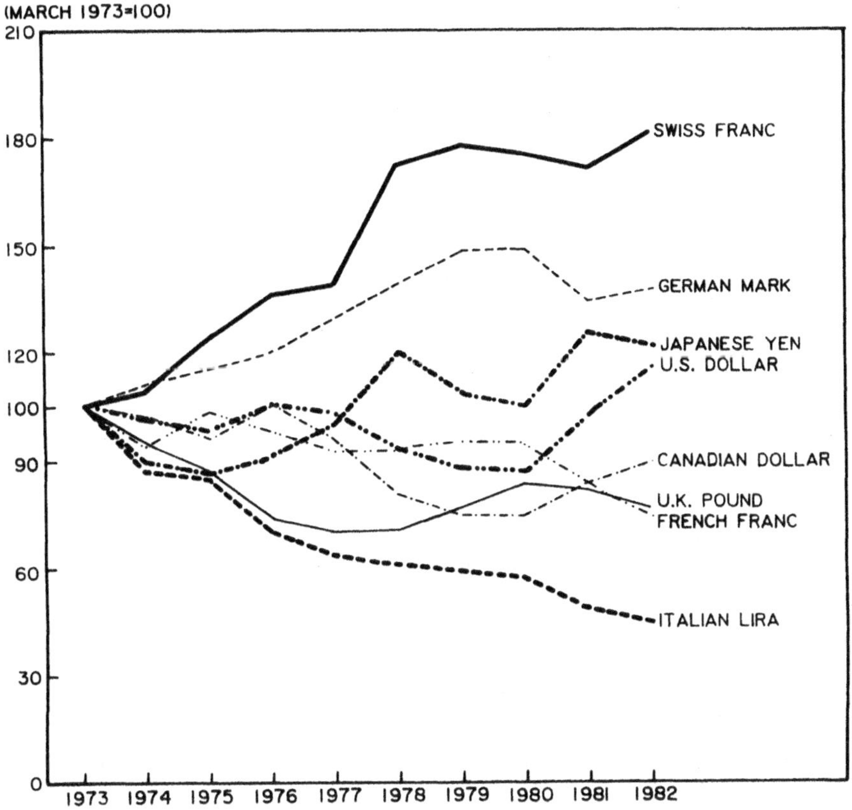

SOURCE: Board of Governors, Federal Reserve System.

The last column is probably more indicative of monetary accommodation. Nominal gross national product growth rates do reflect the relative accommodative stance of monetary policy over the longer run, even if they do not show the extent to which money growth is translated into real output growth versus inflation. (Viewed in the familiar quantity equation context, nominal GNP equals the product of the money stock times velocity. Thus, nominal GNP growth rates measure rates of money growth adjusted for changes in velocity.) By this gauge, it is again the countries with more independent central banks that emerge as less accommodative.

Table 1
Price Level, Money Supply, and Nominal GNP Growth in Eight Major Countries

Country	Implicit deflator inflation	Consumer price inflation	Narrow money supply growth[1]	Broad money supply growth[2]	Nominal GNP growth
	Average annual rates of change, 1960-80 (Percent)				
Germany	4.4	3.9	12.6	13.6	8.3
Switzerland	4.8	4.2	11.4	8.5	8.1
United States	4.9	5.3	5.5	9.6	8.6
Canada	5.8	5.3	7.2	12.2	10.6
Japan	6.3	7.4	18.1	19.3	14.6
France	6.9	6.8	10.9	14.3	12.4
United Kingdom	8.9	8.8	7.9	10.6	11.4
Italy	9.5	8.8	14.6	14.0	14.7

1. Based on M1.
2. Based on M1 plus quasi money.
Sources of Primary Data: International Monetary Fund and the Organization for Economic Cooperation and Development.

CENTRAL BANK REACTION FUNCTIONS

Although the above comparisons are interesting, they leave much to be desired in investigating the underlying importance of central banks' independence. A further step is to consider the various sources of pressure to which a central bank is subject. This step can open the discussion to a wide range of economic and social forces that frame the context within which monetary policy is made. The basic premise is that monetary authorities react to a number of different influences in attempting to deliver an acceptable set of economic conditions. Policy targets, such as interest rates and money supply growth rates, are presumed to be manipulated in response to underlying economic, sociological, or political pressures. In this spirit, many economic researchers in recent years have attempted to estimate central bank 'reaction functions.'(9) These attempts have been aimed at identifying the forces to which particular central banks have responded and at quantifying the magnitude of the responses.

Monetary policy may be influenced by outside forces, but the authorities can still control their operating and intermediate monetary targets with a reasonable degree of accuracy. A monetary policy that resists pressures entering the relevant reaction function simply requires accepting the consequences – for example, higher unemployment or lower economic growth in the short run – if the pressures are not accommodated. The extent to which such pressures are accommodated, however, can depend significantly on the independence of the central bank.

Although cataloging all plausible pressures is not possible, several are frequently mentioned. Commonly cited is the pressure that government fiscal deficits place on interest rates and money growth. If the central bank counteracts alleged 'crowding out' of private investment, resulting from higher interest rates because of government financing needs, it monetizes the public debt. One would expect this option of taxing through inflation, rather than conventionally, to be exercised more the less the independence of the central bank from government.

Central banks also may react to other inflationary pressures. Wage increases may call for monetary validation if unemployment results from wage gains in excess of productivity. And international sources of inflationary pressure may call for accommodation. Typical foreign sources are import price pressure (due to a depreciating exchange rate or rising world prices in general) and unsterilized international reserve flows in the balance of payments.

The response of the monetary authority may not be inflationary, on the other hand. The central bank's reaction may be to combat inflationary pressures by being more restrictive. And any discretionary monetary policy responds to real economic activity, either procyclically to foster an expansion or countercyclically in a fashion that stimulates real growth.

In assessing the importance of factors entering these monetary reaction functions, it is possible to draw upon other work to some extent. One of the relatively few formal studies of central bank independence concluded that the Federal Reserve should be considered a subservient central bank rather than an independent one.(10) That study surveyed 10 industrial countries – Australia, Belgium, Canada, France, Germany, Italy, Japan, Sweden, the United Kingdom, and the United States – on the basis of available reaction function studies. Among the central banks of these countries, only the German bank was found to behave independently as measured by the response to included pressures. This outcome was reinforced by other conclusions on relative central bank inflationary-deflationary stance and observations concerning appointment of bank governors.(11)

Another investigation, some results from which are presented in Table 2, partly supports this finding but yields somewhat different conclusions regarding the United States. The responses of monetary policy to four pressures

Table 2

Significance of Four Pressures for Monetary Accommodation in 12 Industrial Countries

	Domestic		Foreign		Total Number of cases
	Fiscal deficit	Wage increases	Reserve changes	Import prices	
Area	Cases in which variables were significant at the 5-percent confidence level, using a one-tail test that the sign was as hypothesized				
Australia	11	7	6	0	24
Belgium	10	9	3	1	23
Canada	5	3	0	0	8
France	4	8	2	115	
Germany	6	1	0	0	7
Italy	9	5	6	2	22
Japan	7	10	11	0	28
Netherlands	11	9	10	1	31
Sweden	9	0	3	2	14
Switzerland	1	0	8	1	10
United Kingdom	6	10	4	2	22
United States	6	4	0	2	12
12 Countries	85	66	53	12	216

Source: Leroy O. Laney and Thomas D. Willett, 'The Political Economy of Global Inflation: The Causes of Monetary Expansion in the Major Industrial Countries' (U.S. Department of the Treasury, Office of International Monetary Research, Washington, D.C.,.1977, Mimeographed).

Table 2 (Continued)

Reaction Function Specifications Used for the 11 Estimated Equations

Equation	Annual observations (starting with the earliest available year in International Monetary Fund data)

1. Changes in M1 as the dependent variable; the fiscal deficit cyclically adjusted; percentage changes in nominal wages specified as the wage increase term; changes in monetary authority foreign assets as the reserves term; differences in import price inflation and consumer price inflation as the import price pressure term.
2. Same as (1), with changes in the broad money supply as the dependent variable.
3. Same as (1) except the fiscal deficit cyclically unadjusted.
4. Same as (3), with changes in the broad money supply as the dependent variable.
5. Same as (1) but modified to abstract from multicollinearity in annual data (independent variables were regressed on each other; then the residual of this regression was substituted for the basic variable.)

6. Same as (5), with changes in the broad money supply as the dependent variable.
7. Same as (1) except percentage changes in import prices only were substituted as the import price term.

Quarterly observations (starting with the earliest available quarter in International Monetary Fund data)

---

8. Changes in seasonally adjusted M1 as the dependent variable; the fiscal deficit cyclically and seasonally adjusted; other quarterly variables computed the same as in (1).
9. Same as (8), with the fiscal deficit seasonally (but not cyclically) adjusted.
10. Same as (8), with percentage changes in M1 substituted for firstdifference changes as the dependent variable.
11. Same as (8) except distributed lags were estimated on the independent variables.

Note: An example of this general specification is found in T.D. Willett and L. O. Laney, 'Monetarism, Budget Deficits, and Wage Push Inflation: The Cases of Italy and the U.D.,' *Banca Nazionale del Lavoro Quarterly Review* 31 (December 1978): 315-31.

– the fiscal deficit, wage increases, international reserve influences, and import price increases – were examined across a sample of 12 industrial countries. Initial results were sensitive to alternative econometric specifications testing these four factors, so 11 different regressions (described below the table) were estimated for each country. The figures in the table indicate the number of equations in which the respective variables were significant statistically at the 5-percent confidence level.

The outcomes provide two interesting observations. First, the monetary authorities were more responsive to the two domestic pressures than to the two pressures of foreign origin. This suggests that sources of inflation may originate more often at home than abroad even in an open economy and that domestic monetary and fiscal policies must bear most of the responsibility. Balance-of-payments surpluses and deficits may influence monetary expansion when sterilization is not complete. Recent empirical research suggests, however, that even though such developments may have been important for certain countries in particular episodes, the industrial countries have generally been able to sterilize a high proportion of international reserve flows. Thus, secular rates of monetary expansion are primarily a function of domestic considerations, rather than international ones.(12) Likewise, while international commodity price shocks and exchange rate changes can exert independent influences on domestic price levels in the short run, long-run price trends are largely due to domestic macroeconomic policies.

But perhaps more noteworthy, monetary policy was less accommodative overall in the countries in which the central bank has been characterized as more independent. The four countries showing the fewest total cases of significant monetary validation of the pressures covered were Germany, Canada, Switzerland, and the United States. While Sweden and France fell fairly close to the United States, the remaining countries had considerably higher totals.

A STRUCTURAL APPROACH

Beyond the typical economic reaction function arguments is an array of social and political arguments. Considering some of these is appropriate because an examination of central bank independence leads inevitably into this broader realm. Sociopolitical factors are usually more strongly linked to the structure of an individual society than are the behavioral economic variables that are often hypothesized. Is it possible to identify structural aspects that make some societies exhibit greater inflationary tendencies than others? Is the central bank less independent in these more inflationary societies simply because it evolved as part of the underlying social structure, or does the relationship of the monetary authority to government make any separately identifiable contribution?

Again, complete identification of inflationary factors is not possible, but several explanations have been suggested. A frequently mentioned aspect is the growth of government.(13) Some work has even found significant explanatory power from the extent of unionization in the economy.(14) The role of an 'aspirations gap,' both within countries and among countries, has also been hypothesized. According to this reasoning, many attempts to improve real income per capita relative to that in other countries, as well as make income distribution more equal within a country, may be well-intentioned but ultimately result mainly in inflation.(15) And the openness of an economy can be important for internationally transmitted inflation.(16)

The results of an attempt to explain inflation across countries by using several of these structural factors are presented in the accompanying appendix. There, most of the proxies for the factors investigated are only weakly significant statistically or not significant at all. But a variable intended to capture central bank independence is always strongly significant. The implication is that even after several frequently mentioned structural forces are accounted for, the relationship of the central bank to government appears to play an important separate role.

CONCLUSION

These results suggest that independent central banks have conducted monetary policies over the postwar years that have been less accommodative to outside pressures than the policies of their less autonomous counterparts; consequently, their countries have experienced substantially lower rates of inflation. This article has not evaluated monetary policy with respect to other objectives, such as maximization of real growth rates or reduction of unemployment. Even though other segments of society, in the political arena or the policymaking establishment, can be depended on to emphasize the importance of these other goals, often only the monetary authority can be depended on to defend the value of the currency. And most would judge this to be the principal responsibility of a central bank.

Central bankers, therefore, may be doing their best job when they are least popular. Once an inflation-conscious credibility has been established by a central bank, its occasional departure from noninflationary monetary policy may be overlooked as a factor in the formation of inflationary expectations. But it is questionable whether making the bank more answerable to the political process would enhance such credibility.

Because examples of independent central banks are few – only the banks in Germany, Switzerland, and the United States were considered to be so here – and because such categorization is somewhat subjective, these generalizations remain more tentative than might be deemed desirable. Societies with low inflation rates have more independent central banks, but causation may run more from the former to the latter than vice versa. Evidence presented here, however, suggests that central banking arrangements are likely to have made an independent contribution to the lower rate of inflation. The evidence also suggests, contrary to conclusions by some analysts that the U.S central bank fits better with the dependent central banks, that the Federal Reserve should at least be classified in an intermediate position, between the German and Swiss cases on the one hand and the dependent central banks on the other.

APPENDIX

Institutional Independence, Monetary Accommodation, and Inflation

Even when other often-cited structural factors are taken into account, central bank independence appears to be important in explaining monetary accommodation and inflation in developed countries. Using cross-sectional data from 17 industrial countries – Australia, Belgium, Canada, Denmark, Finland, France, Germany, Italy, Japan, the Netherlands, Norway, Spain, Sweden, Switzerland, the United Kingdom, and the United States – central bank institutional independence and several other structural aspects that have been set forth in explaining why inflation rates differ across countries were investigated for the 1960-80 period.

Fiscal deficits relative to savings (DS) can be an important variable, as countries with a low savings ratio are less able to finance deficits privately than are those with a high savings ratio. The percentage of the labor force unionized (U) was also included, perhaps not so much because labor unions cause inflation directly as because they affect political behavior through lobbying and voting. If the aspirations gap hypothesis is valid, variables such as the percentage change in real income per capita (YC) can be important across countries, as well as a Gini coefficient (G) measuring income inequality within countries. Foreign inflationary pressures were proxied by the ratio of imports to gross domestic product (IY). Finally, to capture the influence of probable central bank independence, a dummy variable (CB) set equal to 1 for Germany, Switzerland, and the United States – zero otherwise – was added.(1)

These variables were regressed as independent variables to explain three different gauges of monetary accommodation: two inflation measures – rates of change in implicit price deflators (DI) and consumer prices (CI) – and the growth of nominal gross national products (NGNP). Because price levels over the 1960-80 period rose substantially worldwide and, at the same time, diverged and possibly crossed internationally, cross-sectional data were divided into three sub-periods – 1960-67, 1967-73, and 1973-80 – and then pooled for the actual regressions. This was not done for the unionization or Gini coefficient variables, which are not likely to have exhibited much variation over time. Sources yielded these for the years 1977 and 1970, respectively.

The central bank independence variable was always quite significant, while the other variables generally performed poorly. Real per capita income and the deficit-savings ratio entered significantly in the inflation regressions, the former more strongly than the latter, but not in the regression using nominal income growth as the dependent variable. The coefficients indicate that inflation could be about 4 percent less, on average, in countries with an independent central bank; of course, any such estimate should be regarded with caution.(2)

---

[1] For the 1960-67 period the independence dummy was also set equal to 1 for Canada, because

the Bank of Canada was accorded final authority overmonetary policy during this period.

2 Several variations on the reported regressions were investigated. Regressions were estimated with separate dummies for each country with an independent central bank. Germany and the United States were significant here but Switzerland usually was not, possibly because other variables captured the independence effect for the Swiss National Bank. (For example, the Swiss fiscal balance was in substantial surplus in each period.) In addition, in one set of regressions, the mean global rate for the variables was subtracted in each subperiod to abstract from any trend biasing upward the significance of those independent variables that were so divided. The independence dummy still was dominant, and the results reported here are biased against the relative importance of the bank independence term. Finally, a separate set of regressions was computed substituting fiscal deficits relative to GNP for deficits relative to savings. Results were generally the same but not quite as robust as those reported.

Regression Results

DI =	8.41	+ 5.96 DS	− .02 U	− .88 YC	+ 9.40 G	− .03 Y	− 4.01 CBI
	(1.80)	(1.51)*	(−.66)	(−3.30)***	(.81)	(−.79)	(−3.32)***
	$\bar{R}^2$ = .31; F = 4.69.						
CI =	9.38	+ 7.00 DS	− .01 U	− .98 YC	+ 7.72 G	− .051Y	− 4.03 CBI
	(1.97)	(1.73)**	(−.50)	(−3.57)***	(.65)	(−1.15)	(−3.26)***
	$\bar{R}^2$ = .33; F = 5.15.						
NGNP =	13.14	+ 5.67 DS	− .04 U	+ .14 YC	+ 3.55 G	− .041 Y	− 4.58 CBI
	(2.46)	(1.25)	(−1.47)	(.47)	(.27)	(−.94)	(−3.31)***
	$\bar{R}^2$ = .22; F = 3.33.						

Note: Figures in parentheses are t statistics; * indicates significance of the independent variable at the 10-percent level, ** at the 5-percent level, and *** at the 1-percent level, using a one-tail test that the variable is signed as hypothesized.
$\bar{R}^2$ is the coefficient of determination adjusted for degrees of freedom. F is a test statistic for regression significance; here, all are significant at the 5-percent level.

NOTES

1. For further discussion on alternative monetary constitutions, see Thomas D. Willett, 'A New Monetary Constitution: An Evaluation of the Need and the Major Alternatives,' Claremont Working Papers, no. 71 (Claremont, Calif.: Claremont Graduate School, November 1982), and the references cited there. See also Leland B. Yeager, ed., *In Search of a Monetary Constitution* (Cambridge: Harvard University Press, 1962).
2. An evolving branch of the economic literature investigates the interaction of national politics and macroeconomic policy. Much of this literature does not focus explicitly on monetary policy as it relates to government or partisan politics, but see Bruno S. Frey and Friedrich Schneider, 'Central Bank Behavior: A Positive Empirical Analysis,' *Journal of Monetary Economics* 7 (May 1981): 291-315, and Leroy O. Laney and Thomas D. Willett, 'Presidential Politics, Budget Deficits, and Monetary Policy in the United States, 1960-1976,' *Public Choice* 40, no. 1 (1983): 53-70.
3. See Ira P. Kaminow, 'Politics, Economics, and Procedures of U.S. Money Growth

Dynamics,' in *Political Economy of International and Domestic Monetary Relations*, ed. Raymond E. Lombra and William E. Witte (Ames: Iowa State University Press, 1982, 181-96, along with discussions by Thomas Mayer and John T. Woolley, Comment by Thomas D. Willett and Leroy O. Laney ('Technical Versus Political Causes of Monetary Expansion'), and the rejoinder by Kaminow.

4. As indicated by Lester C. Thurow, for example: 'Whatever its historical merit, the time has come to end the independence of the Fed. If the President is competent enough to have his finger on the nuclear button, he is competent enough to control the money supply. Presidents are elected and defeated on their economic performance. They deserve both the controls and the responsibilities that this implies. No President should be able to hide his failures behind an 'erratic' money supply beyond his control. And if the charge is true, no President should have to put up with an incompetent Fed' (*Newsweek*, 1 March 1982, 29).
5. Some observers have noted that under current arrangements the Administration exercises more de facto influence over the Fed than does the Congress. See, for example, Sherman J. Maisel, *Managing the Dollar* (New York: W. W. Norton & Company, 1973), 108-13, and Robert E. Weintraub, 'Congressonal Supervision of Monetary Policy,' *Journal of Monetary Economics* 4 (April 1978): 341-62.
6. According to Milton Friedman: 'The only two alternatives that do seem to me feasible over the longer run are either to make the Federal Reserve a bureau in the Treasury under the secretary of the Treasury, or to put the Federal Reserve under direct congressional control. Either involves terminating the so-called independence of the system. But either would establish a strong incentive for the Fed to produce a stabler monetary environment than we have had' ('Monetary Policy: Theory and Practice,' chapter 2 in this volume, p. 31).
7. For discussion, see Edward J. Kane, 'External Pressure and the Operations of the Fed,' in *Political Economy of International and Domestic Monetary Relations*, ed. Lombra and Witte, 211-32.
8. Comparatively few attempts have been made to classify central banks according to their independence, but the above categorization is generally supported in work done so far. See for example, Donald R. Hodgman, *National Monetary Policies and International Monetary Cooperation* (Boston: Little, Brown and Company, 1974); Michael Parkin and Robin Bade, 'Central Bank Laws and Monetary Policies: A Preliminary Investigation,' University of Western Ontario, Department of Economics, Research Report no. 7804 (London, Ontario, Canada, 1978), part of which was published in Michael Parkin, 'In Search of a Monetary Constitution for the European Communities,' in *One Money for Europe*, ed. Michele Fratianni and Theo Peeters (New York: Praeger Publishers, Praeger Special Studies, 1978), 167-95; and 'Relations Between Government and Central Bank: A Survey of Twenty Countries,' by D.E. Fair for the U.K. Parliament, Committee to Review the Functioning of Financial Institutions, *Appendices*, Cmnd. 7937 (June 1980), 557-72. A summary of the last work cited is found in Don Fair, 'The Independence of Central Banks,' *The Banker*, October 1979, 31-41 passim.
9. Early examples are G. L. Reuber, 'The Objectives of Canadian Monetary Policy, 1949-61: Empirical 'Trade-offs' and the Reaction Function of the Authorities, *Journal of Political Economy* 72 (April 1964): 109-32, and John H. Wood, 'A Model of Federal Reserve Behavior,' in *Monetary Process and Policy: A Symposium*, ed. George Horwich (Homewood, Ill.: Richard D. Irwin, 1967), 135-66. For comparative international evidence, see also Robert J. Gordon, 'World Inflation and Monetary Accommodation in Eight Countries,' *Brookings Papers on Economic Activity*, 1977, no. 2: 409-68, and T. D. Willett and L. O. Laney, 'Monetarism, Budget Deficits, and Wage Push Inflation: The Cases of

Italy and the U.K.,' *Banca Nazionale del Lavoro Quarterly Review* 31 (December 1978): 315-31.

10. Parkin, 'In Search of a Monetary Constitution for the European Communities,' 180-84.
11. The conclusion for the United States, however, was influenced by at least two aspects of Parkin's analysis that should be noted. First, as his indicator of secular inflationary-deflationary stance, Parkin uses the average rate of change in the exchange rate for the currency of each country in his sample against the U.S. dollar over the 1951-75 period. He finds that the two most institutionally independent central banks – in Germany and Switzerland – rank one and two, respectively, and the United States ranks number nine (that is, eight currencies appreciated against the dollar, while only three – those of France, Italy, and the United Kingdom – depreciated). But use of exchange rate changes as a measure of inflationary trends is questionable, because exchange rates are often influenced substantially by real factors that can cause large deviations from purchasing power parity, both in the short run and the long run. (For discussion and references, see the articles by Richard J. Sweeney and Thomas D. Willett in *The International Monetary System: A Time of Turbulence*, ed. Jacob S. Dreyer, Gottfried Haberler, and Thomas D. Willett [Washington, D.C.: American Enterprise Institute for Public Policy Research, 1982].) Also, while simple comparisons may be misleading, Parkin observes that 100 percent of the Fed's Board of Governors is Government-appointed (compared with fractions in the German and Swiss cases), but he does not account at all for the fact that only a fraction of the policymaking Federal Open Market Committee is composed of that Board.
12. For supporting evidence, see Leroy O. Laney and Thomas D. Willett, 'The International Liquidity Explosion and Worldwide Inflation: The Evidence from Sterilization Coefficient Estimates,' *Journal of International Money and Finance* 1 (August 1982): 141-52.
13. For one analysis, see Alan T. Peacock and Martin Ricketts, 'The Growth of the Public Sector and Inflation,' in *The Political Economy of Inflation*, ed. Fred Hirsch and John H. Goldthorpe (Cambridge: Harvard University Press, 1978), 117-36.
14. See Robert E. McCormick, 'Why Are Inflation Rates Different Across Countries?' (Paper prepared for the Liberty Fund Conference, Long Island, New York, 25-27 September 1980).
15. For investigation, see M. Panic, 'The Origin of Increasing Inflationary Tendencies in Contemporary Society,' in *The Political Economy of Inflation*, ed. Hirsch and Goldthorpe, 137-60.
16. For discussion, see Richard J. Sweeney and Thomas D. Willett, 'The International Transmission of Inflation,' *Kredit und Kapital* 9, special supplement (1976): 441-517.

Chapter 12

A PRIVATE CENTRAL BANK: SOME OLDE ENGLISH LESSONS

By G. J. Santoni

Dissatisfaction with persistent and volatile inflation since the mid-1960s has led to numerous calls for a different approach to monetary policy. In some cases, people have suggested that monetary policy decisions be made more explicitly political, for example, subject to greater control by Congress via congressionally mandated monetary growth targets. In the same vein, Milton Friedman has proposed that monetary policy be set by the Treasury, thus making the President of the United States ultimately responsible for its conduct.

In contrast, come critics of the current system have argued for a return to the constraints of Bretton Woods or the even earlier classical gold standard. Some have suggested that the only lasting solution to the problem entails the private production of money.

Behind these different suggestions is the implication that central bankers will respond systematically and, hence, predictably to the different incentives embodied in these alternative programs of monetary control. If the incentives are changed, so the theory goes, better policy decision will be made.

This paper focuses directly on the theoretical and empirical support for the claim that different incentives induce policymakers to choose different monetary growth rates. This paper does *not* advocate a particular set of incentives or form of organization for the central bank. Rather, it merely points out that the choices of monetary policymakers depend, as all choices do, upon the set of incentives the individual confronts.

Toma, E.F. and Toma, M. (eds.) Central Bankers, Bureaucratic Incentives, and Monetary Policy

ISBN 90 247 3366 9

A verification of this proposition is sought by examining the behavior of the Bank of England over the period from, roughly, 1700 to 1930. This period, which encompasses two significant changes in the incentives facing England's central bankers, provides support for the view that policymakers, like other individuals, respond predictably to changes in the cost-reward circumstances facing them.

WHAT DISTINGUISHES CENTRAL BANKERS?

The central banker is the person (or group) holding the enforceable right to control the quantity of nominal money balances in circulation.(1) This right is valuable. Whoever holds it can, among other things, materially influence the rate of inflation and the flow of profits from money creation (seigniorage), as well as the present value of the right itself.

WHY THE BANK OF ENGLAND

The Bank of England presents an interesting case in studying the effect of different incentives on the behavior of central bankers. There are two reasons for this. First, the original organization of the Bank differed from its modern counterparts in one fundamental respect: the Bank of England was a privately-owned-for-profit central bank from its inception in 1694 until the early 1930s. Further, the Bank was immersed in a set of institutional arrangements that related the wealth of the Bank's owners inversely to the rate of inflation. This paper shows that the costs and benefits of varying monetary growth rates were different for England's private for-profit central bankers than those typically taken into account by modern central bankers.(2) Consequently, a different monetary growth rate emerged.

A second reason for studying this particular case is that control of the money supply by the Bank's owners was interrupted from 1793 to 1821, when the government seized the Bank's monetary control function. For the purposes of this paper, the interruption is important because it allows a contrast of monetary growth outcomes produced by certain identifiable changes in the incentive structure, while other important institutional factors remained roughly constant.

A BRIEF HISTORY OF THE BANK OF ENGLAND: 1694-1832

Prior to 1694, England's money supply consisted mainly of coins. These coins were controlled by the government through regulation of the mint.

The coins were in a continually bad state because the populace persisted in clipping, sweating, filing, washing and boring them. Further, the government resorted to progressive debasement in the form of frequent recoinages, a practice that was particularly pronounced during the reigns of Henry VIII and Edward VI.(3)

In some cases, the government expropriated monetary wealth outright. In 1640, Charles I closed the London Mint and confiscated the funds of the private citizens that had been stored there for safekeeping. Later, in 1672, Charles II expropriated funds deposited with the Treasury by London goldsmiths.(4) This irresponsible behavior had important consequences when, in 1692 and 1693, William III floated long-term loans to finance a war with France. Because of the earlier debasements and expropriations, the interest rates demanded for long-term loans to the Crown contained a substantial premium.(5)

Establishment of the Bank

William's war with France was a costly affair. When additional funds were required in 1694, a proposal that twice previously had been put forward by William Paterson was adopted in the Ways and Means Act of that year. The Act provided that those who subscribed

> for and towards the raising and paying into the receipt of the Exchequer the said sum of twelve hundred thousand pounds part of the sum of fifteen hundred thousand pounds were to constitute jointly the Company of the Bank of England.(6)

The loan was a perpetuity, paying interest at the rate of 8 percent. This was considerably below the interest rates that previously had been charged the Crown. The subscribers, however, received additional rights to 1) form a joint stock banking company, 2) deal in bills of exchange, gold and silver, 3) grant advances on security, and 4) issue promissory notes transferable by endorsement in an amount not exceeding the Bank's capital.(7)

These terms apparently were very attractive. The entire loan was subscribed within 12 days. Every subscriber became a shareholder of the Bank to the extent of his subscription, and all or any fraction of his share could be sold to others.(8)

The bank opened for business on July 27, 1694, in Mercers' Chappell. From its inception, every effort was made by the Governor and Court of Directors (Board of Directors of the Bank) to attract depositors and to promote the circulation of its 'running cash notes.'(9) These notes were convertible into legal tender money, gold coins, at a fixed exchange rate upon demand at the Bank.(10)

Subsequent legislation strengthened the Bank's position. The Bank was granted a monopoly in joint stock banking in early 1697.(11) In 1708, the Bank obtained a monopoly in the issue of joint stock bank notes.(12) Later, in 1742, Act 10 and 11 George II., C. 13 (par. 5), reaffirmed the earlier rights granted to the Bank. Each of these pieces of legislation was accompanied by an additional Bank loan to the government. The Bank subscribed an additional 1,001,017 pounds for loan to the government at 8.0 percent in 1697. In 1707, it extended a 1,500,000 pound loan at 4.5 percent to the government and, in 1742, another 1,600,000 pounds at 3.0 percent.

No further significant legislative changes regarding the Bank's position occurred until 1826. In that year, the Bank's monopoly on joint stock banking was limited to within a 65-mile radius of London.(13) Seven years later, in 1833, its monopoly of joint stock bank note issue was also limited to the same area. However, Bank of England notes were made legal tender at this time.(14) This legislation provided legal force to the practice that had already been adopted by other banks of maintaining their reserves in the form of Bank of England notes.

The Government Steps In: 1793-1821

The Napoleonic Wars between England and France began in 1793. With the exception of a minor truce, the war continued until Napoleon's abdication on April 6, 1814.(15) Governmental demands from the Bank for financing rose substantially during the war. Of course, the Bank's contract with its depositors to redeem its notes at a fixed price in terms of gold got in the way of the government's interest and, on February 26, 1797, the King and Privy Council ordered the Bank to suspend specie payments, a suspension that was to last for more than 20 years.(16)

During the suspension, control of the money supply, which had rested with the Bank's owners, was largely usurped by the government. Clapham notes that

> The minutes of the Court and those of the Committee of Treasury are full of . . . requests for help from Perceval, and the Bank's reluctant but invariable acquiescence.(17)

The Bank apparently acquiesced because of an 'understanding, a gentleman's understanding . . . to do this business and to do it in the way most convenient to the Treasury.'(18)

Given the transfer of monetary control to the government, it is, perhaps, not surprising that the Bank's Board of Directors became unusually lackadaisical in their attention to duties. As a result of absenteeism, the Bank Court experienced difficulty in maintaining a quorum. Letters were sent to a number of directors that 'pointedly asked "when their attendance could be depended upon" for 'too much of the business had been one "by a Single Director with the assistance of the Head of the Discount Office'.'(19)

Return to Private Control

The suspension played an important role in the government's effort to wrest control of the money supply from the Bank. In the absence of suspension, 'control' of the stock of money would have meant little to the government since the requirement to redeem notes at a fixed price in terms of specie eventually would have (and did during 1790-96) placed an effective constraint on note issue.

The public was never keen on the suspension, and the Bank made this the political issue in its fight to regain control of the money supply. In October of 1797, six months after it was ordered to suspend payments, the Bank indicated that it could 'with safety resume its accustomed functions (payments of specie), if the political circumstances of the country do not render it inexpedient.'(20) The Bank's report was virtually ignored by government. In June of 1810, the 'Report from the Select Committee on the High Price of Bullion' recommended to Parliament that the resumption of specie payments (at the old par) begin within two years. The issue was not even taken up for discussion until July of the following year.(21) A vote on the recommendation was taken in the House of Commons in 1811. The House voted 180 to 45 against the issue.

On its own initiative, the Bank began partial resumption of specie payments for notes of 5 pounds or less in January of 1817. Early in 1819, however, Parliament required the Bank to discontinue the practice.(22) Parliament had promised on five different occasions to eventually return to specie payments, but continued to drag its feet on fixing a date. Finally, on July 2, 1819, the House of Commons passed an act permitting the resumption of cash payments (bullion and coin) after May 1, 1822. At the request of the Bank, this date eventually was moved forward to May 1, 1821.(23)

Some Important Observations

There are a number of important points to draw from the previous discussion in analyzing the incentives faced by the central bankers. First, given the one exception noted, the right to control the money supply was held privately. This right, in the form of ownership shares in the Bank, was traded in an organized market. Any expected changes in the future profits of the Bank would be reflected by changes in the price of Bank shares and would immediately affect the wealth of Bank owners.

Second, the owners of the Bank had loaned considerable sums to the government in perpetuity at fixed rates of interest. By 1743, the sum was well in excess of nine million pounds.

Finally, the Bank's contract with its customers to redeem its notes at a fixed price in terms of gold was a voluntary arrangement. An official (established by law) gold standard did not exist in England until 1821. In fact, the gold standard came about largely as a result of the Bank's continuous prods to an unwilling Parliament.

The following discusses how this unique incentive structure faced by England's central bankers influenced the monetary growth rate.

The Profits From the Right to Control Money

Like the right to control the production of any commodity, the right to control the production of money is valuable. The central bank, at the cost of a few cents worth of paper and ink, can produce a $100 bill (or a 100-pound note) that can be exchanged in the market for $100 worth of resources.

The Flow of Profits

The central bank introduces money into circulation by exchanging units of money (which it prints) for commodities. These commodities may be either real or financial assets. Since the bank buys these assets at market prices, the expected flow of nominal profits generated by the purchase of the assets is equal to the nominal interest rate times the price of the assets purchased. This is equivalent to the nominal interest rate multiplied by the quantity of money exchanged for the assets. The flow of real revenue is simply the nominal flow divided by the price level ($i \times M/P$).

Since we are interested in relating the bank's real revenue flow to the rate of money production, account must be taken of the fact that, at higher rates of money production (higher rates of inflation), people will want to hold less of their wealth in the form of real purchasing power (M/P). Other things unchanged, the flow of real revenue would decline at higher rates of money growth because M/P declines. Even though M is rising, the price level rises faster. However, other things are not unchanged. Faster money growth increases the rate of inflation and this raises the nominal interest rate (i).

Faster money production exerts two opposing forces on the bank's real revenue. One force tends to reduce revenue, while the other tends to increase revenue. In general, there is a unique rate of money growth (and rate of inflation) that will maximize the flow of real revenue.

A Simple Example

Table 1 presents a hypothetical example relating different rates of inflation (or rates of monetary growth), π, to the public's demand for real purchasing power, M/P. In order to facilitate the calculation of the rate of inflation that maximizes the bank's revenue flow, suppose that the public knows the rate of inflation with certainty (extreme rational expectations), that changes in the monetary growth rate affect only the rate of inflation and the public's desire for real purchasing power but no other real variables, that the cost of producing nominal units of money is zero (so revenue and profits are identical), that real output and population are stationary, that the real interest rate is 10 percent, and that the nominal interest rate is equal to the sum of the real interest rate and rate of inflation ($i = r + \pi$).

The numbers in the first two columns of table 1 indicate that, as the rate of inflation rises (falls), the public's demand for real purchasing power falls (rises). The third column indicates the nominal rate of interest at the various rates of inflation. The fourth column indicates the profit stream at the different rates of inflation.

As the rate of inflations falls from very high rates, the bank's profit from inflation initially rises because people choose to hold a greater amount of real purchasing power. Reducing the rate of inflation increases total profits up to a point (1.80 real goods per unit of time in this example), after which further reductions in the rate of inflation cause profits to fall. In this example, the profit-maximizing rate of inflation (monetary growth rate), which is the one the central bankers will choose, is 20 percent.(24)

Table 1
The Revenue From Money Production

(1) π	(2) M/P	(3) $i = r + \pi$	(4) $R = i(M/P)$
.50	0	.60	0.00
.45	1	.55	.55
.40	2	.50	1.00
.35	3	.45	1.35
.30	4	.40	1.60
.25	5	.35	1.75
.20	6	.30	1.80*
.15	7	.25	1.75
.10	8	.20	1.60
.05	9	.15	1.35
0.00	10	.10	1.00

where:

π = the rate of inflation (rate of monetary growth)
M/P = the stock of real purchasing power demanded
i(M/P) = the profit from monetary production (inflation)

*indicates maximum profit

THE BANK OF ENGLAND'S UNIQUE CONSTRAINTS

The Flow of Profits

Among other things, the above result depends upon the particular set of operating rules the bank faces. Apart from the particular assumptions expressed above, the foregoing example does not constrain the bank in any way. If additional rules were imposed, the profit function may change. As a result, the central bankers would be confronted with different incentives, causing them to select a different monetary growth rate.

The Bank of England was founded on the condition that the stockholders grant a substantial loan to the government at a fixed rate of interest. By 1743, that loan amounted to almost 10 million pounds. At the point when these loans were made to the government, the interest rate charged was below the market rate. (Recall the 1694 loan at 8 percent when the market rate on long-term loans to the Crown was 14 percent.) This subsidized loan rate is a payment made by the Bank to the government for the lease rights to the production of money. The right was never granted to the Bank in perpetuity. Rather, as indicated above, the Bank's charter came up for review periodically.

The cost to the Bank of its government loan depends upon the market rate of interest. If the coupon rate is c and the amount loaned is L, the nominal value of the lease payment per unit of time is (i - c)L. The real value is the nominal amount divided by the price level, (i - c)L/P. The higher the nominal rate of interest, i, relative to the coupon rate, c, the larger the cost of the lease to the Bank.

An additional constraint is relevant. The quantity of notes the Bank could issue was restricted by law to an amount less than or equal to the capital invested by stockholders. Since the capital represented the loan to the government, M must be less than or equal to L. Given this constraint, the Bank's owners will choose M = L because the flow of real profits is highest in this case, other things the same (see appendix). Consequently, the Bank's profit is simply the coupon rate earned on the loan, c, times the loan (which is equal to the quantity of notes issued, M), divided by the price level, P.

Table 2 illustrates the effect of this set of rules on the profit-maximizing rate of inflation for the Bank. The first three columns of table 3 simply reproduce the first three columns of table 1. Column 4 calculates the real profits of the Bank under the new set of rules where the coupon rate, c, is assumed to be 10 percent. Note that profits are maximized at a zero rate of inflation rather than the 20 percent rate obtained previously.(25)

Table 2

An Example of the Bank's Profit Function

(1) π	(2) M/P	(3) $i = r + \pi$	(4) $R' = c(M/P)$
.50	0	.60	0.00
.45	1	.55	.10
.40	2	.50	.20
.35	3	.45	.30
.30	4	.40	.40
.25	5	.35	.50
.20	6	.30	.60
.15	7	.25	.70
.10	8	.20	.80
.05	9	.15	.90
0.00	10	.10	1.00*

*indicates maximum profit

The Role of Specie Payments: A Contract for Price Level Stability

It is in the interest of Bank owners to inform the public of their intention to maintain a relatively low inflation rate. Demand for the Bank's product does not rise until the anticipated rate of inflation declines. This eventually will result from the Bank's policy of maintaining a relatively low monetary growth rate. The owners of the Bank, however, chose to hurry the adjustment of expectations by 'marketing' their bank notes in a particular way.

In marketing its notes, the Bank guaranteed its customers a low rate of price inflation. This guarantee took the form of a contract to redeem Bank notes at a fixed price (a fixed weight in gold). The contract can be thought of as insurance against the overissue of Bank notes, because it pledged the original investment of the Bank's stockholders as surety for meeting the contract.(26) If bank notes were issued in such quantity as to cause their market price in terms of gold to fall below the price promised by the Bank, people would arbitrage the difference by trading gold for notes in the market at the low price and exchanging the notes for gold at the Bank for the higher price. In the process, wealth would be transferred away from the stockholders to those engaging in the arbitrage. The guarantee was believable because customers knew that stockholders would lose wealth if the Bank overissued its notes relative to the supply of goods in general and gold in particular.(27)

DIFFERENT CONSTRAINTS FOR THE GOVERNMENT

When, for all practical purposes, the government took control of the money supply in 1793, the constraints facing the decisionmakers changed substantially. Recall that the government did not expropriate ownership rights in the Bank outright. Had they done so, it would have been a clear (and, possibly, politically unsavory) transfer of wealth from stockholders to the government. The government, however, did the next best thing from its point of view. It expropriated the wealth from stockholders by a more circuitous route.

When the government took over, the Bank held a loan which, while an asset to the Bank, was a liability to the government. In terms of the example used here, an increase in the rate of inflation increases the nominal interest rate, i, and increases the Bank's opportunity cost of the government loan, $(i - c)L/P$. In effect, accelerating the rate of inflation raised the lease payment the Bank made to the government.

Further, during its period of control, the government continuously violated the constraint that the quantity of notes in circulation not exceed the capital of the Bank. The government did not wish to be bound by the same rule that it believed appropriate in regulating the behavior of the Bank's stockholders.

As a result of the different constraints faced by Bank owners vs. the government, we should expect to observe relatively low rates of monetary growth and inflation during periods when the money supply is controlled by the private owners of the Bank of England and more rapid rates of monetary growth and inflation during the periods of government control. In addition, the demand for real purchasing power should be lower during the period of government control and the price of Bank stock should decline.

EVIDENCE

The Behavior of English Prices

One of the more interesting pieces of evidence concerning the effect of different incentives is England's history of inflation during the period of private monetary control. England's money supply was under private control for almost 200 years, and the rate of inflation during this period was statistically indistinguishable from zero.

From the establishment of the Bank in 1694 until the beginning of the Napoleonic Wars in 1793 when the government usurped control of the money supply, the annual average rate of inflation in England was .01 percent. In 1821, after the Napoleonic Wars, the government returned control of the money supply to the Bank and, at the Bank's insistence, established an official gold standard. During this period, 1822-1913, England's annual average rate of inflation was .42 percent which, again, is statistically indistinguishable from zero. In contrast, by 1931, the England government had taken complete control of the money supply. Since that date, the annual average rate of inflation has been significantly positive at 6.47 percent.(28)

The Napoleonic Wars: Additional Evidence

The above data regarding the history of English inflation are consistent with one of the implications of the theory. Other aspects of the theory can be examined by considering data from the period immediately before, during and after the Napoleonic Wars. The war is important because the transfer of control of the money supply during the war was accomplished through a 'gentleman's understanding' rather than an outright government expropriation of Bank ownership. As a result, ownership shares in the Bank continued to be exchanged by private individuals, and changes in the value of these shares along with changes in the demand for real purchasing power provide further evidence in regard to the theory.

The Market Price of Bank Stock

Table 3 presents an estimate of the effect of the government takeover and suspension of specie payments on the real price of Bank stock. The estimate controls for the effects of business cycles (proxied by average annual real weekly earnings of men in full-time employment) and the interest rate, and

Table 3
The Real Price of Bank Stock, 1780-1832[1]

Estimate[2]

Ps/P =	1.375	−	.232r	+	.005RW	−	$.141D_0$
	(7.40)*		(8.22)*		(7.27)*		(2.21)*
Rho =	.70						
	(7.02)*						
$\bar{R}^2$ =	.72						
DW =	2.02						

where: P_s/P = the real price of Bank stock.
r = the yield on 3 percent consols.
RW = real weekly earnings.(3)
D_0 = a dummy variable for the period subsequent to government's seizure control. D_0 = 1 for the years 1793-1832 and zero otherwise.

[1] The price of Bank stock is the annual average calculated from the daily price quotes reported in *Gentleman's Magazine* for the years 1780-1832.

[2] Corrected for first-order autocorrelation. t-values in parentheses.

[3] The E.W. Gilboy series for average weekly earnings is spliced to the A.L. Bowley and G.H. Wood series by a factor which is the ratio of the average levels of the two indexes over the years 1791-93 and then divided by the price level. See R.B. Mitchell, *Abstract for British Historical Statistics* (Cambridge University Press, 1962), pp. 347-48.

* Significantly different from zero at the 5 percent level.

includes a dummy variable for the period subsequent to the suspension. The coefficients of the business cycle proxy and the interest rate are significant and have the expected sign. The coefficient of D_0 is negative and significant. Its magnitude implies that the government takeover caused the real price of Bank stock to fall 'permanently' by about 11 percent.(29) In short, the government chose a rate of inflation that was inconsistent with maximizing the real flow of Bank profits (from all sources) and this was reflected in the price of Bank stock.

The price of the stock did not return to its original level when monetary control was returned to the stockholders in 1819.(30) This was tested by including a second dummy variable that assumes the value of 1 for the period 1793-1818 and zero otherwise, along with D_0 that assumes a value of 1 for the period 1793-1832 and zero otherwise. The coefficient of the second dummy is insignificant, indicating that the variable is redundant. That is, singling out the 1793-1818 period adds nothing to the explanatory power of the equation.

In addition to this evidence, monthly data for the price of Bank and India Company stock are available for the period 1780-1801.(31) There appears to be a break in the ratio of the price of Bank stock to India Company stock in 1793. Before then, the mean of the ratio was .93 with a standard deviation of .11. After 1793, the mean fell to .83 with a standard deviation of .03. The decline in the ratio is statistically significant.(32) The price of Bank stock apparently declined relative to India Company stock by about 11 percent, virtually identical to the estimated decline produced by the regression in table 3.

Disgruntled Stockholders

Understandably, the stockholders were restive during the suspension. In 1801, Alexander Allardyce, spokesman for the critics, moved that a complete accounting of the Bank's financial condition be presented to the stockholders so that the Court might 'declare a dividend of the whole profits, the Charges of Management only excepted, as the Law directs.'(33)

Real dividend payments, inclusive of bonuses, did not increase during the suspension and the real value of Bank stock declined. These two factors along with interest-free loans made by the Bank to the government must have appeared to critics as a thinly veiled expropriation of wealth.(34) They no doubt recognized the spirit of Charles II lurking in the government.

Prices

As was the case for the more extended period discussed above, the rate of inflation is indistinguishable from zero (see table 4) in the years immediately preceding the government takeover and those following resumption of specie payments in 1821. In contrast, the price level rose significantly (at an

Table 4
Growth of Bank Money and Inflation, 1780-1832

Time period	Money growth[1]	t-score	Inflation[2]	t-score
1780 - 1792	1.96	.41	.72	.60
1793 - 1813[3]	4.04*	2.20	4.85*	2.67
1814 - 1821	−2.95	1.05	−6.99	2.06
1822 - 1832	.47	.16	−.87	.41

[1] B. R. Mitchell (1962), pp. 442-43.
[2] *Ibid*, pp. 469-70. The Schumpeter index for consumer goods is spliced to Gayer, Rostow, Schwartz index of domestic and imported commodities by a factor which is the ratio of the average levels of the two indexes over the years 1821-23.
[3] The period of the Peace of Amiens (the year 1802) is excluded from this period.
* Significantly different from zero at the 95 percent confidence level.

average annual rate of 4.85 percent) during the years 1793-1813.(35) This was a result of a significant increase in the monetary growth rate. Note that the rate of inflation closely corresponds to the rate of growth in the money supply during this period.(36)

The Real Value of Bank Money

The theory implies that the demand for real purchasing power will fall if the guarantee regarding the low rate of inflation is broken.(37)

Table 5 presents a regression that estimates the effect of the government's seizure of control over the money supply on the demand for real purchasing power by controlling for the effect of business cycles, population and the alternative cost of holding money. Annual population data are not available back to 1780, so time is used as a rough proxy to control for population growth. The interest rate on 3 percent consols was included as a measure of the alternative cost of holding wealth in the form of money. In addition, a dummy variable is included to test for a shift in the relationship in the period subsequent to the government takeover.

Table 5
The Demand for Real Purchasing Power, 1780-1832

Estimate[1]

M/P =	1.535	2.002t	.573RW	18.678D
	(.08)	(5.88)*	(5.00)*	(1.88)
Rho =	.56			
	(3.92)*			
$\bar{R}^2$2 =	.70			
DW =	1.97			

where: M/P = the stock of real purchasing power.
t = time in years.
RW = real weekly earnings.
D_0 = a dummy variable for the period subsequent to government's seizure of monetary control. D_0 = 1 for the years 1793-1832 and zero otherwise.[2]

[1] Corrected for first-order autocorrelation. t-values in parentheses.
[2] Since the hypothesis excludes positive values for D_0, a one-tailed t-test is employed.
* Significantly different from zero at the 5 percent level.

The coefficients of the proxies for the business cycle and population are significant and have the expected signs. The interest rate proved insignificant and was excluded from the estimate. The coefficient of D_0 is negative and significant. Its magnitude implies that the demand for real purchasing power fell by about 12 percent when the government seized control of the Bank.(38)

Conclusion

The above analysis suggests that decisions regarding the control of money depend more on the incentives individuals face in making choices than on the particular individuals who make the choice. Various methods of organizing monetary control produce distinct policy outcomes insofar as they confront policymakers with different incentives. Since it is unclear, for example, that the incentives confronted by the policymaker would be much different if monetary control were placed in the hands of Congress or the Treasury instead of the Board of Governors, it is unclear that the adoption of either of these alternatives would cause a noticeable change in policy. Additional research along these lines may prove helpful in suggesting a system of incentives that will induce the present-day equivalents of the Court of Directors to assign the desired weights (whatever they happen to be) to present and future consequences in reaching decisions regarding monetary control.

APPENDIX

The Profit Function and Sharing Arrangement

Bank Profits

The Bank's flow of real profit is i(M/P), as in the text, minus the opportunity cost of the government loan, (i - c)L/P.

$$(1)\quad R' = i\frac{M}{P} - (i - c)\frac{L}{P} = i\frac{M}{P} - i\frac{L}{P} + c\frac{L}{P}$$

Given the constraint that $M \leqslant L$, it is clear from expression 1 that the Bank's owners will choose $M = L$. The Bank's profits are highest in this case, other things the same. As a result, the profit function reduces to

$$(2)\quad R' = c\frac{L}{P} = c\frac{M}{P}$$

Sharing the Gain from Money Production

The capitalized value of the nominal profit stream is

$$(3)\ \frac{PR}{P} = \frac{c}{P}\ L$$

Since the above expression takes account of the opportunity cost of issuing the government loan, expression 3 is the net increase in stockholder wealth that derives from the right to issue money. The increase is proportional to the loan (L) where the proportion is determined by the ratio c/i. The higher is c relative to i, the greater is the stockholders' share and the lower is the government's share. For the initial loan of 1,500,000 pounds, the stockholders' share was 857,142 pounds (1,500,000 x .08/.14) in terms of the prices that existed in 1694. The government's share was 642,857 pounds.

Long-term interest rates fell dramatically after the formation of the Bank.[1] In part, this was due to the eventual effect of the Bank's choice of a zero rate of inflation on price expectations. Of course, the decline in the nominal interest rate had the effect of raising the Bank's share of the net wealth derived from issuing money (c/i in expression 3 rises as i falls). As noted above, the government renegotiated c downward each time the Bank's charter was renewed in an effort to maintain relative shares.

[1] See Homer, pp. 131 and 161; Martin (1865), pp. 24-25; and Rogers (1887), p. xiv.

NOTES

1. More precisely, they control the issuance of 'high-powered money' or base money. Since the long-run link between base money and the transaction balances of public (money) is so close, the paper treats the right to control base money as synonymous with the right to control money. See Balbach (1981); Johannes and Rasche (1979).
2. Alchian (1977), pp. 127-50.
3. Kemmerer (1944), pp. 34-36.
4. Charles finally acknowledged one-half the debt, but the promise to pay was never kept. Payments, at the rate of 6 percent, were made only during the period 1677-83. Charles explained the reason for his action as follows:

   > Whereas since the time of our happy Restoration We have been involved in great Forreigne Warrs as well for the Safety of our Government as the vindication of the Rights and Privileges of our Subjects. In the prosecution whereof we have been constreyned for some years past, contrary to our Inclinacions, to postpone the payment of the moneys due from Us to several Goldsmiths and other upon Tallys struck . . ., And although the present Posture of Our affaires cannot reasonably spare so great a sum as must be applied to the satisfaction of those debts, Yet considering the great difficulty which very many of our Loving Subjects (who putt their moneys into the hands of those Goldsmiths and others from whom we received it) doe at present Lye under, almost to their utter ruine for want of their said moneys, We have rather chose out of our princely care and compassion towards Our people, to suffer in Our owne Affaires than that our loving subjects should want soe reasonable a Reliefe.

   Bisschop (1967), p. 48. Incidentally, tallys were pieces of wood upon which government indebtedness was recorded. The government issued tallys when it borrowed from individuals. Goldsmiths regularly accepted these tallys and credited the accounts of the depositors.
5. Homer (1977), p. 126. Both loans were 1 million pounds. The first was a life annuity paying interest of 10 percent until 1700 and 7 percent thereafter on a semitontine basis (surviving subscribers split one-half the proceeds due decedent subscribers). The second loan paid interest at the rate of 14 percent.
6. Bisschop, 74, and Clapham (1958), vol. 1, pp. 16-20.
7. Bisschop, pp. 70-71, and Macleod (1897), pp. 773 and 776. The Bank employed three methods of accounting for the transaction accounts ('running cash') of its depositors and these methods define how the balances were transferred in the exchange process. The

methods were by 'Notes payable to Bearer, to be endorsed,' by 'Books or Sheets of Paper, wherein their Account to be entered,' or by 'Notes to persons to be accomptable.' The first method was the forerunner of central bank notes. The third was essentially equivalent to a present-day checking account. The second was much like modern passbook accounts. See Clapham, vol. 1, p. 21.

8. Bank shares exchanged hands regularly and, in 1747, *Gentleman's Magazine* began publishing daily price quotes for Bank of England shares of stock. In 1773 New Jonathan's Coffee House printed the words, 'The Stock Exchange' over its door and admittance was permitted only by fee.
9. Clapham, vol. 1, pp. 20-23.
10. It is interesting to note that an official (established by law) gold standard was not enforced in England at this time. The Bank's commitment to redeem its notes at a fixed price in terms of gold was not foisted upon the Bank by the government. Rather, this was a voluntary contract established by the Bank with its customers. England's official gold standard was not established until 1821 (more than 100 years later) and then only as a result of the Bank's insistence.
11. Clapham, vol. 1, pp. 46-50.
12. Bisschop, pp. 82-83. Act 7 Anne, C.7, provides 'that during the continuance of the said corporation of the Governor and Company of the Bank of England, it shall not be lawful for any body politic or corporate whatsoever, created or to be created (other than said Governor and Company of the Bank of England), or for any other persons whatsoever, united or to be united in covenants, or partnership, exceeding the number of six persons, in that part of Great Britain called England, to borrow, owe, or take up any sum or sums of money on their bills or notes payable at demand, or at a less time then six months from borrowing thereof.'
13. Bisschop, p. 198.
14. Andreades (1924), p. 261; Bisschop, p. 198.
15. There was, of course, Napoleon's 'Campaign of 100 Days' between his escape from Elba on March 1, 1815, and his defeat at Waterloo on June 18, 1815. Due to its brevity, it is ignored in this analysis.
16. The wording of the order ran as follows: The Bank will 'forbear issuing any Cash in Payment until the Sense of Parliament can be taken on that Subject.' Clapham, vol. 1, p. 272.
17. Clapham, vol. 2, p. 33; see, as well, Viner (1937), p. 122; Cannan (1919), p. xi.
18. Clapham, vol. 2, p. 11.
19. Clapham, vol. 2, p. 31.
20. Clapham, vol. 1, p. 272. See, as well, Cannan, p. xi.
21. Viner, p. 171.
22. Viner, p. 172.
23. Viner, pp. 172-73.
24. Since $R = i \times (M/P) = (r + \pi)(M/P)$, real profits are maximized when

$$\frac{dR}{d\pi} = \frac{M}{P} + \frac{d(M/P)}{d\pi}(r + \pi) = 0, \text{ or } \frac{d(M/P)}{d\pi}\frac{\pi}{M/P}\frac{(r + \pi)}{\pi} = -1.$$

Hence, $n_m (\frac{r}{\pi} + 1) = -1,$

where n_m = the elasticity of demand for real purchasing power with respect to the rate of inflation. When r = 0, this result reduces to $n_m = -1$ which is the familiar result obtained by others.

See Friedman (1953), pp. 251-62; Friedman (1971), pp. 846-56; and Bailey (1956), pp. 93-110.

25. This result is completely general as long as the demand for real purchasing power is inversely related to the rate of inflation. In this case,

$$\frac{dR}{d\pi} = c\frac{d(M/P)}{d\pi} < 0.$$

Since the derivative of the profit function with respect to the rate of inflation is negative, it does not pay the Bank to generate an inflation by continuously expanding M and, of course, the constraint that $M \leqslant L$ will eventually become binding. Given that profit maximization requires M = L from expression 1, a deflation would not benefit the Bank because it would require M to fall below L. As a result, the Bank will choose a zero rate of inflation.

In addition, the Bank's owners tended to be net monetary creditors as a class and this further reduced their incentive to inflate. There were about 1,300 original subscribers to the Bank stock. Many of them were London businessmen who were 'linked sneeringly with the rather ill-famed money-lending scriveners.' Others were Gentlemen and Esquires, 'people who . . . live idly as "gentlemen".' See Clapham, vol. 1, pp. 273-89.

26. 'That double event, (1) a low identification cost to everyone about the intermediate commodity and (2) specialist-experts who provide quality assurance and information more cheaply than novices can provide for themselves, explains the use of a low identification cost commodity as a general intermediary medium of exchange-money. It permits purchase of information from lower cost sources, a cost reduction that exceeds the added cost of using an intermediary good for indirect exchange.' Alchian, pp. 117-18.

27. Of course, the guarantee is not perfect. New gold discoveries or improvements in mining technology would cause the price of gold and Bank notes to fall in terms of, say, a standard commodity basket. However, the guarantee, while imperfect, was operational. It provided a relatively low-cost method of metering the Bank's rate of note production and policing the guarantee.

28. This period includes the Depression and World War II. If these years are excluded and the inflation rate is calculated over the period 1946-82, the mean rate of inflation is 6.87 percent (t-score = 9.10). The t-scores for the periods 1694-1793, 1822-1913 and 1931-82 are .145, .489 and 6.62, respectively.

29. The estimates are adjusted for first-order autocorrelation. They were checked for second-order autocorrelation with the result that Rho 2 was insignificant.

30. During the later part of the suspension, various moves to resume specie payments were afoot. As early as 1810, the *Bullion Report* advocated a return to specie payments in 1812. In addition, the Bank had begun a partial resumption in 1817, and in 1819 Parliament finally committed itself to a specific date for resumption. For purposes of the following test, I terminate the period in 1818, the year prior to Parliament's decision to return control to the Bank.

31. See Sinclair (1803), pp. 22-48.

32. The t-score = 10.78.

33. Clapham, vol. 2, p. 40.

34. In 1799, when the market rate of interest stood at 5.07 percent on long-term securities, the Bank made a 'loan' to the government of 3 million pounds interest-free for six years. The

present value of this gift was, roughly, 770,000 pounds. In addition, when the loan came due in March of 1806, the government asked that the loan be renewed until a point in time six months after a 'Definitive Peace.' The government offered to pay 3 percent interest. At the time, the long-term interest rate was considerably higher and 3 percent consols were selling at about a 40 percent discount.

35. The years 1814-21 are treated separately in table 4. During this period, various steps were being taken to return to specie payment (see end note 30).
36. The issue of private vs. government control of the money stock might seem to be a red herring since the money supply and price level always rise during wars. This, however, was not the case in two previous instances. During the Seven Years' War (1755-63), the government did not tamper with the Bank's control over the money supply, and the mean rates of growth in money and prices were 2.94 and 1.18 percent, respectively. Neither of these magnitudes differs significantly from zero. Similarly, during the War of Jenkin's Ear (1739-43), the mean rates of growth in money and prices were -1.62 and .66 percent, respectively. Again, neither of these differs significantly from zero.
37. Exactly when the public became aware of a break in the trust is problematical. They certainly were aware of it by 1797 when the government ordered the Bank to suspend specie payments. The data, however, suggest an earlier date. Prices began rising rapidly in 1790 and, shortly afterwards, the public began arbitraging the difference between the price of gold in terms of notes at the Bank and its price in the foreign market. The Bank's bullion account began to decline in 1791, then fell substantially in 1792. The following assumes the public became aware of the break in 1793 when the war with France began.
38. As was the case with the price of Bank stock, the demand for real purchasing power did not return to its original level when the government returned monetary control to the Bank and the guarantee was reinstated. This was tested by the same procedure as that employed in the case of the price of Bank stock. The results were the same. The coefficient of the second dummy was insignificant, indicating that it is redundant.

REFERENCES

Alchian, Armen A., 'Some Economics of Property Rights,' *Economic Forces at Work*, Liberty Press, 1977.

Andreades, A., *History of the Bank of England*, P. S. King and Son, 1924.

Bailey, Martin L., 'The Welfare Cost of Inflationary Finance,' *The Journal of Political Economy*, April 1956, pp. 93-110.

Balbach, Anatol B., 'How Controllable is Money Growth?' Federal Reserve Bank of St. Louis *Review*, April 1981, pp. 3-12.

Bisschop, W. R., *The Rise of the London Money Market: 1640-1826*, Burt Franklin, 1967.

Cannan, Edwin, *The Paper Pound of 1797-1821*, P. S. King and Son, 1919.

Clapham, Sir John, *The Bank of England a History*, vols. 1 and 2, Cambridge University Press, 1958.

Friedman, Milton, 'Discussion of the Inflationary Gap,' *Essays in Positive Economics*, University of Chicago Press, 1953.

-----, 'Government Revenue from Inflation,' *Journal of Political Economy*, July/August 1971, pp. 846-56.

Homer, Sidney, *A History of Interest Rates*, Rutgers University Press, 1977.

Johannes, James M., and Robert H. Rasche, 'Predicting the Money Multiplier,' *Journal of Monetary Economics*, July 1979, pp. 301-25.

Kemmerer, Edwin W., *Gold and the Gold Standard*, McGraw-Hill, 1944.

Macleod, M. A., *The Theory of Credit*, vol. 2, part 2, 2nd ed., Longmans, Green and Co., 1897.

Martin, Frederick, *Stories of Banks and Bankers*, Macmillan and Co., 1865.

Rogers, Thorold, *The First Nine Years of the Bank of England*, Clarendon Press, 1887.

Sinclair, Sir John, *The History of Public Revenue of the British Empire*, A. M. Kelly: New York, 1803.

Viner, Jacob, *Studies in the Theory of International Trade*, Harper and Brothers, 1937.

IV. CONCLUSION

Chapter 13

CENTRAL BANKERS AND THE ISSUE OF INDEPENDENCE

by Eugenia Froedge Toma and Mark Toma

In democratic systems of government, a hierarchical system of control governs the activities of bureaucratic agencies, including central banks. At the top of the central bank hierarchy are the taxpayers, who assume the role of the principal. Because of the high costs of direct participatory democracy, taxpayers elect (either directly or indirectly) a smaller body of individuals to represent their interests in governmental decision making. Taxpayers grant to this elected legislative body a wide range of powers including the right to decide how the officials at the central bank will be selected. It is the legislature's task to oversee the central bank's operations to insure that it conducts monetary policy to serve the interests of taxpayers.

The introductory chapter emphasized that economists traditionally assume the link between the principal and agent (the central bank official) is perfect. Implicitly, taxpayers costlessly signal their preferences to legislators, and costless mechanisms insure that the legislators translate those preferences into policy. This traditional assumption also implies that legislators can monitor the activities of the central bank at zero cost and thereby guarantee that bank officials serve the legislative interest. The conclusion emerging from this framework is that central bankers' decisions passively reflect taxpayers' interests.

The chapters in CENTRAL BANKERS reflect a dissatisfaction with these traditional deus ex machinas of the political process. The theoretical and empirical analyses suggest that central bank officials may not passively reflect the public interest because of transaction costs in the political process. There are information and monitoring costs not only between tax-

Toma, E.F. and Toma, M. (eds.) Central Bankers, Bureaucratic Incentives, and Monetary Policy
© 1986, Martinus Nijhoff Publishers, Dordrecht,
ISBN 90 247 3366 9

payers and the legislature but also between the legislature and the central bank.

Consider these costs from the taxpayers' point of view. There are costs to becoming informed as well as to signaling their preferences to the representatives. If dissatisfied with agent behavior, taxpayers confront three choices – each of which involves costs. The ultimate expression of dissatisfaction is exiting the political jurisdiction (Hirschman, 1970). At the federal level, however, the costs associated with this option tend to be prohibitive. A lower cost option is to vote for a new representative and, by implication, for new agent members. Finally, taxpayers may choose to lobby their political representative. Because each of these activities is costly, the democratic process may sometimes generate policy outcomes that are at odds with the preferences of the general taxpayer. There is no reason, however, to conclude that this type of signaling problem would systematically bias outcomes toward either too much or too little money production by the central bank.

Within the framework developed thus far, the interests of the body politic can be summarized by a single objective function. This singular treatment of all taxpayers, however, tends to oversimplify the way transaction costs affect outcomes. Individual taxpayers may find that their interests on any particular issue naturally coincide with the interests of a narrow subset of the taxpaying population, thus motivating interest group formation. In a world of costly information, those individuals who can organize into interest groups at relatively low cost have an advantage in the political process.

Politicians act as entrepreneurs by entering into contracts with these interest groups to provide them with favors (McCormick and Tollison, 1981). Fulfilling these contracts generally requires a revenue source. With additional revenue comes additional brokerage opportunities for politicians and, thus, more votes or private income.

Although politicians benefit from increases in revenue from any source, their ability to raise revenue will be limited by the willingness of differentially affected groups to organize and lobby against such increases. The amount of revenue raised from a tax base will depend upon the organization costs of those groups affected – either favorably or adversely. Again, *a priori*, there is no reason to conclude that the amount raised from a given base, such as real money holdings, would be systematically too high or too low from the perspective of the general taxpayer.

Consider the possibility that politicians somehow could raise revenue without motivating interest group formation; that is, without imposing concentrated costs on a particular subgroup. Under those circumstances, an important constraint on political behavior would be removed. The absolute dollar magnitude of revenue from this specific source may be significantly higher than what would be chosen by the general taxpayer under an idealized setting of zero transaction costs.

Money creation represents a revenue source that tends to satisfy this condition. Consider first how money creation would be used as a tax instrument in the idealized setting. To the extent that other tax instruments impose some deadweight losses on the general taxpayer, he will choose to raise some government revenue from money creation. Of course, the inflation tax affects the public's real money holdings and thus has its own deadweight loss. Given a certain amount of revenue to be raised, the general taxpayer in an idealized setting will employ the different tax instruments until distortionary costs are equalized across instruments at the margin. Under these idealized conditions, the general taxpayer may request *some* inflation as a means of minimizing deadweight losses.

When we move out of the zero transaction cost setting, the generalized way the inflation tax raises revenue becomes important. Inflation imposes costs on all money holders. While any one episode of monetary stimulus redistributes wealth, it does not appear to do so in any systematic fashion. At one time those with a preference for present rather than future consumption may experience a wealth decrease after monetary expansion; at another time, a completely different group may be affected. Across numerous episodes of money creation these wealth redistribution effects will tend to cancel one another.

It is precisely because money creation does not give rise to interest group opposition that politicians find it a tempting tax instrument to exploit. In a setting characterized by transaction costs, money creation can be used to extract revenue above the idealized level. Politicians will not be unconstrained in their desire to increase inflation tax revenue. The politician can never raise so much revenue from money creation that the general taxpayer perceives he would be better off under some feasible alternative monetary regime.

We have emphasized the signaling problems between taxpayers and their representatives, but a similar type of problem arises between the legislative body and its bureaucratic agent. Given that the legislature wants to raise a certain amount of inflation tax revenue, legislators face the task of translating this objective into policy actions by the central bank. Legislators traditionally exercise control over the agents' actions through the budgetary process. The budget awarded to the bureaucratic agency generally serves as a reward mechanism: behavior that is consistent with legislators' objectives translates into bigger budgets.

Assume, for the moment, that the cost of monitoring the central bank's money production activities are zero or negligible. Politicians can then elicit precisely the monetary policy desired by manipulating the budget of the central bank. With zero monitoring costs, the government's optimal rate of base production will be produced at least cost. As long as the cost of monitoring remains small, direct monitoring and the traditional budget appropriation process will lead to the government's desired inflation rate.

The budgetary reward system can be reinforced with other tools possessed by the legislator that enable him to control the bank's actions. Included among these mechanisms of control are the government's power to fire the central bank chairman (or at least to threaten removal) and to appoint a management team more willing to do as the government desires. More radical, the government could remove (or again threaten to remove) from the central bank some or all of its monetary functions. Any of these sanctions could be imposed if the central bank behaves contrary to the long run interests of the government.

Almost any reward system can be successful if monitoring costs remain insignificant. A problem arises, however, when monitoring costs increase. Suppose, for example, the central bank possesses information about the public's real demand for money that can be discerned by the legislative body only with the expenditure of substantial resources. Without this information, how will the legislature know whether the central bank is producing an inflation rate that corresponds to the seigniorage solution desired by the legislature? There is no obvious way of constructing a schedule of budgetary rewards and penalties that induces the central bank to use its information advantage to pursue legislative objectives.

A potential solution to this principal-agent problem involves replacing the traditional budget appropriation method with a system whereby the central bank finances its own activities out of its earnings from open market operations. This revenue structure of financing automatically makes total government seigniorage an object of central bank concern. More to the point, it creates an incentive for the central bank to increase seigniorage to the point that the median voter perceives that an alternative management team could make him better off. Every dollar of inflation tax revenue produced, up to this critical point, adds directly to the funds the central bank earns to cover the costs of its operations. As long as the central bank and government share (marginal) revenues from the inflation tax, the revenue system of financing creates a mutuality of interests by allowing both parties to benefit anytime seigniorage increases. Unlike the budgetary process, the mutuality of interests is achieved without the legislature's using costly monitoring resources.

Governments will choose the revenue structure of financing central bank activity only if they expect it to be effective, an outcome that depends in part upon the monetary authority's power to make decisions. Consider as an example the evolution of the power of the monetary authority in the United States. The original Federal Reserve Act created a Federal Reserve Board and twelve district Federal Reserve Banks with monetary policy responsibilities. The Act gave the Federal Reserve Board only limited monetary powers. In open market operations all twelve banks could buy and sell government securities on their own behalf – without the consent of the Board. This meant that the Board's influence over government seigniorage was indirect at best in those early years.

The financing method chosen by the legislature for the Board reflected this limited influence. Congress did specify that the individual Reserve Banks could finance their operations out of their earnings. The original Federal Reserve Act granted the Board considerably less financial independence. Although its expenses were financed from assessments against the Reserve Banks' earnings, the funds were considered 'public moneys' as they were to be deposited in the Treasury and then paid out by a disbursing agent (Willis, 1923, pp. 665, 673). Consequently, the Board was subject to government audit and, in effect, was 'organized and operated like other government bureaus' (Willis, 1923, p. 673).

Gradually, open market operations became more centralized. The New York Fed began executing the transactions of several banks simultaneously during the 1920s. Similar changes were occurring 'through agreement and consent of the twelve regional banks and of the Federal Reserve Board, but without the sanction of any specific provisions of law' (Weyforth, 1933, p. 106). The Banking Act of 1933 legalized many of these informal arrangements: 'no reserve bank was to engage in open-market operations except in accordance with regulations adopted by the Federal Reserve Board' (Weyforth, 1933, p. 107).

Not coincidentally, the increase in the monetary powers of the Federal Reserve Board was accompanied by a change in its method of funding. The Banking Act of 1933 eliminated government's oversight of the Board's operations. Instead of depositing funds in the Treasury where their use was subject to government audit, the Board was allowed to deposit its assessed funds in the Federal Reserve Banks and to control their use. The amended Federal Reserve Act explicitly stated that the 'funds derived from such assessments shall not be construed to be Government funds or appropriated moneys' (Banking Act, 1933, Sec. 6(b)). Congress was no longer a watchdog over the Board's expenditures.

The switch to a pure revenue structure for financing the Board's operations came about only when the Board gained control over the Federal Reserve System's monetary policy decisions. The revenue structure was not arbitrarily chosen but was chosen by the government as an incentive mechanism that yielded benefits to itself.

To be sure, there was a cost to government from creating the revenue structure. Because the revenue structure insulated the Fed from the monitoring process, its officials would be in a better position to extract discretionary profits for themselves. As long, however, as the consumption of perks by central bank officials is low relative to the expenditure of resources that would be required for successful legislative oversight, government will select the revenue method of financing.

The Fed continues to operate under a form of the revenue structure. Since the Banking Act of 1933, the Fed has not been required to transfer any open market operation revenue to the government. Indeed, from 1933 to 1947, it made no transfers of any significant size. Then, in 1947, the Fed announced that it would transfer a portion of its revenue to the Treasury. During that year, the Fed remitted $75 million out of $159 million in current earnings. As discussed in previous chapters, these Fed-initiated transfers have continued annually since 1947.

Michael Parkin and Robin Bade (1979) have examined the financing structure of the central banks in twelve industrialized countries and have concluded that the U.S. Congress is not unique in its method of financing bank operations. With the exception of Japan, the industrialized democratic countries have chosen some version of the revenue structure. The countries differ slightly in the sharing schema in that some (including the United States) allow the central banks to turn over excess revenue voluntarily. In other countries the government dictates the percentage of the bank's earnings that must be turned over, and still in others, the profits are paid to the government after meeting prior claims specified by statute. Regardless of details, the various arrangements to pool central bank revenue between the bank and the national treasury have the same economic effect as a merger of the bank and the treasury.

That most countries have chosen some form of the revenue structure is not surprising when considered within the principal-agent framework outlined in this chapter. The revenue method proves to be an efficient way for the legislature to satisfy the objective of increasing seigniorage when continuous monitoring of the central bank is relatively costly. The revenue structure is attractive because it is self-regulating, that is, government can reduce the monitoring costs inherent in the budgetary process.

Consider the implications of the principal-agent framework for the age old question of the central bank's independence. If we forego this framework and take the revenue structure as given, the central bank can reasonably be viewed as a highly autonomous agency. Certainly the absence of budgetary oversight, along with relatively long terms of office, gives central bank decision makers a degree of day-to-day independence that is not enjoyed by the typical bureaucrat.

The conclusion that central bankers are independent is only one part of the story. In fact, an appreciation that the central bank is an agent of the legislature changes the whole notion of what it means to be independent. It is almost inconceivable that in the long-run the central bank could continue to behave in a way that is contrary to the basic interests of its principal, the legislature. Instead of viewing the revenue structure as a badge of central bank independence, we may more usefully look at this financing method as a tool, designed by the legislature, that creates a mutuality of interests between the legislature and the central bank.

This is not to argue, of course, that monetary policy outcomes are necessarily optimal in some global sense. In a world where information cannot be costlessly acquired, there will be signaling problems – particularly between taxpayers and their political representatives. Reformers of the present system of central banking must explicitly recognize these problems and be aware that the present method of financing central bank operations provides both the treasury and the central bank with a vested interest in maintaining the status quo.

REFERENCES

Hirschman, Albert O., *Exit, Voice, and Loyalty*, Harvard University Press: Cambridge, MA, 1970.

McCormick, Robert E. and Robert D. Tollison, *Politicians, Legislation, and the Economy*, Martinus Nijhoff Publishers: Boston, 1981.

Parkin, Michael and Robin Bade, 'Central Bank Laws and Monetary Policy,' Unpublished working paper, University of Western Ontario, September, 1979.

Weyforth, William O. *The Federal Reserve Board: A Study of Federal Reserve Structure and Credit Control*. Johns Hopkins Press: Baltimore, 1933.

Willis, Henry Parker, *The Federal Reserve System: Legislation, Organization, and Operation*, The Ronald Press Company: New York, 1923.

LIST OF CONTRIBUTORS

Keith Acheson, Carleton University and Claremont Graduate School

King Banaian, St. Cloud State University

John F. Chant, Simon Fraser University

Milton Friedman, Hoover Institution

Edward J. Kane, Ohio State University

Leroy O. Laney, Federal Reserve Bank of Dallas

Thomas Mayer, University of California, Davis

Wm. Stewart Mounts, Jr., Mercer University

Gary J. Santoni, Federal Reserve Bank of St. Louis

William F. Shughart II, George Mason University

Neil T. Skaggs, Illinois State University

Clifford Sowell, Berea College

Robert D. Tollison, George Mason University

Eugenia Froedge Toma, University of Kentucky

Mark Toma, Miami University

Cheryl L. Wasserkrug, Millikin University

Thomas D. Willett, Claremont Graduate School

FINANCIAL AND MONETARY POLICY STUDIES

1. Multinational Enterprises – Financial and Monetary Aspects.
   Editors: J.S.G. Wilson and C.F. Scheffer, with 16 contributors.
   1974. ISBN 90-286-0124-4
   (SUERF Colloquium Nottingham University, England, April 1973)
2. Floating Exchange Rates – The Lessons of Recent Experience.
   Editors: H. Fournier and J.E. Wadsworth, with 14 contributors.
   1976. ISBN 90-286-0565-7
   (SUERF Colloquium Venice, October 1974)
3. The Development of Financial Institutions in Europe, 1956–76.
   Editors: J.E. Wadsworth, J.S.G. Wilson and F. Fournier, with 26 contributors.
   1977. ISBN 90-286-0337-9
   (SUERF Colloquium Brussels, April 1976)
4. New Approaches in Monetary Policy.
   Editors: J.E. Wadsworth and F. Léonard de Juvigny, with 29 contributors.
   1979. ISBN 90-286-0848-6
   (SUERF Colloquium Wiesbaden, September 1977)
5. Europe and the Dollar in the World-wide Disequilibrium.
   Editor: J.R. Sargent, with 17 contributors.
   1981. ISBN 90-286-0700-5
   (SUERF Colloquium Basel, Switzerland, May 1979)
6. Bank Management in a Changing Domestic and International Environment: The Challenges of the Eighties.
   Editors: Donald E. Fair and F. Léonard de Juvigny, with 25 contributors.
   1982. ISBN 90-247-2606-9
   (SUERF Colloquium Helsingør, Denmark, October 1980)
7. International Lending in a Fragile World Economy.
   Editors: Donald E. Fair in co-operation with Raymond Bertrand, with 25 contributors.
   1983. ISBN 90-247-2809-6
   (SUERF Colloquium Vienna, April 1982)
8. Currency Competition and Monetary Union.
   Editor: Pascal Salin.
   1984. ISBN 90-247-2817-7
9. Government Policies and the Working of Financial Systems in Industrialized Countries.
   Editors: Donald E. Fair in co-operation with F. Léonard de Juvigny, with 24 contributors.
   1984. ISBN 90-247-3076-7
10. Jelle Zijlstra, A Central Banker's View.
    Editors: C. Goedhart, G.A. Kessler, J. Kymmell and F. de Roos.
    1985. ISBN 90-247-3184-4
11. Monetary Conditions for Economic Recovery.
    Editors: C. van Ewijk and J.J. Klant.
    1985. ISBN 90-247-3219-0
12. Shifting Frontiers in Financial Markets.
    Editor: D.E. Fair.
    1985. ISBN 90-247-
13. Central Bankers, Bureaucratic Incentives, and Monetary Policy.
    Editors: E.F. Toma and M. Toma.
    1986. ISBN 90-247-3366-9

GPSR Compliance

The European Union's (EU) General Product Safety Regulation (GPSR) is a set of rules that requires consumer products to be safe and our obligations to ensure this.

If you have any concerns about our products, you can contact us on ProductSafety@springernature.com

In case Publisher is established outside the EU, the EU authorized representative is:

Springer Nature Customer Service Center GmbH
Europaplatz 3
69115 Heidelberg, Germany

Batch number: 10761599

Printed by Printforce, the Netherlands